HYPERPROFITS

HYPERPROFITS

Beat the Pros with this New,
Proven Investment System

by David A. Goodman, Ph.D.
and John W. Peavy III, Ph.D.

Doubleday & Company, Inc. Garden City, New York 1985

For Glenda and Deanna

Library of Congress Cataloging in Publication Data

Goodman, David A.
  Hyperprofits: beat the pros with this new, proven investment system.

  1. Speculation.   2. Stock-exchange.   3. Stocks.
I. Peavy, John W.   II. Title.
HG6041.G56   1985   332.63'22
ISBN: 0-385-19599-0

Library of Congress Catalog Card Number 85-4504
Copyright © 1985 by David A. Goodman and John W. Peavy III
Printed in the United States of America
First Edition

Foreword
Why We Wrote This Book

Every investor has a lifelong goal of achieving the coveted status of being wealthy. But in today's fast-paced financial world, many a would-be investor has decided that investing personally is too complex and treacherous. "I would rather let an expert invest my money for me" is a commonly heard phrase today.

Recent statistics confirm this attitude. The giant financial institutions (banks, mutual funds, insurance companies, etc.) have largely replaced individual investors as the dominant participants in the stock market. Individuals, who as recently as the sixties accounted for nearly three fourths of the stock market activity, now initiate less than a fourth of all trades on the New York Stock Exchange. Apparently, more and more individuals have conceded that competing against the financial pros is a no-win proposition.

You may agree that it is futile to try to beat the professionals at their own game of picking attractive stocks. After all, many highly educated and experienced pros spend seventy or more hours each week striving to discover stock market bargains. How can you possibly survive financially against such intense competition?

We wrote *Hyperprofits* specifically to answer this important question. After several years of exhaustive stock market research, we concluded that the individual investor is not headed for rapid extinction—far from it. Instead, we are convinced that the small investor has unique opportunities that often escape the pros' attention. *Hyperprofits* shows you how to identify those very special investment opportunities.

We readily concede that you can't win if you compete head-on with the financial giants. It's highly unlikely that you will ever make a find among the stocks that the Wall Street pros most closely follow. But Hyperprofits steers you away from these institutional favorites and directs your attention to stocks which go largely unnoticed. That's right, Hyperprofits focuses on small, out-of-favor stocks—just the type of investment the pros typically neglect. Why would you ever desire to own a security that is shunned by the pros? The answer to this query is quite elementary: Because extensive computer research by the authors and others reveals these outcasts to be the real money-makers.

The Hyperprofits approach to investing rests firmly on three solid investment pillars. In this book we fully develop and explain each pillar and show how each can individually enhance your wealth-building opportunities. However, the real benefit comes when the three pillars are combined into one cohesive investment technique. This is what Hyperprofits is all about. The synergistic effect of the three pillars offers an investment opportunity that enables you to compete in the financial arena and win. Our research reveals that over the long run the Hyperprofits investment approach has yielded gains far in excess of those achieved by the typical investment professional.

Hyperprofits stands above other investment strategies in that it not only offers the opportunity for high profits but also scientifically documents the performance of the system. As such, Hyperprofits provides four important advantages:

1. *High Profits.* We find that over a long period of time the Hyperprofits approach provided a 32 percent annual profit rate—more than triple the overall stock market performance. On the surface this profit rate may not seem so enticing, but the long-term effect is staggering. For example, $5,000 invested at this rate in a tax-deferred account would swell to the awesome sum of approximately $80,000 in only ten years.

2. *Risk Management.* No investment technique is risk-free, Hyperprofits included. We readily admit that Hyperprofits stocks decline when the overall stock market is falling. However, Hyperprofits stocks tend to fall less than the average stock. And, when the market advances, the Hyperprofits selections really perform. We carefully identify how to moderate investment risks, making sure that you don't fall victim to the numerous "foolish" risks which continually confront us all.

3. *Small Outlay.* You don't have to be a millionaire to use Hyperprofits. About $5,000 can get you started. This sum allows you to purchase five different Hyperprofits stocks, a minimum level of diversification. Of course, larger amounts can be employed even more effectively because diversification can be increased, thus further reducing risk.

4. *Ease of Use.* You don't have to be an investment wizard or a mathematical genius to use Hyperprofits. We lay out this remarkable investment approach clearly so that even the novice investor can participate. We provide a

simple step-by-step procedure for selecting and reviewing your Hyperprofits portfolio. We also identify the necessary data sources and how to use them. Throughout, numerous examples are provided to facilitate your journey through Hyperprofits.

We are convinced that, when used properly, Hyperprofits offers you the opportunity to achieve attractive long-term investment results and thus be well on the way toward achieving your goal of financial wealth. But you must keep Hyperprofits in perspective. This is not a get-rich-quick scheme, nor is it a no-risk technique. Rather, Hyperprofits combines three proven investment pillars, prudent risk management, and a process we call "the magic of compounding" into a rewarding investment approach.

To document our belief in Hyperprofits, we have already invested our own funds in a Hyperprofits portfolio. In this regard we are indebted to Kit Werlein, the senior trust officer at the First National Bank of Kerrville, Texas, for graciously aiding us in the formation of the portfolio and for serving as the portfolio's custodian. We believe that after you read *Hyperprofits* you will have as much confidence in this unique approach as we do. Best of all, you will see that Hyperprofits is not only profitable, it's fun!

Acknowledgments

We never realized the magnitude of the task of writing this book. This project would have never begun without the assistance and encouragement of numerous individuals. We especially thank Dr. Mick McGill at Southern Methodist University for his early advice and assistance and Dominick Abel, our agent, for his continuing help. We also wish to express our gratitude to the many academic colleagues, student assistants, investment practitioners, and journal reviewers who provided insightful advice and counsel. The cast is too large to name individually, but each person's contribution is appreciated more than we can express.

Many of our initial findings occurred as a result of an extensive research project which was partially sponsored by a Research Grant Fellowship from the Edwin L. Cox School of Business at S.M.U. We are most appreciative of this support and the environment for exploring investment occurrences. We are grateful to Kit Werlein at the First National Bank of Kerrville, Texas, for providing the opportunity for us to build our own Hyperprofits portfolio and for serving as the custodian for the portfolio. Dr. Goodman also wishes to acknowledge Terri Hoffman's inspiration and support.

The perceptive comments and steadfast encouragement of Adrian Zackheim, our editor at Doubleday & Company, are sincerely appreciated. His efforts greatly enhanced this book. And, of course, we could not have completed this project without the patience and encouragement of our wives, Glenda Goodman and Deanna Peavy. For the support they provided no words of appreciation would be adequate.

Contents

LIST OF TABLES

LIST OF FIGURES

1

The Complete
Action Strategy
for Hyperprofits

The lifelong dream of countless Americans is to become wealthy. And why not? All it takes is money! To most, however, the notion of becoming really wealthy is almost as remote as being elected president. But it really shouldn't be. In today's fast-paced financial world, anyone with enough time, knowledge, and perseverance can achieve financial independence. Sound ridiculous? Well, let's take a closer look.

There are three basic ways to accumulate personal wealth: (1) receiving a windfall gift or inheritance, (2) selling your labor or services for pay, and (3) using your existing money (no matter how limited) to create even more money. The first route is the quickest and simplest, and we highly recommend it. But, unfortunately, few of us will ever be the beneficiaries of such a windfall. The second road to riches is also very unlikely. If you're seven feet tall and able to dunk a basketball or have the opportunity to become chairman of the board of General Motors, then you may be able to amass wealth from your pay.[1] But the typical worker faces an entirely different situation. After meeting soaring living expenses and deducting the bite of taxes usually there's not much of your paycheck left—certainly not enough to propel you to financial independence.

That leaves only the third route for you to pursue. It is this final concept —letting your money work for you—on which you must concentrate if you want to become truly wealthy. That's what *Hyperprofits* is all about. We intro-

---

[1] GM chairman Roger Smith earned $1,490,000 in 1983 and nearly seven-foot-tall Moses Malone signed a six-year, $13.2-million contract with the Philadelphia 76ers in 1982. We concede that both of these gentlemen can attain financial independence from their salaries (and bonuses) alone.

duce a remarkably profitable investment strategy, called Hyperprofits, that will show you how to take a modest sum of money and build financial security.

What Is Hyperprofits?

Hyperprofits is a scientifically proven stock investment strategy which has been shown to yield spectacular financial rewards over long periods of time. Hyperprofits synthesizes several profitable investment techniques into one harmonious strategy which any investor can readily employ. The effect of this strategy is to generate a level of profit performance well above that which any of its component techniques could produce alone. In a sense Hyperprofits is based on the premise that two plus two equals five.

Hyperprofits was derived from exhaustive computer research by the authors as well as other investigators. It stands above other investment strategies in that it not only offers the investor remarkable profits but also scientifically documents the performance of the system. Hyperprofits is not just empty promises. It really works!

To illustrate the attractiveness of Hyperprofits, $1,000 invested in the Dow Jones industrial average stocks in 1970 would have grown to less than $2,000 by 1980. Meanwhile the same $1,000 invested using Hyperprofits would have exploded to the awesome sum of $16,060—sixteen times the original investment and more than eightfold the Dow Jones results.

Getting Rich Quick

Will Rogers once advised, "Take all your savings and buy some good stock and hold it till it goes up, then sell it. If it don't go up, don't buy it." No one can question the soundness of this advice; it always works. Of course, we all know that Will's investment strategy is impossible to implement and therefore has no more value than a Ouija board for generating stock market profits.

Yet investment techniques with no more merit than Will Rogers's advice or a Ouija board abound throughout Wall Street. Some get-rich-quick schemes seem remarkably tempting and may even work for a while. But inevitably any promise of instant riches is doomed to fail, often resulting in financial disaster to the unsuspecting investor.

If you're looking for some risky new get-rich-quick scheme, then read no further. This book is not for you. But if you desire a scientifically proven investment strategy that will enable you to steadily accumulate a financial fortune, then you've come to the right place. Hyperprofits is designed specifically for you. In the following paragraphs of this chapter we describe the foundation on which the Hyperprofits concept firmly rests and then introduce the three financial pillars which interact to make Hyperprofits work.

The "Magic" of Compounding

Remember, your goal is to become wealthy. Until now you have resigned yourself to the belief that such a lofty financial status is reserved only for the likes of Rockefellers, Kennedys, and du Ponts. But that's not so! According to *Time* magazine, approximately half a million Americans are already millionaires. That's one out of 453 people. With that many financial successes why can't there be more? Of course, there can be more millionaires—indeed many more. And, more importantly, you can become one. The ingredients required for such financial success are straightforward: a modest initial capital, strict adherence to the Hyperprofits investment strategy, and a little time. The "magic" of compounding will do the rest.

The magic of compounding is behind nearly all great fortunes accumulated in history. Einstein considered it humanity's greatest invention, since it allows for the systematic, reliable increase of wealth. So great is the power of compounding that if the Indians who sold Manhattan Island back in 1626 had invested their $24 at 10 percent and let it compound, today they could buy back the entire island (skyscrapers and all) and still have over $100 billion left over. No wonder Baron de Rothschild, one of the wealthiest men ever, when asked to name the seven wonders of the world, responded, "I cannot. But I know that the eighth wonder is compound interest."

The principle of compounding has existed for as long as there's been money. Simply stated, compounding means that you earn interest on previously earned interest so that your money grows at an ever increasing pace. The effect of compounding is that your money grows at a higher rate than is apparent. For example, suppose you invest $100 in a savings account at 5 percent compounded annually. Your money will grow to $162.90 in ten years. So your average interest rate is really 6.29 percent.

How dramatic the impact of compounding is depends on two things: first, how high your rate of return is, and second, how long your money is allowed to build. Take the same $100 and invest it at 20 percent instead of 5 percent and you will accumulate $519.17 at the end of the same ten years. This is $519.17 as opposed to $162.90! Imagine how even higher rates would further intensify this effect.

4   *Hyperprofits*

Now suppose you allowed your $100 to grow for twenty-five years at 5 percent. You would amass a total of $338.64 in contrast to the $162.90 for ten years. Let's combine the two features and invest your $100 at 20 percent for twenty-five years. Now your small nest egg will produce a remarkable $9,439.62. At 30 percent for twenty-five years your wealth would soar to an astonishing $70,464.08! Table 1 shows you how long it will take you, riding the compounding vehicle, to become a millionaire using different starting amounts and profit rates.

Table 1

Years Required to Become a Millionaire

Starting Amount	Compound Rate of Return			
	5%	10%	20%	Hyperprofits*
$ 1,000	141.6	72.5	37.9	24.8
5,000	108.6	55.6	29.1	19.1
10,000	94.4	48.3	25.3	16.6
50,000	61.4	31.4	16.4	10.8

* Assuming the 32 percent historical Hyperprofits return.

It may be hard to believe, but only $1,000 will multiply to $1 million in just 24.8 years if you can compound your money at the same rate of return that the Hyperprofits system has produced.[2] Now you can see the importance of compounding as a foundation for Hyperprofits. You don't have to find stocks that double overnight. A steady, yet achievable, rate of return will lead you down the path to financial security. The dynamic profit power of Hyperprofits is that it captures the magic of compounding, thus enabling your money to multiply at a high rate over a sustained period of time.

[2] We assume that your funds are compounding in a tax-deferred account such as an Individual Retirement Account or a Keogh Plan (see Chapter 8).

Why Hyperprofits Is for You

The Hyperprofits strategy detailed in this book is designed to provide you with four powerful investment benefits: (1) windfall profits, (2) relatively low risk, (3) small initial investment outlay, and (4) ease of use. Let's look briefly at each of these.

Windfall Profits. Our computer research findings reveal that by adhering strictly to the Hyperprofits investment strategy, an investor would have earned an average historical profit rate in excess of 32 percent per year. Over the same historical period the stock market as a whole averaged less than 8 percent annually. These returns were achieved during a period that included both up (bull) and down (bear) markets. Since Hyperprofits performance is related to overall market performance, in good years Hyperprofits yielded well above the 32 percent average. Because all gains are reinvested, the effect of compounding produces spectacular results.

Relatively Low Risk. Risk or the chance of diminishing stock value is measured in relation to the market as a whole. The risk of the total market is average risk. Our research shows that Hyperprofits entails relatively low downside risk. This means that the risk is less than that of the market or a random selection of stocks.

We can measure the risk of Hyperprofits by observing its performance whenever the market declines. Over a long period of time we find that, in general, Hyperprofits does decline when the market falls; however, typically not as much. Significantly, in over half the years in which the market falls, Hyperprofits outperforms the market. That is, Hyperprofits falls less than the average selection of stocks. So while the long-run historical returns of Hyperprofits are more than double that of the market, the risk of decreasing stock value is lower than that of the market.

Small Initial Investment. About $5,000 will enable an investor to use Hyperprofits. This sum allows the purchase of five stocks, a minimum level of diversification. If you elect to pursue a mutual fund specializing in Hyperprofits stocks, then an even smaller amount can be invested. Larger amounts can be employed even more effectively because diversification can be increased, thus reducing investment risk.

Easy to Use. You do not need to learn anything complex or make sophisticated calculations. No charts or graphs are used. All that is needed is a small base of data and some simple arithmetic. Later, we shall indicate the specific pieces of information needed and where to obtain them. We shall also show you a simple step-by-step procedure for selecting and reviewing your Hyperprofits portfolio. By the end of the book, you will be an expert in Hyperprofits. Even if you have never invested in stocks before you will be in a position to be a highly successful investor by using Hyperprofits.

The Three Pillars
of Hyperprofits

Hyperprofits is founded on three crucial principles, or pillars, which have been shown to be indicative of superior investment performance. When resting upon a foundation of profit compounding, these pillars serve to create a highly profitable financial structure. Each pillar alone yields high performance. But when the three pillars are blended together, they form a single cohesive investment strategy which achieves far more than any one pillar alone.

The first of these pillars is called the Price–Earnings Relative, or PER. This factor measures how good a buy a particular stock is in relation to other stocks in the same industry grouping. The details on how to get this and other key factors will be given to you later in the book.

Industry groups are very important because prices of stocks within groups have a strong tendency to move together. Whether or not a stock is a bargain depends on how it stands in comparison to other similar stocks. If you are shopping for a tennis racquet, you want to compare price and quality among competing brands. Comparing a racquet with a pool cue doesn't tell you anything. The PER gives you this information for stocks.

The second pillar of Hyperprofits is called the Discounted Price–Earnings Ratio, or DPE. This factor too enables you to measure whether or not a stock is a bargain and to what extent. But in this case the measurement is made in a different way from the first pillar.

To know whether a stock is a bargain or even an outright steal, it is vital to know how the stock stands in relation to its own history. If your racquet normally sells for $45 but is on sale for $25, then this could be a steal. But if the racquet has been on sale for $25 for the past year and no one's buying, then maybe it's not a bargain. By measuring the DPE you can determine this for stocks.

The final pillar of Hyperprofits is size of the firm whose common stock you are contemplating purchasing. This is called the firm-size factor. The size factor enables you to determine how genuine an apparent stock bargain really is. Take, for example, two companies, both highly successful and profitable. One company is a large, established "blue chip." The other is a small, relatively obscure company which has been in business for only a few years. Will the two companies' stocks be equally sought after by investors? Probably not, because very few investors even know about the small company whereas almost everyone has heard of the profitable corporate giant. Many investors buy the recognized blue chip's stock while the small company's stock goes unnoticed. The net result: the large stock soars to a price where it is not a bargain, but the small stock's price remains at a bargain level. Of course, not all small stocks are bargains. Nevertheless, if you can uncover *attractive* small companies before others discover them, you will be well on your way to achieving Hyperprofits. On the other hand, it is highly unlikely that you will find such a bargain among the stocks of corporate giants.

The three financial pillars harmonize into a unified investment strategy which produces a synergetic profit effect. First, we want to invest in stocks which are rock-bottom-priced compared to similar stocks. Therein lies the role of the first pillar. We do not want, however, to invest in stocks which are always relatively low-priced. We want only those stocks which are unusually good bargains so that they have a high chance to pop up in price. This is where the second pillar comes in to interact with the first.

Finally, we want to find stocks that are overlooked so that we can buy them before the cash-laden institutions enter the scene. Here is where the third pillar enters to synergize with the other pillars. As we shall describe later in more detail, the three pillars of Hyperprofits blend into a cohesive investment strategy which produces extraordinary financial rewards for you.

Hyperprofits Really Works!

Now you know what Hyperprofits is and you have a general idea of how it works. But the big question is, does it work? And if so, does it work well enough to fulfill your financial dreams?

To answer these questions we turned to our trusty computer. We programmed the computer to follow the Hyperprofits system precisely as presented in this book. Using historical stock market data from 1970 to 1980, the computer bought, held, and sold stocks in accordance with the simple Hyperprofits rules. The computer also kept track of all profits.

The results were extraordinary. Over the ten-year period, Hyperprofits averaged approximately 32 percent annual profits before commissions and taxes. What does this mean in terms of dollars? If you had started with $5,000 in 1970, by 1980 you would have accumulated the grand sum of $80,298. If you had been fortunate enough to have $10,000 to invest in 1970, it would have grown to $160,596. Not a bad start for your wealth-building program.

How does this performance compare with the profits of an average stock portfolio? Over the same period of history, the average $5,000 investment in the market would have grown to the meager total of $10,795. The Hyperprofits gains are more than seven times greater.

As a further illustration of the magical power of Hyperprofits, consider a sample Hyperprofits portfolio published in the Dallas *Times Herald* on August 30, 1982. This portfolio utilizes only the first pillar of Hyperprofits by itself. Table 2 shows the resulting percentage profits after only one year.

Table 2

One-Year Hyperprofits Returns

Stock	Buy Price	Sell Price	Percent Profit
Honeywell	741/8	1151/4	55.5
Schering-Plough	331/2	415/8	24.2
Applied Magnetic	157/8	27	70.0
Borden	341/4	521/4	52.6
Standard Oil—Ohio	313/4	561/4	77.2
Simmonds Precision	175/8	511/4	190.9
Manhattan Industries	115/8	203/4	78.6
Average Profit			78.4

The portfolio as a whole yielded 78.4 percent profit. This would turn your $10,000 into $17,840 in a single year. Imagine what the profits would be combining the other two pillars. Of course, the Hyperprofits strategy will not produce these spectacular results in every year, but in the long run Hyperprofits offers you the opportunity to build more wealth than you ever imagined.

In the chapters that follow, we will give you a thorough understanding of Hyperprofits and show just how to use it. In Chapter 10, we put our computer to work applying Hyperprofits to the current universe of stocks. There, we present ten top Hyperprofits picks for the future.

From Risk
to Riches

In the first chapter, we introduced the Hyperprofits investment strategy. In following chapters, we will detail exactly how to employ this profitable strategy. But before we begin our exciting financial venture you should become acquainted with the concept of investment risk. In this chapter, you will discover how to transform calculated or intelligent risk into stock riches. Notice that we did not say high or foolish risk, nor did we say no risk. Every self-made millionaire has discovered the secret of utilizing calculated, sensible risk to amass a fortune. Hyperprofits is a system that capitalizes on the principles of intelligent risk and superior stock selection to produce a financial bonanza for you.

The mere mention of the stock market evokes a strong reaction from the many Americans who believe that Wall Street is nothing more than a legalized gambling arena. Why would anyone so foolishly risk his or her hard-earned savings on such a gambling device? After all, no one wins in the long run at gambling, except, of course, the dealer. So why play the stock market when, sooner or later, you are bound to lose? Isn't Las Vegas a lot more fun than Wall Street and not nearly as treacherous?[1]

We will show you that the stock market is not a gambling arena. Sure, there are risks involved in buying stocks and not everyone wins; but as long as you carefully manage those risks, you will be a winner and thus well on your way toward Hyperprofits.

---

[1] Actually Wall Street may be less treacherous today than earlier. It wasn't until 1764 that the dreaded whipping posts were removed from Wall Street—a short distance from where the New York Stock Exchange now resides.

You Can Be the Dealer

If you have ever been to Las Vegas, you are probably painfully aware that the only winner in the long run is the dealer. Why? Because the rules of the game are firmly set so that the dealer has a slightly higher chance of winning each game than the player does. This favored dealer status can be expressed according to the law of probability. Now, don't get concerned. We're not going to delve into a detailed mathematical discourse. A simple example will suffice. Take, for instance, the game of roulette. There are 38 equal slots on a roulette wheel—18 black, 18 red, and 2 green. If you bet on either black or red, then you have 18 chances of winning, but alas you have 20 chances of losing. It doesn't take an Einstein to figure that on each spin of the wheel you have a greater chance of losing than winning. Expressed as a probability, you should, on average, win 18 out of every 38 plays, or 47.4 percent of the time (18 divided by 38). But that means that you must lose the rest of the time so your probability of loss is 52.6 percent.

Now you see the problem. On each roll of the wheel you have a slightly higher probability of losing. Of course, you won't lose every time and you may even ride a "hot" streak and win several times in a row. But one fact becomes vividly apparent: the longer you play, the greater the chance of losing your money. You simply can't override the law of probability in the long run.

Now let's turn the table. What if you are the dealer? That means that every time a player loses, you win. And, keep in mind, the player is going to lose 52.6 percent of the time. As a dealer, therefore, you should win approximately 526 out of every 1,000 games. Admittedly, that doesn't appear to be an earth-shattering result, but the main point remains: as a dealer you will win in the long run. And, furthermore, the more you play, the more dollars you will win. You don't have to win all the time, just most of the time, to ensure financial success.

"So what?" you may exclaim. "I can never be a Las Vegas dealer." That's true. But what you can become is a participant in the stock market. And, even more importantly, your probability of winning in stocks can be higher than the dealer's probability of winning at roulette. In effect, you can assume the role of the dealer and have the odds stacked in your favor. Now don't take this to mean that we view the stock market as a legalized gambling device, because we don't. Just the opposite; we contend that stocks represent solid investment opportunities which in the long run offer you a high probability of winning financially. Read on, because in the following paragraphs we reveal why stocks are so desirable. And in subsequent chapters we explain the Hyperprofits investment strategy that will dramatically increase your probability of winning in this exciting investment arena.

The Long Haul

We've all heard stories about how some innocent soul invested a sum of money in a "can't-lose" stock only to see that stock rapidly plummet to a mere fraction of its original value. Such horror stories make you think long and hard before taking a chance on stocks. But to judge stocks based on such scanty hearsay would be both unfair and unfortunate. It's much like the roulette dealer abandoning the game just because he or she lost on the first spin of the wheel. What's really important is how stocks perform over the long haul. We already know that the roulette dealer, even though he or she may have an occasional bad day, profits handsomely over time. Now let's observe the long-term track record for stocks.

Fortunately, a pair of University of Chicago researchers have provided exhaustive stock market performance results over a very long time period. Roger Ibbottson and Rex Sinquefield analyzed common stock returns from 1926 to 1981.[2] Their findings conclusively document the attractiveness of stock investments. A portfolio consisting of all exchange-listed common stocks appreciated an average of 9.1 percent each year (compounded) over this fifty-six-year period. Now, 9.1 percent may not seem so enticing, especially in today's world of double-digit interest rates. But over the period observed, this was a truly exceptional rate of return. Inflation, as measured by the Consumer Price Index, increased an average of only 3.0 percent yearly. Stock returns, therefore, were more than triple the rate of inflation over this era—a result that virtually any investor would be elated to achieve.

Common stocks also substantially outperformed every other type of security. Over the same 1926–81 period U.S. Treasury bills, presumably the lowest-risk investment you can own, provided an average annual return of only 3.0 percent—exactly the same as the average inflation rate. If you pay income taxes (and who doesn't?), then part of your Treasury bill return goes to Uncle Sam, thus leaving you with a yearly after-tax gain somewhat less than the inflation rate. By owning bills, you would actually have seen your assets erode in purchasing power. Sure, you would have more assets at the end of each year, but

---

[2] See Ibbottson and Sinquefield's *Stocks, Bonds, Bills and Inflation: The Past and the Future* (Charlottesville, Virginia: The Financial Analysts Research Foundation), 1982.

they would buy less. That's the problem with low-risk assets: they don't allow you to maintain your purchasing power. On the contrary, you will actually lose ground in *real* terms by adopting and implementing a very low risk investment philosophy. Such performance should repulse even the most conservative investor.

Stocks also outpaced bonds over this era. Long-term government bonds also returned a paltry 3.0 percent average annual return and the slightly riskier corporation bonds provided an average gain of 3.6 percent each year. Still you can see the plight of the tax-paying investor. On an after-tax basis bond returns did not provide a sufficient cushion to hedge against inflation. Only through common stocks was the investor able to make significant headway against inflation. And keep in mind, this period witnessed only a 3.0 percent annual inflation rate. Today, an asset's ability to hedge against inflation is even more crucial.

Clearly, common stocks were the place to be over this era. If you invested $1,000 in a diversified portfolio of stocks in 1926, you would have accumulated $133,615 by year-end 1981 (assuming no taxes). Meanwhile the cost of a basket of assorted goods and services would have inflated from $1,000 to $5,242. Whereas your $1,000 would have purchased only one market basket in 1926, by the end of 1981 your original portfolio could acquire more than 25 baskets. But this is for the average stocks. Imagine how well off you would have been with Hyperprofits stocks.

Bills and bonds, although considerably "safer," did not afford the opportunity to substantially outpace inflation. The moral is clear: if you're too conservative in your investments, then you're bound to be relegated to meager investment results and thus highly vulnerable to the ravages of inflation—a sure way not to attain your goal of financial independence.

Risk—Another Four-Letter Word?

What first pops into your mind when someone mentions the word risk? If you're like most Americans, your initial response is that risk is something that is potentially harmful and should be carefully avoided. Evel Knievel takes risks, but then he has probably landed hard on his head a few too many times. Most of us, however, are not daredevils; in fact, we're very cautious in our approach toward risk. Generally we would prefer to avoid a risk rather than be exposed to it. Why take an unnecessary chance when such an action could cause personal harm? A recent New York Stock Exchange survey confirms this attitude by revealing that 70 percent of the investors questioned were found to be unwilling to accept more than the very smallest amount of risk.

Risk aversion, however, is just the factor that has caused many an investment portfolio to flop. That's right, avoiding risk is a certain way to achieve mediocre investment results. Contrary to the message implied by a recent investment book entitled *No Risk,* we assert that to earn superior returns you must accept some *reasonable* amount of risk. Or, more succinctly stated, risk (when properly managed) has its rewards. A no-risk approach is also a no-reward approach.

We realize that the notion of willingly accepting risk is alien to most individuals, but before you conclude that we're prime candidates for some sort of crazy investors' asylum, permit us to further develop our case.

Risk has always been an elusive and tricky concept and investment risk is no exception. The only certainty about risk is that there is considerable uncertainty in how to define it. More and more investors and financial researchers, however, are agreeing that investment risk is the possibility that the actual return you realize from an investment will differ from the return you expected when you acquired the investment. Maybe an example will best illustrate this concept. If you purchase a one-year-maturity Treasury bill to yield a 10 percent interest rate, then you are almost certain to earn that 10 percent return over the year. Remember, the Treasury runs the printing presses so you're unconditionally guaranteed to get your money back with interest. Or, stated in terms of the law of probability, you have almost a 100 percent probability of earning 10 percent for the year.

Now assume that you buy a twenty-year-maturity Treasury bond with a 10 percent annual rate of interest. In this instance you may *not* earn the 10 percent rate of return. As interest rates fluctuate, your bond's value will also change. Sure, you'll earn 10 percent in interest that first year, but this gain does not paint the entire picture. What you really want to know is your total return, not just your total interest. Total return has two components: current income (interest or dividends) and change in value. Therefore, for instance, if interest rates increase during the next year, your long-term Treasury bond will become proportionally less attractive because its fixed 10 percent interest rate is no longer as enticing to investors. Because investors can obtain a higher interest rate on new Treasury bonds, they will buy your bond only if you sell at a lower price than you originally paid. This price loss offsets some of your interest income and thus lowers your total return. If the bond's price falls, say, 6 percent in the year, then your total return is only 4 percent (e.g., 10 percent interest minus 6 percent price change)—not 10 percent.

In the previous example, you expected to earn 10 percent but achieved only a 4 percent return. That's what risk is all about. You fell short of your expectation. When you purchased the Treasury bond you should have realized that, unlike the Treasury bill, there was some probability that you would not attain your return expectation. Riskier assets such as common stocks have an even higher probability of not earning exactly what you expected.

Why then would you ever buy a risky asset if there is a higher probability of your not earning what you expected to earn? The answer is elementary: because in the long run the years in which you earn less than expected will be offset by those years in which you earn more than expected. The net result is that in the long run you should earn approximately what you anticipated, assuming, of course, that your original expectations were reasonable.

When carefully and intelligently managed, moderate-risk acceptance can enable you to progress down the path to financial independence. Moreover, intelligent risk is absolutely essential to building your fortune. Think about this. Have you ever heard of a single self-made millionaire who didn't build his or her fortune through intelligent risk? In the next paragraphs we reveal how you should evaluate and manage risk to best facilitate your financial journey.

Taking Calculated Risks

One of the most widely acclaimed phenomena in finance is that, on average, investors earn higher returns when they bear greater risks. The Ibbottson and Sinquefield performance results clearly document this risk–return relationship. Remember, investment risk is the possibility that the actual return from an investment will differ from the expected return. Or, stated another way, the amount of investment risk depends on the degree to which a security is likely to fluctuate in price. Accordingly, you can gauge risk by estimating the probability that fluctuations of varying magnitudes will occur.

Earlier we relied on the law of probability to determine that in the long run the game of roulette is profitable for the dealer but not the player. Now let's apply that same law to security investments. No doubt you are now wondering, "How can I determine the probability that a security will fluctuate by a given amount?" Certainly stocks are more difficult to analyze because, unlike with the roulette wheel, there are more than thirty-eight possible outcomes, e.g., the stock's value a year from now can be at any one of innumerable prices—each of which has some (albeit typically small) probability of occurring.

Fortunately, the painstaking work of Ibbottson and Sinquefield takes much of the guesswork out of determining the probability of stock investment outcomes. We have already shown the historical returns for various asset categories, but these researchers went one giant step further when they computed the amount of historical risk associated with each asset group. A simple mathematical expression, known as the "standard deviation" of returns, provides information on both the probability and the magnitude of variations from the expected return. A standard deviation, therefore, measures the "average" volatility of a security's return. The larger the standard deviation the greater the risk, but typically also the greater the expected return.

Table 3 summarizes the historical returns and standard deviations detected by Ibbottson and Sinquefield from 1926 to 1981.

Table 3

Returns and Risk of Asset Categories
1926–1981

Category	Annual Return	Standard Deviation
Common stocks	9.1%	21.9%
Long-term corporate bonds	3.6	5.6
Long-term Treasury bonds	3.0	5.7
Treasury bills	3.0	3.1
Inflation	3.0	5.1

As you can clearly see, stocks provided the highest return, but at the greatest risk. Stocks had an average annual variability in returns of 21.9 percent. This means that, statistically speaking, stocks' prices may deviate in an "average" year by as much as 21.9 percent more or less than the average annual 9.1 percent return. Therefore, in a bad year stocks may lose 12.8 percent (9.1 percent minus 21.9 percent), but in a good year stocks may return 31 percent (9.1 percent plus 21.9 percent). Because the good and bad years, on average, cancel out, your long-run annual return in stocks equals exactly 9.1 percent.

On the other hand, Treasury bonds did not have as much risk as stocks, as indicated by their 5.7 percent standard deviation. But that lower risk translated to a much lower annual rate of return. In an average bad year your Treasury bond return would equal −2.7 percent (3.0 percent minus 5.7 percent), but in a typical good year you would earn only 8.7 percent (3.0 percent plus 5.7 percent). The net result: a compound annual return of only 3 percent—far inferior to stocks' 9.1 percent yearly gain. Even in a very good year, the return on a Treasury bond would not match an average year's return for common stocks.

Avoiding Foolish Risks

While taking calculated risks is a prudent way to enhance your investment performance, the acceptance of unnecessary risk is just the opposite. You take a risk every time you cross the street, but you don't take an unnecessary risk by stepping out in front of an oncoming bus and hoping the bus will stop. The same concept applies to investment risk. Taking a calculated risk is fine as long as you avoid the unnecessary risks. Yet most investors fail to achieve financial independence not because they refuse to bear risks but because they foolishly expose their assets to unnecessary risks.

The high rates of return on common stocks reported by Ibbottson and Sinquefield were achieved by taking calculated risks; indeed, stocks had a considerably higher standard deviation than other investment alternatives. Equally important, however, is the notion that this stock portfolio was not exposed to unnecessary risks. In particular, the following three characteristics of the Ibbottson and Sinquefield stock portfolio combined to shelter the portfolio from unnecessary (and incredibly expensive) risks.

1. The portfolio, once constructed, remained relatively static. Individual stocks were not actively "bought" and "sold." This feature prevents the portfolio from falling victim to various fads, manias, and speculative binges.

2. The portfolio consisted of many different stocks so that the occasional "dog" would be offset by the stellar performer. Too few stocks in a portfolio opens the possibility of that occasional dog's dominating the entire portfolio's performance.

3. The portfolio's performance was gauged over the long run so that the full-return capabilities of stocks could be captured. Both good and bad years occurred, but these unusual years averaged out so that overall stocks returned a high compound annual return.

Had the stock portfolio not adhered to these three factors, the portfolio's standard deviation would probably have been higher with no associated increase (and probably a decrease) in the rate of return. Each of these characteristics is crucial to your investment survival. Fortunately, Hyperprofits incorporates each of these features in designing the best investment strategy for you. Let's now observe how disastrous unnecessary risks can be to your investment performance and, more importantly, how the adherence to Hyperprofits automatically protects you from those foolish risks.

Who's Left Holding the Tulip Bulb?

Investors are only human and, as such, suffer human failings. One of the greatest of these human deficiencies, at least in regard to investing, is the tendency to follow the actions of the crowd. This kind of crowd psychology often leads otherwise rational investors to abandon all logic and fanatically enter a game of "psychic" investing. Tempted by the promise of riches, these investors forget the intrinsic worth of an investment. What's really important is participating in the action. After all, if the crowd approves, the investment must have substantial merit. But these fads are like investment black holes— just waiting to suck in anyone who becomes involved.

History teaches a convincing lesson about following crowd psychology, namely that crowds tend to violently overreact. When a crowd deems a particular item to be "fashionable," then mass hysteria often ensues. Everyone wants in on the action and, as a result, prices skyrocket to unconscionable (and, we might add, unsustainable) heights. Investment merits have long since been discounted; now only a kind of psychic phenomenon precariously props the price at such a pinnacle. Unjustifiably high prices may persist for months, even years, but typically just when the masses have rationalized these lofty price levels, the price plummets with the intensity of a falling meteor. Few participants escape these reversals without suffering astronomical financial losses. And the more frenetic the binge, the more disastrous the fall.

Speculative binges, fueled by greedy investors striving to get rich quick, have tempted investors for centuries. Charles Mackay captured the essence of crowd hysteria in his 1841 epic, aptly entitled *Extraordinary Popular Delusions and the Madness of Crowds,* by describing the events of the great tulip bulb mania of 1634–38. During that period, certain rare strains of tulip bulbs became enormously popular in Holland, causing rich and poor alike to engage in heroic efforts in attempts to acquire these fashionable items. No self-respecting Dutch family would be caught without a tulip bulb portfolio.

The ensuing frenzy drove tulip bulb prices skyward. Skeptics gradually became believers as tulip prices rapidly escalated. The "easy" profits were just too tempting to resist. Over this period the rarest variety, the now infamous Semper Augustus, soared from a paltry 50 florins to an astonishing 5,500 florins—a *10,900* percent increase! Tulipmania existed in epidemic proportions. Everyone believed that a new tulip buyer could always be found and at a higher price. And indeed this phenomenon did continue for several years. No matter what price you paid, someone always seemed eager to pay an even higher one. After all, if the bulb's price went from 1,000 to 2,000 florins, what's to stop it from rising to 3,000 or even 4,000 florins?

But unsuspecting investors, as is the case with most speculative crazes, failed to realize that at some point all the buyers would be gone. If everyone already owns tulips, who's left to buy at higher prices? Finally some investors realized the market was saturated and decided to sell. Soon others followed. As a result, tulip prices plummeted at an ever increasing pace. Almost overnight, the bloom vanished from the tulipmania and public panic abounded. Families saw their entire fortunes wilt before their very eyes. So severe was the great tulip bulb crash that it forced Holland into a prolonged depression.

Okay, now we've convinced you not to pay exorbitant prices for tulip bulbs. "So what?" you say. You've never owned a tulip bulb, you think they're ugly, and you have a severe allergic reaction to them.

Please consider that our message is directed at speculative crazes, not just tulip bulbs. And please remember that speculative madness is not confined to the seventeenth-century Dutch nor is it confined to the ignorant. Sir Isaac Newton, most noted for his formulation of the law of universal gravitation, lost a considerable sum when participating in a speculative mania.[3] His losses led him to discover that the principle of gravity was not confined to heavenly bodies. Indeed, prices propped up merely by psychic support invariably succumb to the financial laws of gravity. Or, as a financially humbled Newton exclaimed, "I can calculate the motions of heavenly bodies, but not the madness of people." Hopefully, the tulip bulb binge vividly illustrates what happens when otherwise sane investors lose control and fall victim to crowd hysteria.

[3] Sir Isaac fell victim to the South Sea Company speculative binge. Shares of this company (organized to explore for New World riches) skyrocketed from 120 pounds in April 1720 to over 1,000 pounds in July 1720. By year's end, however, the company lay in ruins and its shares were worthless.

Efficient Markets and
Investor Psychology

Surely, today's investors are not so gullible as to fall prey to another tulipmania. Investors are currently more informed and sophisticated than their seventeenth-century counterparts. In fact, the business of investing has become so fiercely competitive that some observers contend that all securities are fairly valued. The legions of highly trained M.B.A.s and other investment gurus who migrate to Wall Street so carefully analyze securities that they make the market "efficient." This is because undervalued investments are so sought after that, once found, their prices are quickly bid up by eager purchasers seeking to earn a profit. On the other hand, overvalued investments are so avoided that their prices decline until they are no longer too highly priced. Because of the intense competition among skillful buyers and sellers, these adjustments occur very rapidly.

The implications of this efficient market theory are striking: securities are priced "fairly" and thus an investor cannot make above-average profits unless he takes above-average risks. Efficient markets imply a direct return–risk relationship: the higher the desired return, the greater the risk that the actual return will not be what you desired. The now well-known "beta" factor, named after the second letter in the Greek alphabet, was developed to gauge the risk of a security. A beta of 1 designates a stock with average price fluctuations comparable to those of the overall stock market, while a beta larger than 1 indicates price volatility that is greater than the market's (vice versa for a beta less than 1).

Efficient-market disciples claim that the intense competition among investors causes securities to be fairly priced. They further assert that the increased presence of large financial institutions with their hordes of skillful security analysts leads to more efficiency. The eyes and ears of numerous security analysts, each actively seeking out mispriced situations, cause security prices to move toward some consensus value. In the absence of these market participants, public investment information would not be acted upon as quickly and security prices would be slow to respond. But as long as security analysts rapidly and accurately react to all pertinent news, securities will be fairly priced. In that event, there is no need for individuals to spend time and effort in seeking out undervalued securities: they simply don't exist.

The efficient-market theory has sobering implications to investors. If, indeed, the securities markets really are efficient, then in the long run you won't be able to earn superior returns and you might as well stop reading this book. The key question becomes, How effective and rational are security analysts and investors in detecting undervalued and overvalued stocks? Can't even the best trained and most experienced analyst fall victim to occasionally following the crowd? If so, then the markets can't always be efficient and you should continue reading.

Benjamin Graham, appropriately designated the father of security analysis, argued rather convincingly against the complete efficiency of markets. In his 1949 classic *The Intelligent Investor,* Graham concluded that even professional investors are susceptible to following the leader and, in the process, tend to overreact to future corporate prospects. These analysts, therefore, often engage in the same type of psychic investing that the tulip bulb freaks pursued centuries ago. These experts still rally around the most favorably viewed stocks, frequently chasing those coveted issues to exorbitant prices based on the premise that another buyer can always be found at an even higher level. Meanwhile, the stocks considered least attractive are relegated to an investors' graveyard— to be avoided regardless of price.

Graham's overreaction theory directly contradicts the much publicized efficient-market theory. So who's right? A look at recent stock market history provides a clue.

Modern-Day Tulip Bulbs

Admittedly, tulipmania is a thing of the distant past. A recurrence of this speculative binge is highly unlikely, but one thing is sure: other investment manias will continue to happen and, just like the tulip craze, cruelly part unsuspecting investors from their money. You find that hard to believe? How could today's sophisticated investors be so naïve? Well, a recent example may convince you that investors still have human desires and thus are susceptible to almost any kind of investment scheme or fad.

During 1971–72, American financial institutions (primarily bank trust departments, large pension funds, mutual funds, and the like) singled out approximately fifty large growth companies and engaged in a titanic buying warfare for those precious securities. Prices of these so-called nifty fifty growth stocks soared to dizzying heights. In 1972, the shares of Avon, Disney, and Polaroid, to name a few, all sold at prices in excess of eighty times earnings. That's right, the experts paid over $80 to acquire a single dollar of earning power. At one point the total market value of Avon exceeded that of the entire domestic steel industry. Sound excessive? Only two years earlier, the average price–earnings ratio (known as the P/E ratio) for these same stocks was less than twenty times. Obviously a speculative excess had occurred. But it would have been undignified to own anything else and, besides, you would have looked foolish if you hadn't gotten in on the action. Investors became convinced that only through the nifty fifty could one achieve lasting financial success. How could anyone lose money by owning shares of such high-quality and fast-growing corporations?

Of course, you can probably guess what happened to this modern-day speculative binge. The collapse of the nifty fifty was as sudden and cruel as the tulip bulb descent. By 1974, such popular growth stocks as Avon, Disney, and Polaroid had lost more than 80 percent of their peak market values. Even regal IBM, the epitome of the "one-decision" stock (you only decide when to buy them, never when to sell), had more than half its market value lopped off.

The experience of the 1970s suggests that just possibly the experts aren't always fully rational in their investment activities: even Wall Street can become so greedy that it chases a fad beyond the realm of reasonableness. However, the efficient-market theory rests firmly on the assumption that investors do always respond rationally and rapidly to any relevant news and, in so doing, force prices to their fair values. But, as one perplexed manager put it, "If markets are so efficient, at what price was Polaroid fairly valued? At 149½ in 1972 or at 14 in 1974?"

The rise and fall of the nifty fifty vividly portrays the risks of driving prices to extremes, no matter how attractive the underlying company. Speculative bubbles will continue to occur and in each instance will be suddenly burst.

As we document in later chapters, Hyperprofits is built on a foundation that specifically avoids investment fads and manias. In fact, the three pillars of Hyperprofits force you to buy only those stocks which are out of favor—yes, those which Graham considered to be relegated to the investors' graveyard. You won't be popular at cocktail parties because you won't be in on the latest investment fad. To the contrary, your portfolio will consist of many out-of-vogue stocks—certainly not a way to be the life of the party. But be patient, because when your stocks do become fashionable (and invariably they always do), you will reap financial rewards that will more than compensate for your cocktail party boredom. The risk of buying a stock at the peak of its speculative spiral is one which you must not tolerate. Such unnecessary risks, if taken, can destroy your investment results. Hyperprofits, however, ensures that you won't expose your financial resources to this foolish risk.

Diversify, Diversify, Diversify

You may have heard about the three most important ingredients in determining the investment worthiness of a parcel of real estate: location, location, location. Well, diversification is just as important to your financial success as location is to selecting attractive real estate.

Even the most ideal investment strategy will eventually produce a "loser," and the best way to guard against a loser's crippling your investment performance is to diversify. Simply stated, diversification means "Don't put all your eggs in one basket." Spread your investment dollars across several different stocks so that if one stock performs poorly, the others can come to the rescue. And, furthermore, proper diversification requires that the stocks you acquire be subject to different economic, social, and political risks. For instance, a portfolio of ten different oil stocks does not provide adequate diversification. As we have seen, if oil prices drop unexpectedly, all oil stocks fall. In fact, the proper choice of basically unrelated stocks may be more important than how many issues you own. A study by Richard Brealey, a finance professor at the London School of Economics, dramatically portrays the advantage of selective diversification. He documents that only eleven stocks, if properly selected for their diversification traits, would be less risky than a portfolio of 2,000 stocks randomly selected without regard to risk.

Diversification is a mandatory component of the Hyperprofits investment strategy. We readily admit that this strategy does not select only winners; some losers will emerge. Rather, Hyperprofits thrives on the ability to select proportionally more winners than losers. Therefore, if you are sufficiently diversified, your winners should easily compensate for some losers and still leave a handsome profit. We do not advocate the purchase of only one or two individual stocks. Who knows, either or both of those stocks could just be that occasional loser. Without diversification, such a loss has no chance to be offset by other, winning stocks.

You may be wondering, "How many different stocks must I own to be sufficiently diversified?" To respond to your query, we turn to a scholarly research effort by W. H. Wagner and S. C. Lau, published in the November-December 1971 issue of the *Financial Analysts Journal*. Their findings, based upon the performance of a large number of common stocks over an eleven year period, revealed that a portfolio consisting of only five unrelated stocks achieved approximately 79 percent of the diversification advantages of the entire stock market. A ten-stock portfolio was 85 percent "diversified" and a twenty-stock portfolio, 89 percent. These findings are most encouraging, particularly for the smallest investor. By purchasing as few as five unrelated stocks your portfolio will be substantially diversified. Of course, a ten- or twenty-stock portfolio achieves even more diversification.

Sounds simple, doesn't it? Even a five-stock portfolio can be highly diversified. Therefore, you would logically expect that everyone would practice the concept of diversification. Well, you are seriously mistaken. Three professors at the University of Pennsylvania's Wharton School discovered in a survey of federal income tax return data that over one third of stock-owning families in America held only one stock, and another 16 percent owned only two. That's right, approximately half of all individual stock portfolios contained only one or two stocks. Apparently many Americans subscribe to the all too familiar "Put all your eggs in one basket and watch the basket." But, unfortunately, most Americans aren't capable of properly watching that basket.

The above finding is certainly not a very strong testimony to the belief in and practice of diversification in America. But to ensure the long-run success of your investment program you must diversify. Look at it this way: by owning five or more different stocks you will be far more diversified than most. This factor alone will give you a meaningful head start compared to other investors, and, when combined with the Hyperprofits investment strategy, will enable you to reap significant financial rewards without the ultra high risk exposure of an undiversified portfolio.

Let us summarize our discussion of diversification by citing three important rules of diversification:

Rule 1: If you own stocks, make absolutely sure that your portfolio consists of at least five different issues and, whenever possible, the ownership of ten or more stocks is even better.

Rule 2: Purchase stocks whose risks are not highly related. This typically means buying the stocks of companies which participate in different industries. This rule is especially crucial if your portfolio contains very few issues.

Rule 3: Do not overdiversify. Except for the very largest portfolios, the advantages of diversification tend to disappear after you have acquired twenty to twenty-five different stocks. Beyond that number, your portfolio becomes unwieldly and you will experience extreme difficulty in following so many securities. Furthermore, it is far more difficult to select, for example, thirty excellent stocks than ten.

As you will see later, Hyperprofits incorporates all three of these rules and more to maximize your protection.

The Patience of Job

One thing that history has taught us is that stock prices do not march in the same direction forever. Bull markets eventually turn into bear markets and, conversely, bear markets also reverse. We shall illustrate this observation by returning to the comprehensive Ibbottson and Sinquefield performance results.

As you recall, common stocks provided a 9.1 percent compound annual return over the 1926–81 time period. Of course, you would not have earned that 9.1 percent every year—far from it. In fact, if you had purchased a market portfolio of stocks in 1926, you would have experienced a compound yearly return of −3.3 percent for the first seven years. The net effect: after seven years over 25 percent of your original funds would be lost. Such disastrous results would discourage even the most diehard investor. But here is where patience yields its rewards. The highest stock market returns typically occur immediately following a major bear market. Had you in your frustration abandoned the stock market in 1932, you would have missed several exceptionally profitable years of stock performance: 1933, +54 percent; 1935, +47.7 percent; and 1936, +33.9 percent (1934 was down 1.4 percent).

These high returns of the mid-1930s more than offset the losses experienced during the stock market crash of 1929–32. The compound annual return for stocks from 1926 to 1936 was an attractive 8.1 percent and that was over a period that encompassed the worst stock market decline in America's history! The message is clear: even the worst stock market decline will reverse. The patient investor profits in the long run.

Yes, risk, when prudently managed, does have its rewards. In the next chapters you will be exposed to a rewarding stock investment strategy which has been shown to produce handsome returns while at the same time carefully managing risks in order to provide you with the best risk-reward combination possible.

Building a Hyperprofits Foundation

We have shown that over the long run stocks have proved to be the right route to achieving financial rewards. But remember, even in the best of all possible markets, many stocks will not be big winners and, worse yet, some will even be losers. To illustrate just how dramatic this effect can be, consider the period July 1, 1982, to June 30, 1983. During that year, the average share on the New York Stock Exchange rose a resounding 58.2 percent, while on the neighboring American Stock Exchange the average share appreciated a staggering 81.0 percent.

You Can't Lose—or Can You?

By all accounts this was one of the most magnificent periods in stock market history. So any dummy can make big bucks in such a strong bull market, right? Well, before you jump to a conclusion take a look at the price performance of the stocks from ten different major industries over this same time period (Table 4).

Table 4

Price Performance of Stocks by Industry
July 1, 1982–June 30, 1983

Company	Industry	Price Change
Tony Lama	Shoe	−42.0%
Scope, Inc.	Electronics	−54.9%
Texon Energy	Investments	−57.1%
Pizza Time	Restaurant	−40.7%
Rich Tank Car	Freight	−48.1%
American Resource Management	Oil producing	−77.3%
Baldwin United	Insurance	−63.5%
Pettibone Corp.	Machinery	−38.8%
MGF Oil	Oil service	−71.9%
Warner Communications	Recreation	−38.1%
	Average	−53.2%

Amazing, isn't it? While the market was skyrocketing to scintillating heights, this diversified portfolio was plummeting a depressing 53 percent. What does this prove? It shows that even if the market's hotter than a fire-cracker, you can still get severely burned if you have not invested in the right stocks.

Blue Chips to the Rescue

"All right," you might say, "but these stocks are not exactly household names. What if I protect myself by investing only in well-known, blue-chip stocks?" Good thought. Let's take a closer look. In 1983, the price of the 30 Dow Jones industrial stocks rose an average of 29.1 percent. Not too shabby. Now take a look at the list of stocks below. Do you recognize any of these? Of course you do. They are all well-known, large companies. Blue chips through and through.

Company	Industry
Digital Equipment	Computers
MCI Communications	Communications
Mary Kay Cosmetics	Cosmetics
Procter & Gamble	Soaps
Paine Webber	Brokerage
Pennzoil Co.	Oil
Eastman Kodak	Photography
Mattel, Inc.	Toys
AMF, Inc.	Sporting goods
Disney Studios	Motion picture
Tandy Corp.	TV distribution
Goodyear Tire	Tires

If your portfolio consisted of these stocks, you certainly ought to prosper in a buoyant market. After all, these are among the largest and most secure companies in America. What would you imagine the price appreciation of this portfolio was in 1983? Twenty percent, 30 percent, maybe even 40 percent? Not quite! Check Table 5 to see the results stock by stock. It's hard to believe, but every one of these industrial pillars lost value in 1983, averaging a pitiful −19 percent return in a good market year.

Table 5

Price Performance of Selected Blue Chips

Company	1983 Price Change
Digital Equipment	−28%
MCI Communications	−21%
Mary Kay Cosmetics	−39%
Procter & Gamble	−4%
Paine Webber	−11%

Pennzoil Co.	−3%
Eastman Kodak	−11%
Mattel, Inc.	−70%
AMF, Inc.	−2%
Disney Studios	−17%
Tandy Corp.	−15%
Goodyear Tire	−13%
Average	−19.5%

So not even the giant so-called superstars can completely protect you. Now can you see why it is absolutely imperative for you to invest in the *right* stocks even when the market is on your side? You need to be in the big winners, not the big companies, if you want to create wealth. This is precisely the purpose of Hyperprofits: to identify the winners for you. In this chapter you will begin your trek down the road to Hyperprofits. By the end of the chapter, you will understand the foundation on which Hyperprofits firmly rests. This foundation will enable you to see how and why Hyperprofits works. Armed with this knowledge, you will easily be able to learn and apply Hyperprofits to create wealth for you.

Wall Street Revolution

During the 1970s a startling development burst onto the investment scene. This was the advent of the low-P/E investment strategy. We say startling because it turned traditional investment thinking upside down. But before we show you why, let us digress for a moment. First, what is a P/E, and, more important, what is the low-P/E strategy? A P/E is the simple ratio of a stock's current market price divided by its company's earnings per share for the past year. So the P/E ratio is a stock's price in relation to the underlying company's earnings per share. It is also known as the earnings multiple.

The low-P/E investment strategy simply says to buy stocks whose P/E ratios are *low,* the lower the better. What's so startling about this? The fact is that this strategy runs completely contrary to traditional investment philosophy. The established thinking has always been to buy the stocks of the fastest growing companies—the ones whose earnings are most likely to expand at a rapid pace. But the experts readily identify and purchase the shares of these growing entities. Therefore, as you would expect, the shares of the companies with the brightest prospects often sell at prices that are high in relation to current earnings, i.e., high earnings multiples. So the traditional story line reads: If you want high price appreciation, then buy high P/Es, the "growth" stocks.

Growth Company or Growth Stock?

If asked the question, "Would you prefer to invest your money in a fast-growing or a slow-growing company," how would you respond? If you're like most Americans, you would select the fast-growth alternative without hesitation. That's exactly the question we recently presented to the senior undergraduate students in one of our investments courses at Southern Methodist University. Their overwhelming choice? The fast-growth companies, of course. To complete our survey, we posed the same question to several of our older investing friends. "Fast growth," they readily replied.

How would you respond? If you recall the message in the previous chapter, you would probably answer something like the following: "I'm not concerned whether I buy the stock of a fast- or a slow-growth company. To the contrary, my overriding concern is to buy an *undervalued* stock, no matter whether it be that of a fast- or slow-growth company." If indeed that was your answer, then mark yourself a perfect score. You're well on your way toward Hyperprofits!

That very question helps explain the basis for the Hyperprofits system of investing. Hyperprofits strives to select growth stocks, not growth companies. What's the difference? A lot! Upon your ability to distinguish between these two growth categories rests your entire financial future. Enough said? Then let's proceed onward.

As a matter of record, let's provide a couple of important definitions.

Growth company: A company whose sales and earnings are expected to increase at a rate in excess of that of the average company.

Growth stock: A stock whose market price is expected to increase at a rate in excess of that of the average stock.

Now you see the difference. What you really desire is a growth stock, not a growth company. This is very important because growth companies are not necessarily growth stocks. Why? Because many investors in their haste to acquire the stocks of growth companies drive the prices of those stocks to lofty levels. Remember the nifty fifty in the 1970s. Growth companies but certainly not growth stocks. Ben Graham was aware of the risks involved in paying too much for the stock of even the fastest-growing company. In fact, he widely touted the merits of investing in undervalued (growth) stocks, not growth companies. But, at the same time, he realized that most investors would not follow his advice. And he was right.

Those Coveted High Multiples

You probably recall that a P/E is also known as an earnings multiple because it represents the number of times (or multiple) that a stock's price exceeds the company's earnings per share. We shall now explain why the magnitude of these multiples is so crucial to your investment success.

The emphasis many investors place on earnings growth in selecting stocks often results in the earnings multiples of growth companies becoming very large when compared to the P/Es of average or slow-growth companies. When investors flock to those high-growth companies, they can't help but drive the prices (and thus the P/E ratios) of those coveted issues to lofty heights.

The notion that high-P/E stocks are the ones on which to build a fortune seems almost self-evident to many investors. Consider the two groups of stocks listed in Table 6. As of January 1, 1984, the group on the left had high earnings multiples while the group on the right had low P/Es. Which of these two groups of stocks do you think most investors would stake their hard-earned dollars on, the high- or the low-P/E group? Who in his or her right mind would be crazy enough to risk precious savings on those low multiple stocks which no one's heard of (much less cares about) when they could just as easily grab hold of the coattails of those glamorous high-P/E giants with outstanding earnings growth prospects. Well, to tell you the truth, at one time we certainly wouldn't have gone for the low P/Es. But that was before the revolution.

Table 6

High- and Low-P/E Stocks

High P/Es	Low P/Es
Motorola	Teleconcepts
Black & Decker	Webcor
RCA	Technical Tape
International Paper	Grolier Publishing
Wal-Mart	Thor Corp.
Weyerhaeuser	Buell Industries
Georgia Pacific	Susquehanna
Burroughs Corp.	Turner Construction
Wang Labs	Vinco Manufacturing
Union Carbide	Andal Corp.
Sony Corp.	Stepan Chemical
Dr. Pepper	Century Telephone
Hewlett-Packard	American Israeli
Polaroid Corp.	Sandgate Corp.

Science and the Superstars

Hold on to your hat. The shocking truth is that, on the average, low-P/E stocks yield much higher profit returns than high P/Es. Much higher! How much higher? Let us cite just one example for openers. We called upon our computer to analyze the performance of 125 diverse common stocks from the beginning of 1970 to the end of 1980. These stocks were arranged into five separate portfolios, or quintiles, ranked according to their P/E magnitude. The first quintile contains the lowest 20 percent of P/Es; the fifth quintile, the highest. We noticed that the stocks of some industries tended to cluster in specific quintiles (for example, banks in the low-P/E quintile and electronics in the high-P/E quintile)—a problem which we remedy in the next chapter.

Portfolios were adjusted at the end of each year to reflect shifts in P/E rankings. Thus, for example, if a stock's earnings multiple increased beyond the boundaries of its group, that stock would be "sold" at year end and replaced with the lowest-multiple issue from the next highest quintile. The "sold" stock would then advance to a higher-P/E quintile and be "bought" for that portfolio. Table 7 presents the annual return, and average P/Es.

Table 7

Annual Returns of Low- and High-P/E Stocks

	Low P/E Quintile 1	High P/E Quintile 5	Total Portfolio
Annual return	19.8%	4.1%	9.0%
Average P/E	7.0×	20.8×	12.6×

As we said, the widely touted investment axiom contends that a P/E ratio is no more than a barometer gauging collective investor expectations regarding a stock's outlook. The higher the multiple, the more favorable the prospects. Then doesn't it follow that securities in the first quintile receive low multiples because investors envision less than desirable prospects for those issues? One would certainly think so.

But how perceptive are these investors? A look at our table provides a surprising answer. The lowest-P/E portfolio provided a remarkable 19.8 percent compound annual return over the selected period, far exceeding the relatively meager 4.1 percent compound yearly return of the highest-multiple group.

These findings may come as sacrilege to investment disciples who preach a strategy of accumulating only the securities of highly visible companies with superior earnings prospects. But often too many disciples worship too few stocks. The implication is obvious. Those sacrosanct issues may be driven to heavenly heights, while the cast-outs languish in an investor purgatory.

In the Beginning

But this is merely the beginning. Although the low-multiple investment strategy was popularized in the 1970s, evidence of its validity came to light well before its acclaim. As early as 1960, an industrious bank vice-president named Francis Nicholson uncovered the high profit potential of low-P/E stocks. Of course, 1960 was like prehistoric days as far as computers are concerned. Nicholson, working without benefit of a computer, followed the price appreciation of 100 industrial stocks from 1939 to 1959. He divided the stocks according to their P/E ratios into five groups of twenty. He then kept track of their performance over separate five-, ten-, fifteen-, and twenty-year periods.

Table 8 shows what he found. In every time period tested, the low-multiple stocks beat not only the averages but all other categories as well. If you had held the low group from 1939 to 1959, for example, you would have earned a whopping 1,175 percent on your investment. Not bad! Meanwhile the so-called growth companies, the high-multiple group, earned 542 percent, less than half the low-P/Es' return.

Computer to the Rescue

There it was, solid evidence for the performance of the low-P/E strategy sustained over a twenty-year history. But who paid any attention to it? Certainly not most investors. However, James McWilliams, an investment officer at a Chicago bank, took heed, even if no one else did. In 1966, McWilliams, armed with the latest in high-powered computers of the day, set out to determine whether Nicholson was right. He utilized a much larger sample of companies, 390 in all, and tested performance from 1952 to 1964. Instead of five groups, McWilliams arranged the stocks into ten portfolios, or deciles, ranked in order of P/E ratios.

His results appear in Table 9. Although less spectacular, they confirm those of Nicholson. As you can see from the right-hand column, the lowest-multiple portfolio averaged 23 percent profit return per year, higher than that of any other group.

Now this is important. McWilliams also showed what would have happened to $10,000 invested in each portfolio over the twelve-year period. For instance, Portfolio 5 averaged 16 percent appreciation per year. After twelve years, the $10,000 initial investment would have grown to $51,000. Next consider Portfolio 1, the lowest-P/E group. We have already seen that it yielded an average profit return of 23 percent per year, a little less than one and one half

Table 8

Price Appreciation by Price-Earnings Groups:

	1939–1944	1939–1949	1939–1954	1939–1959	1944–1949	1944–1954	1944–1959	1949–1954	1949–1959	1954–1959	1957–1959
Price-earnings ratios at beginning of each period	%	%	%	%	%	%	%	%	%	%	%
Lowest 20 P/E ratios	48	102	444	1,175	56	307	691	188	470	123	56
Next lowest 20 P/E ratios	16	76	237	524	37	238	540	91	273	95	42
Middle 20 P/E ratios	–5	25	114	329	36	152	570	122	328	88	40
Next highest 20 P/E ratios	–4	18	140	378	26	100	305	84	291	79	26
Highest 20 P/E ratios	5	43	206	542	33	156	508	51	273	115	39
Average for 100 stocks	12	53	228	589	38	191	523	107	327	100	40

Source: Francis Nicholson, "Price-Earnings Ratio," *Financial Analysts Journal*, July–August 1960.

Table 9

Average Returns by P/E Deciles

P/E Deciles	1964*	1963	1962	1961	1960	1959	1958	1957	1956	1955	1954	1953	Average Return
Low 1	20%	12%	15%	28%	2%	64%	−5%	8%	27%	68%	25%	15%	23%
2	21	8	5	27	0	66	−9	4	25	77	11	24	22
3	21	12	2	28	−2	53	−4	6	21	61	10	15	18
4	22	9	3	24	−0	67	1	2	20	51	20	17	20
5	19	4	− 2	28	−2	52	−3	1	24	49	12	9	16
6	12	2	− 1	27	−4	39	−1	2	24	42	14	9	14
7	11	5	− 1	23	1	51	2	8	19	43	21	12	16
8	17	5	− 6	32	−4	43	−2	9	21	41	12	11	15
9	14	1	− 6	29	−5	47	−2	3	31	35	10	9	14
High 10	27	7	− 12	20	−1	65	−5	−1	28	43	10	8	15
Average return	19	6	0	27	−1	55	−3	4	24	51	14	13	17

* Years ending April 30.

Source: James McWilliams, "Prices, Earnings, and P-E Ratios," *Financial Analysts Journal*, May–June 1966.

times the highest-P/E group. Therefore, the low-P/E portfolio should have accumulated one and one half times $51,000, or around $75,000, right? Well, the fact is that the value of the low-multiple portfolio actually catapulted to a lofty $103,000, more than double the figure for Portfolio 5.

You say how can this be so when there's only about a 50 percent difference in annual rate of return. You already know the answer because you read about it in Chapter 1. That's right, the magic of compounding enabled the lowest-P/E portfolio to show such attractive results. Compounding can turn a small percentage advantage into a colossal monetary advantage. Remember this point, because, as you will see, here's where Hyperprofits spells the difference between merely turning a tidy profit and generating a real fortune for you.

What About Risk?

For most investors like us, these studies would surely demonstrate proof that the low-P/E strategy really works. But no, not for some doubting Thomases in the academic community. They still didn't believe it. Their argument ran like this. Maybe low-multiple stocks do beat the market, but, if so, it's only because they're riskier. If they're riskier, it's only fair that the investor should be paid more in the form of higher profit returns for shouldering the burden of this risk. If somehow this extra profit for risk-bearing were removed, then low-P/E stocks would be no better than any others. So went the argument.

Enter an enterprising professor with the uncommon name Sanjoy (Joe) Basu. In 1977, he designed a very scientific test of the performance of low-P/E stocks including a method for dealing with risk. Basu took an even bigger sample, 753 industrials, all traded on the New York Stock Exchange. He studied them over the fourteen-year period from 1956 to 1969.

At the beginning of each year, Basu sorted all stocks by their P/E ratios and arranged them into five equal portfolios. After ranking all stocks from highest to lowest P/E, Quintile 1 was constructed to contain the highest 20 percent of P/Es, Quintile 2 the next highest 20 percent, and so on. Each year the stocks were re-sorted to form the five portfolios again. Basu accumulated the profit returns for each year into the respective quintile groups.

Now for the most important part. Recall that the argument against the previous test results was that risk was not taken into account. Basu countered this by utilizing the risk index called beta. You may recall from Chapter 2 that the average stock has a beta-risk index of 1. Highly risky stocks have indexes greater than 1, while low-risk stocks have indexes less than 1.

Basu kept track of the beta-risk indexes of all stocks entering each P/E portfolio. At the end of the experiment, he was able to report not only the profit return of each portfolio but also the average risk index for the portfolio as well. So we should be able to find out not only if the low-multiple strategy beats the market but also how risky these stocks are. And what are these results? Take a look for yourself at Table 10, which summarizes Basu's historic study.

Table 10

Return and Risk for P/E Portfolios
Basu Study
P/E Portfolios

	Quintile				
	1	2	3	4	5
Median P/E ratio	35.8	19.1	15.0	12.8	9.8
Average annual profit percentage	9.34	9.28	11.65	13.55	16.30
Average Risk index	1.11	1.04	.97	.94	.99

Source: S. Basu, "Investment Performance of Common Stocks in Relation to their Price Earnings Ratios: A Test of the Efficient Market Hypothesis," *The Journal of Finance*, June 1977.

What a result! Not only did the low-P/E stocks produce higher profit returns, but they did it at slightly lower than average risk and certainly much lower risk than the high-P/Es. The average high-multiple stock produced a beta-risk index of 1.11 and yielded a 9.34 percent annual profit. Meanwhile the low-multiple counterparts with a .99 risk index yielded a handsome 16.30 percent annual profit. So not only do low-P/E stocks generate more profit than the glorious high-P/E growth companies, they do it at lower risk to the investor to boot. This is the best of all possible worlds. Remember what the McWilliams results showed about compounding. Correspondingly, the difference between 9 and 16 percent compounded over a period of years can produce a material difference in the thickness of your wallet.

Stock researchers were left in a state of shock. They were prepared to believe that you could make more money on one stock than another if you were willing to take a higher risk. But to make more money at a lower risk is like living in a fantasy world, and everyone knows that Wall Street is no Disneyland. To add insult to injury, the sacrosanct high-multiple growth stocks all along were producing lower profits at high risk. What was the world coming to? Could it really be that the smart money is riding on Teleconcepts and the dumb money on RCA? Could it really be that for these many years the stock experts didn't know what they were talking about?

Seeing Is Believing

You say you're still a bit skeptical. All right, then let Marc Reinganum, a finance professor at the University of Southern California, do his number on you. Playing devil's advocate, some skeptics cited the fact that Basu introduced a bias by using only the large New York Stock Exchange companies in his test. He thus neglected the smaller, less established companies. Professor Reinganum rectified this situation by using a sample of 1,200 companies drawn from both the Big Board and the much smaller American Stock Exchange. He even went so far as to calculate the profit returns on a daily basis over the fifteen-year period 1963 to 1977. His convincing results appear in Table 11.

Table 11

Return and Risk for P/E Portfolios
Reinganum Study

P/E Portfolio	Daily Return Relative to the Average*	Risk Index (Beta)
Highest 1	−.124%	1.12
2	−.176	1.00
3	−.227	.96
4	−.209	.90
5	−.109	.90

P/E Portfolio	Daily Return Relative to the Average*	Risk Index (Beta)
6	−.147	.83
7	−.070	.86
8	.058	.82
9	.103	.88
Lowest 10	.165	.95

* Multiplied by 100 for ease of observation.

Source: Marc Reinganum, "Misspecification of Capital Asset Pricing: Empirical Anomalies Based on Earnings, Yields and Market Values," *The Journal of Financial Economics*, March 1981.

The results are a little tricky to interpret since the profit returns are stated relative to the average return and are on a daily basis. A negative sign indicates profits lower than average, while positive is above average. The key thing to note is that the highest-P/E portfolio yielded a significant negative return while the lowest P/Es provided the highest returns. So high P/Es produced below-average profits while low P/Es produced by far the highest profits of the ten portfolios. But what about risk? A quick look reveals that the high P/Es had the highest risk level of all portfolios with beta indexes of 1.12, while the low P/Es were below average in risk at a .95 index reading.

The Last Word

Here is independent confirmation of Basu's startling findings. Low P/Es have higher profit returns at lower risk than high P/Es. What about the current authors? Can we attest firsthand to the validity of the low-multiple strategy? Well, just for good measure we observed an even larger portfolio consisting of 2,600 companies from the beginning of 1970 to mid-1980. We included over-the-counter issues along with New York and American Exchange companies. Our findings put the icing on the cake (Table 12).

Table 12

Return and Risk for P/E Portfolios

Goodman and Peavy Study

	1	2	3	4	5
Average P/E	20.4	12.8	10.1	8.4	6.6
Average annual profit return (%)	2.21	5.53	8.76	11.35	16.24
Average beta risk	1.12	1.02	1.01	.97	.96

This caps it off. Low-P/E stocks earn higher profits than high-P/E stocks and the stock market in general. And they do it consistently over every time period tested. In our own research, we found that low-multiple stocks averaged an annual profit return of 16.24 percent. Over this same time horizon the Standard & Poor's 500 stocks averaged approximately 8 percent. So the low P/Es were about double the index. Further, the low-multiple stocks generated these attractive returns at lower-than-average risk. There's no doubt about it. The low-multiple strategy really works.

To Burst a Bubble

"All right," you might say, "I'm a believer. But if the low-multiple investment strategy is so great, why the next hundred pages of this book?" Good question. The answer is because the low-P/E investment strategy isn't perfect—far from it. It can make you some money for sure, but it won't make you financially independent. And, after all, that's what you're here for. So please read on, and we'll try to make the experience an enjoyable as well as profitable one for you.

Now let's look a little closer at this. Our extensive P/E test using the 2,600 companies showed that over an extended period of time the low-multiple portfolio yielded an average yearly profit return of approximately 16 percent. Meanwhile, a typical Hyperprofits portfolio over the same time period generated an average annual profit of about 32 percent. "Great," you say, "so Hyperprofits will make me twice as much money as the low-multiple strategy will."

Nope, not even close. Remember the McWilliams example presented earlier in the chapter.

Suppose you invested $10,000 at the same time in both the low-P/E strategy and Hyperprofits. Assuming constant growth rates of 16 percent and 32 percent, respectively, how would your estate grow over the next fifteen years? Table 13 answers your question.

Table 13

Performance of Low-P/E and Hyperprofits Portfolios

Year	Low P/E	Hyperprofits
1	$11,600	$13,200
2	13,456	17,424
3	15,609	22,999
4	18,106	30,359
5	21,003	40,075
6	24,364	52,899
7	28,262	69,826
8	32,784	92,170
9	38,030	121,665
10	44,114	160,598
11	51,172	211,989
12	59,360	279,826
13	68,857	369,370
14	79,875	487,568
15	92,654	643,590

For the low-multiple strategy, you would end up with a tidy estate worth $92,654. Not bad! Now for Hyperprofits. By the end of those same fifteen years your estate would have skyrocketed to the awesome total of $643,590. So instead of merely doubling your money, Hyperprofits would have garnered nearly seven times as much as the low-P/E strategy. What an incredible difference! How is this possible? That's right, the magic of compounding.

Putting Your Eggs in One Basket

This is all well and fine, but then why have we spent all this time learning about the low-P/E strategy? Recall that at the beginning of the chapter, we said that you would learn the foundation of Hyperprofits. Further, this foundation would enable you to understand how and why Hyperprofits really works. Well, we weren't fibbing because the low-P/E investment strategy *is* the foundation for Hyperprofits. We developed Hyperprofits using the low-multiple strategy as our starting point.

How did we go about it? We started by realizing that the low-P/E strategy was *the* one sound and profitable investment strategy which was solidly proven to work. But can it make more money? Could there be something wrong or something missing? If so, what could it be?

Ultimately, we detected three shortfalls which could be remedied by the three pillars of Hyperprofits. We proceeded to really investigate the low-multiple strategy. The first thing we discovered was that the low-P/E stocks had a strong tendency to cluster together in a few industry groups. That is, in some industries a great majority of stocks have high multiples while in other industries nearly all the stocks may have low multiples.

Let us illustrate. The well-known *The Value Line Investment Survey* lists the 100 lowest-P/E stocks each week (excluding public utilities). We took a recent issue and examined the 50 lowest-P/E stocks. Table 14 shows these low-P/E stocks and their corresponding industries.

Table 14

The Fifty Lowest-P/E Stocks

Stock Name	P/E Ratio	Industry Group
Grolier Inc.	1.5	Publishing
Atlas Corp.	1.8	Coal, uranium
De Beers Consol.	2.1	Gold, diamonds

Stock Name	P/E Ratio	Industry Group
Tosco Corp.	2.3	Petroleum
Borman's, Inc.	2.6	Grocery store
Tubos De Acero (ADR)	2.7	Foreign stocks
Northwest Industries	2.8	Multiform
Algoma Steel	3.0	Steel
Global Marine	3.0	Oilfield services
Massey-Ferguson	3.0	Agricultural equipment
Chemical New York	3.1	Bank
First Wisconsin Corp.	3.1	Bank
Zapata Corp.	3.1	Oilfield services
NL Industries, Inc.	3.2	Oilfield services
Rowan Cos.	3.2	Oilfield services
Salant Corp.	3.2	Apparel
Southmark Corp.	3.2	R.E.I.T.
Anglo Energy Ltd.	3.3	Oilfield services
Fidelcor, Inc.	3.3	Bank
United Energy Resources, Inc.	3.3	Natural gas
Anglo American	3.4	Gold, diamonds
Bankers Trust NY Corp.	3.4	Bank
Cameron Iron Works	3.4	Oilfield services
Leucadia National Corp.	3.4	Finance
McDermott, Inc.	3.4	Oilfield services
Nortek, Inc.	3.4	Unassigned
Puritan Fashions	3.4	Apparel
Swift Independent	3.4	Food processing

Blyvoor Gold ADR	3.5	Gold, diamonds
Irving Bank Corp.	3.5	Bank
Marine Midland Banks	3.5	Bank
NBD Bancorp, Inc.	3.5	Bank
Royal Dutch Petroleum	3.5	Petroleum
Security Pacific Corp.	3.5	Bank
Wells Fargo & Co.	3.5	Bank
Ameron, Inc.	3.6	Building
CCI Corp.	3.6	Multiform
Gen'l Bancshares	3.6	Bank
Manufacturers Hanover	3.6	Bank
Maryland National	3.6	Bank
Phila. Nat'l Corp.	3.6	Bank
United Jersey Banks	3.6	Bank
Alaska Airlines	3.7	Air transport
First Interstate BNCP	3.7	Bank
First Nat'l Boston Corp.	3.7	Bank
First Nat'l St. Bancorp	3.7	Bank
Fremont General	3.7	Insurance
Girard Co.	3.7	Bank
Offshore Logistics	3.7	Oilfield services
Parker Drilling	3.7	Oilfield services

Source: The Value Line Investment Survey.

Note that you can count no fewer than eighteen banks out of the fifty. That's 36 percent of the lowest fifty P/Es. Out of ninety-three industries listed, 36 percent of the low P/Es fall into just one of those industries. Now take a look at oilfield services. You will find nine of these, or 18 percent of the total. So the combined banks and oilfield services stocks account for well over half the low P/Es. If the typically low multiple utilities had been included, the industry clustering would be even worse. This means that if you were to select a portfolio of low-P/E stocks, you might wind up with over half your stocks in just two industries—a lousy way to diversify.

Let's take a further illustration of how dramatic the grouping of P/Es into industries really is. As of the beginning of 1984, the average P/E ratio for all twenty-three machine tool and accessory stocks as reported by *The Media General Financial Weekly* was an astronomical 107.9. The lowest P/E in the group belonged to Ex-Cell-O Corp. at a relatively tame 13.4. Now at this very same point in time, the average P/E for seventy-five electric utilities was a meager 6.4. Nevada Power sported the very highest multiple among these at 10.8. So the highest P/E in the entire electric utility industry was lower than the lowest P/E in the machine-tool industry. A low-P/E portfolio composed from these groups would not contain a single machine-tool stock.

You can certainly see how strongly P/Es tend to cluster by industry. But so what? What does this have to do with your wealth-building program? The answer is plenty. For one thing, buying into a low-P/E portfolio can be like putting a lot of your eggs in one basket. If your portfolio is heavily weighted toward one industry, then your fate rides on just how well that one industry performs. You don't have diversification to protect you against disasters. This can be highly risky.

Remember Three Mile Island? Suppose you were heavily invested in public utility stocks. When the crunch hit, where would you be? It would be devastating, to say the least. Because when the news of the Three Mile Island nuclear disaster hit, all utility stocks suffered. These repercussions would wreak havoc on a low-P/E portfolio selected without regard to the principle of diversification.

Lest you think that only bizarre occurrences like the Three Mile Island debacle can spell trouble for a portfolio heavily concentrated in a single industry, consider what happened in a relatively tranquil year like 1983. On January 1, 1983, three of the lowest-multiple ratio industries were communications, oil and gas services, and electric utilities. Suppose you had composed a low-P/E portfolio "diversified" among these three industries. How would you have fared during 1983? As a measure of comparison, the Media General index of 3,112 stocks showed an average price appreciation of 18.5 percent for the year. Not a bad year for investors.

What about our three-industry low-P/E portfolio? Well, for openers, oil and gas services came in at a paltry 6.3 percent price appreciation for the year.

And this was the winner of the bunch. From there on it was downhill. Communications staggered in at 4.4 percent, while to top it off (or should we say bottom it out), the average electric utility climbed a yawning 1.3 percent. So if you had put equal dollar amounts into stocks of these three industries, you would have garnered an uninspiring 4.0 percent return. Just to put this in perspective, if you had selected your portfolio by throwing darts at the financial page instead of using the low-P/E method, you would have earned over four times as much.

This just illustrates what can happen with a low-P/E portfolio that clusters your holdings into a few industries. If those industries don't perform, you're out of luck. So in our research to uncover the deficiencies of the low-P/E strategy, this was our first important finding. Low-P/E stocks tend to aggregate by industry. In the next chapter, we will show how to overcome this problem and increase your profits.

But before moving on, we need to point out two other limitations of the low-P/E strategy. Remember, as we have documented, the low-multiple strategy works well, certainly better than the market average. But you're not looking for something that works well. You're looking to achieve financial independence. That's why we feel it's necessary to dissect the low-P/E strategy.

When a Low P/E Is Not a Low P/E

Having found one barrier to overcome, we attempted to determine whether any other deficiencies existed. And, sure enough, we eventually discovered a second major shortcoming of the low-P/E strategy. We were perplexed as to why some low-P/E stocks did so well while others performed poorly. Our efforts revealed that some stocks persisted in having low P/Es over very long periods of time.

You know from our discussion earlier about Benjamin Graham that low-P/E stocks often tend to be underpriced because investors overreact on the negative side. Well, if investors have overreacted to some unfavorable news or expectations, then why should a P/E be consistently low over a long period of time? If, indeed, overreaction has set in, shouldn't the P/E eventually rebound to a normal level? Shouldn't sooner or later there be a correction to the overreaction? Since it is this very correction which gives the low-multiple stock an advantage over the run-of-the-mill stock, we figured that we should pursue this curiosity even further.

Could it be that if a stock has languished in the low-P/E doldrums for an extended period perhaps it wasn't the victim of overreaction to begin with?

Maybe the quality of the company and its prospects are such that the stock deserves to be in the low-P/E category and stay there. If so, how can we turn around and expect these stocks to be the big winners of the future, the get-rich stocks?

First of all, do stocks with a long and consistent history of low P/Es really exist? Take a look at Table 15, which shows the earnings multiples for selected property and casualty insurance stocks on January 1, 1984. Each company's current P/E and its average P/E ratio over the last five years is listed. As a point of reference, the average P/E of all stocks at this time was 13.2.

Table 15

Property and Casualty Insurance Stock P/Es

Company	Current P/E	5 Year Average P/E
American General	7.5	5.6
American International Group	8.5	8.5
American Plan	NE	5.0
AVEMCO	12.3	7.4
Berkely, W. R.	NE	8.0
Chubb Corp.	8.7	5.4
Cincinnati Financial	9.7	6.0
CNA Financial	7.3	5.8
Continental Corp.	17.9	7.3
Farmers Group	10.5	9.1
Foremost Corp.	12.3	7.3
GEICO	9.2	6.1
General RE Corp.	14.5	8.6
Hanover Insurance	5.4	3.9
Hartford Steam Boiler	9.1	6.7

Kemper Corp.	6.1	4.7
Mission Insurance	9.2	6.0
Motor Club of America	8.1	7.2
Ohio Casualty	8.4	5.8
Physicians Insurance	7.9	6.2
Progressive Corp. of Ohio	9.5	6.8
Safeco	8.4	5.9
St. Paul Cos	6.4	5.2
Seibels Bruce Group	4.7	7.9
Stewart Information Services	8.0	6.3
USF&G Corp.	8.5	6.2
Western Casualty	11.0	5.2
Zenith National	9.4	7.8

NE = no earnings; therefore no P/E calculated.

Source: The Media General Financial Weekly.

Now, scan down the column entitled "Current P/E." For two of the stocks, American Plan and W. R. Berkely, a P/E cannot be calculated because these companies have no earnings (denoted NE). Two other stocks, Continental and General RE, have P/Es which exceed the overall average P/E. But every other stock in the group (twenty-four of them) has a current P/E less than the market average. Note that most of these multiples are considerably below the market average. For instance, twenty stocks have P/Es below 10. Clearly the property and casualty stocks, on average, have low P/Es.

Are we to believe that all these stocks are good buys just because they sport low P/Es? The low-P/E strategy claims they are. But does it make any sense that at least twenty out of these twenty-eight property and casualty stocks are hot prospects? To shed some light on this question, take a look at the five-year-average P/Es for these stocks. Behold, every single stock in the group has a five-year-average P/E below 10. Further, of the twenty stocks whose P/Es are currently below 10, eighteen actually have current P/Es which exceed their long-term average P/E.

If investors overreact thus driving P/Es down below their rightful levels, why have these P/Es wallowed in the depths for five years? If overreaction was really the cause, shouldn't a correction have taken place which would restore them to their true values? Alternatively, could it be that overreaction never took place? Could it be that these P/Es are low because it's an accurate assessment of their worth?

We wanted to discover the answers to these questions. We already know that low P/Es in general do quite well. But what about low P/Es which are nearly always low? To find out, we studied our 2,600 stocks over the period 1970 to midyear 1980. At the beginning of each year we sorted all the stocks in rank order of their P/E ratios and then retained only the lower half. Next, among the lower 50 percent of P/Es, we looked to see what the average P/E had been during the previous five years. We then retained only those stocks in our portfolio whose five-year-average P/E was in the lower half. Hence, our portfolio consisted of below average P/Es which also were below average over the last five years.

The average yearly return for our portfolio turned out to be 8.37 percent. Compare this to the Standard & Poor's 400 industrials which averaged 7.93 percent during the same period. This low-multiple group performed only slightly better than the market index. Recall that we found that the 20 percent lowest P/Es overall yielded 16.24 percent per year. Therefore, this evidence supports our theory. Low P/Es which tend always to be low are not super money-makers. So we uncovered a second major defect in the low-P/E investment strategy. Low P/Es which have for a long time been low are not truly depressed stocks. To the contrary, they are merely selling at low multiples because that's what they deserve.

The Blue-Chip Blues

Having exposed these two major shortcomings of the low-P/E strategy, we felt we were well on our way toward making an important investment breakthrough. But we still weren't satisfied. We already discovered that low P/Es group together by industry. This at best fails to provide you with the adequate safety and protection of diversification and at worst concentrates your money in a few disastrous industries. Next, we found that all low P/Es may not be the depressed supervalued stocks that investors have overreacted to.

But what about the giant glamour stocks like the 30 Dow Jones industrials or the Standard & Poor's 500? Aren't there some low P/Es among these? According to Graham, the father of stock market wisdom, low P/Es may be stocks which investors have overreacted to driving their prices down into the bargain basement. Yet there was something which made us suspicious. There are literally thousands of stock analysts out there who constantly scrutinize the minutest happenings of the so-called blue-chip stocks.

If hundreds of pros are alert to even the slightest changes in these companies, how can overreaction set in? Wouldn't it make sense that the instant one of these superstars became so much as even a minibargain the big institutions would know about it? Wouldn't they then rush in to take advantage of the value, thereby driving the price back up to its rightful level? If so, how much of a bargain can the glamours become? we wondered.

Take a look at Table 16, which shows two groups of stocks as of January 1, 1984. What's the difference between the two? Certainly they're both low P/Es. Recall that the average P/E ratio for all stocks at that time was 13.2. Probably the biggest difference between the two groups is that you've heard of all the stocks on the left and none of the stocks on the right.

Table 16

P/E Ratios of Selected Stocks

Company	P/E	Company	P/E
Allied Corp.	8.7	Washington Homes	6.3
American Brands	9.0	Supreme Equipment	7.9
AT&T	8.7	Gemco National	9.4
Exxon	6.7	REDM Industries	9.1
General Foods	9.0	CHB Foods	7.9
General Motors	9.1	USR Industries	5.1
Standard Oil Cal.	7.3	Mor-Flo Industries	8.7
Texaco	7.2	Decorator Industries	8.4
Average	8.2	Average	7.9

This is our point. Both groups fit into the low-P/E strategy. Only there's a difference. The pros watch the big guys night and day while paying little or no attention to the little guys. Therefore, maybe it's possible for big bargains to develop unnoticed for stocks like those on the right while such occurrences may be impossible for the giants like those on the left.

"Well," you might say, "can't professional stock analysts take note of superbargains in small companies?" Here is the Catch-22. They can know about them, but they really can't do anything about them. You see, the big institutions buy and sell in such huge quantities that there just isn't enough stock in small companies for them to trade. But you can. That's why we developed Hyperprofits.

So our theory is that big companies with low multiples are not the get-rich stocks. But is our reasoning correct? We put it to the test. We turned to our trusty computer and analyzed our 2,600 stocks from 1970 to 1980 once again. First, we sorted the stocks to get the lowest half of P/Es. Next, of these low P/Es we sorted to collect the largest half of companies. The result: an average yearly profit return of 9.19 percent. This is a little better than the Standard & Poor's average of 7.93 percent but nowhere near the overall low-P/E quintile's average of 16.24 percent. Thus we learned that our theory holds water. Low-P/E stocks of large firms were not the big winners we were looking for. These large firms are so closely watched and analyzed that they hardly have a chance to become bargains.

The View from on High

We have now uncovered the three principal weaknesses of the low-P/E investment strategy. To recap, these limitations are: (1) clustering by industry, (2) historically low P/Es, and (3) large, overanalyzed firms. It's startling to think that even with these important shortcomings the low-P/E strategy is still able to perform well beyond the overall market average. Imagine how great the wealth-building potential might be if these limitations were overcome.

Enter Hyperprofits. This is precisely what Hyperprofits is all about. It is firmly based on a most effective and proven stock investment method, the low-P/E strategy. But this is only the base. The real work and potential of Hyperprofits is just beginning. We add to this base three important investment pillars. Each pillar replaces a weakness with a strength. One by one the shortcomings of the low-P/E strategy tumble, enabling your profits to mount. Hyperprofits turns a profitable investment strategy into a superwealth builder, one that can make you financially independent.

In the following chapters you will see just how this structure is erected pillar by pillar. More important, you will see how much money each pillar can add to your bank account, ultimately leading to the majestic profit pinnacle of the full Hyperprofits system. After you have seen it, you will look back in amazement at how easy it is. So let's get to it.

The First Pillar: Industrious Opportunities

The Hyperprofits strategy consists of three harmonious investment techniques which we call pillars. Each pillar is designed to overcome a specific deficiency of the low-P/E stock-selection method. You will recall that the first deficiency of the low-P/E approach is that this technique often leads you to build a portfolio which is heavily concentrated in just a few industries. In this chapter, we introduce the first Hyperprofits pillar, which is designed to overcome the industry concentration defect. You will see how adding this one pillar alone is meaningful enough to increase profits substantially.

High or Low? That Is the Question

You already know that low-P/E stocks display a pronounced tendency to cluster in certain industries. In addition, at a given point in time, each industry itself will be typified by either high, average, or low multiples. That is, the average P/E for all stocks in that industry will be high, average, or low compared to the average of all stocks in the market. To see what we mean, examine Table 17, which shows the average P/Es for fifteen major industry groups in 1984.

Table 17

Average P/Es by Industry, 1984

Industry	Average P/E
Aerospace	12.2
Banking	7.5
Building	23.5
Business equipment	15.2
Chemicals	13.8
Electronics	33.2
Food	13.1
Insurance	8.4
Investments	7.0
Light machinery	40.5
Rare metals	24.3
Oil services	29.8
Retail	13.5
Savings and loan	8.6
Utilities	7.7
Total market	13.2

The average P/E for all stocks at that time was 13.2. But look how widely the P/Es from different industries vary from the overall P/E average. Some industries' average P/Es are quite low, like life insurance at 8.4 and public utilities at 7.7. Others are more than twice the market's average, such as electronics at 33.2 and light machinery at 40.5. Still others are quite typical, such as retail at 13.4 and chemicals at 13.8. The key thing for you to see is that each industry has its own norm for what investors perceive as the typical P/E ratio at that time. These norms are determined by investors' expectations for the future prospects of that industry. The greater the expectations are, the higher the P/E.

Now let's take a closer look at some of the individual companies in these industries. Table 18 lists a representative ten companies from each of the banking and electronics industries together with their P/E ratios.

Table 18

Bank and Electronics P/Es

Banking		Electronics	
Company	P/E	Company	P/E
Chase Manhattan	4.2	Augat	32.9
Texas Commerce	7.5	National Semiconductor	91.9
Northern Trust	12.8	Varian Associates	27.6
Banc Texas	66.7	Tektronix, Inc.	29.4
Security Pacific	7.1	Diodes, Inc.	12.7
Mellon National	6.8	Argosystems	28.6
NCNB Corp.	7.4	Regan Corp.	97.9
Hartford National	7.4	SFE Technology	33.9
Manufacturers Hanover	4.6	Aydin Corp.	12.4
First Interstate	6.9	Unitrode Corp.	27.3
Industry average	7.5	Industry average	33.2

Some interesting points emerge from Table 18. First, a look at the banks. Note that Banc Texas's P/E of 66.7 is clearly very high by any standard. Conversely, Chase Manhattan at 4.2 and Manufacturers Hanover at 4.6 are certainly low P/Es by all accounts. What about the rest? Observe that Texas Commerce, Security Pacific, Mellon National, NCNB, Hartford National, and First Interstate have P/E ratios which are low by total market standards but normal for the banking industry. This leaves only Northern Trust. At a P/E of 12.8, Northern Trust's stock is slightly lower than the market's P/E (13.2), but its P/E is unusually high for the banking industry. How should we classify Northern Trust? Is it a high-P/E or a low-P/E stock? We shall soon find out.

Let's now focus our attention on electronics, a high-P/E industry. There's certainly no doubt about National Semiconductor and Regan with their astronomical P/Es of 91.9 and 97.9, respectively. They're high P/Es through and through. Note that all the rest, save Diodes and Aydin, are high-multiple stocks by market standards but normal by electronics industry standards. Finally, Diodes at 12.7 and Aydin at 12.4 are about average for the market but quite low for the electronics industry.

Sound confusing? Well, it is. But don't become discouraged, because as you read on the mystery will unfold before your very eyes. We already know that low P/Es have provided the best results. Now for the important question: Which stock really has the low P/E ratio, Northern Trust (a bank) at 12.8 or Aydin (an electronics) at 12.4? On the surface their P/Es appear to be very similar. But should we compare these P/Es to the overall market P/E or should we compare them to the P/Es of their own industries?

Take Northern Trust, for example, with its 12.8 P/E. What should its P/E be compared to? We could compare to the overall market, which consists of stocks from many industries having widely varying businesses and products. Or we could observe only those stocks which are most similar to Northern Trust, e.g., the bank stocks.

Now for the important question: Can Northern Trust be a good buy when its P/E is substantially higher than its industry norm, just because the P/E is slightly lower than the market average? Of course not. If it was a good buy, then each bank with a P/E lower than Northern Trust's, which is most of them, would also have to be a good buy.

Don't Bank on It

We have noted that with the sole exception of Banc Texas, each of the bank stocks observed in Table 18 has a low P/E when compared to the overall stock market. Conversely, none of the electronics stocks qualified as a low-multiple security. Therefore, as you can plainly see, the low-P/E investment approach concentrates heavily on banks while virtually ignoring the electronics stocks. That strategy works just fine while bank stocks are climbing. But what happens if bank stocks falter? Let's look at recent history to answer this question.

The year 1984 was fraught with problems for the nation's banks. Energy-loan losses, troublesome Argentine and Brazilian loans, intensified competition, and volatile interest rates, to name only a few problems, combined to make life difficult for bankers. The bottom line: bank stocks, although possessing low multiples, performed miserably. For example, the ten representative bank stocks listed in Table 18 declined an average of 20 percent each in the first six months of 1984 alone—more than double the market's decline.

And guess where the low-P/E approach would have directed a large chunk of your money? That's right, into those low-multiple bank stocks. Your financial position would have soured considerably, even though you adhered to the seemingly attractive low-multiple strategy.

The Pure Play

Recognizing the popularity of the low-P/E approach, *Forbes* magazine called on its computer to create a portfolio consisting of the twenty-five lowest-P/E stocks in the 3,100-stock Institutional Brokers Estimate System Universe. This so-called Pure Play Price/Earnings Fund appears in Table 19.

Table 19

The Pure Play Price/Earnings Fund

Company	Industry	P/E
Public Service New Hampshire	Utility	1.4
Long Island Lighting	Utility	1.8
Consumers Power	Utility	1.9
United Illuminating	Utility	2.2
Public Service Indiana	Utility	2.2
Continental Illinois	Bank	2.4
Maine Public Service	Utility	2.4
Financial Corp. of America	S&L	2.5
Ford Motor	Auto	2.5
American Century	Real estate	2.7

Manufacturers Hanover	Bank	3.1
Golden West Financial	S&L	3.1
Kansas City Power & Light	Utility	3.3
First American Financial	Insurance	3.5
Cincinnati Gas & Electric	Utility	3.5
Gibraltar Financial	S&L	3.5
DWG	Gas	3.5
First Western Financial	S&L	3.6
Chase Manhattan	Bank	3.7
El Paso Electric	Utility	4.0
Middle South Utilities	Utility	4.0
Central Maine Power	Utility	4.0
Commonwealth Energy	Utility	4.1
Toledo Edison	Utility	4.1
Chemical New York	Bank	4.1

Source: Forbes, July 30, 1984, p. 96.

The ultimate low-P/E portfolio? Not quite! Sure, it's a low-P/E portfolio through and through. But look at the industries represented. No fewer than thirteen of the twenty-five stocks are public utilities and yet another nine are financial intermediaries (banks and S&Ls). How could anyone feel comfortable concentrating money in only two industries, both of which are highly vulnerable to rising interest rates? Only Ford, Amercan Century, and DWG fall outside the confines of these two industries. What a blatant violation of the concept of diversification!

Hyperprofits, though resting on the low-P/E investment strategy, guards against such potentially harmful industry concentrations. Sure, Hyperprofits might select an occasional bank or utility stock, but it won't place a disproportional amount of your funds in any single industry. As such, Hyperprofits guarantees diversification—something the low-P/E approach does not provide.

And, as you recall from Chapter 2, diversification is a necessary ingredient in any successful investment technique.[1]

Building a Better P/E

You now see that it's a stock's P/E in relationship to the P/Es of other stocks in the same industry which is most important. Next, you must know how to profit from this knowledge. To do so, you need a stock-rating technique which identifies the truly high P/E stocks and, more important, which singles out the lowest P/Es. How can you do this considering the fact that industry multiples vary so drastically?

To accomplish this, so that all stocks are on an even footing and can be compared directly, we constructed the *Price–Earnings Relative,* hereafter known as the PER. To calculate a given stock's PER we first average all of the P/Es in a given industry. Then we take the individual stock's P/E ratio and divide it by the average P/E ratio for the relevant industry. This is the PER. Simple, isn't it? Wait until you see how effective it is in enhancing your investment performance.

To illustrate, let's take another look at our bank and electronics stocks, only this time we'll replace the P/Es with PERs. If you glance back at Table 18, you will see that every bank stock except Banc Texas has a lower P/E ratio than even the very lowest electronics' P/E ratio. Now let's see how the PER clears the picture (Table 20).

Table 20

Bank and Electronics PERs

Banking		Electronics	
Company	PER	Company	PER
Chase Manhattan	.56	Augat	.99
Texas Commerce	1.00	National Semiconductor	2.77

[1] A detailed discussion of the importance of industry considerations for P/E ratios appears in: John W. Peavy and David A. Goodman, "The Significance of Price-Earnings Ratios on Portfolio Returns," *The Journal of Portfolio Management,* Winter 1983.

Northern Trust	1.70	Varian Associates	.83
Banc Texas	8.89	Tektronix, Inc.	.89
Security Pacific	.95	Diodes, Inc.	.38
Mellon National	.91	Argosystems	.86
NCNB Corp.	.99	Regan Corp.	2.95
Hartford National	.99	SFE Technology	1.02
Manufacturers Hanover	.61	Aydin Corp.	.37
First Interstate	.92	Unitrode Corp.	.82

First, note that by definition the average PER has to be 1. The P/E of the average stock within an industry divided by the average P/E for that industry must equal 1.0. If a stock has a typical P/E ratio for its industry, its PER will be close to 1. Right away we have some valuable information. Those stocks with PERs above 1 are actually high P/Es for that industry while stocks sporting PERs below 1 are low. Next, observe that all stocks from both industries can now be compared on an even keel. For example, our previous comparison between Northern Trust and Aydin becomes crystal-clear. The score: Northern Trust is 1.70, Aydin is .37. What could be more definitive? Northern Trust's PER is well above 1, while Aydin's PER is considerably below 1. Although these two stocks have similar P/Es, their PERs vary substantially.

You can also make a quick comparison among the lowest P/Es of each industry. Which is lower, Chase Manhattan's P/E at 4.2 or Aydin's at 12.4? On the surface you would think that Chase was clearly the lower-multiple stock. A glance at Table 20, however, reveals otherwise. Chase with a .56 PER is actually a higher-multiple stock for its industry than Aydin with its .37 PER. So the electronics firm is lower in the PER sense than the bank. In contrast, note that there's no way that Aydin could make it into a purely low-P/E portfolio. But in a low-PER portfolio Aydin would clearly emerge as a likely candidate. You can see what a dramatic difference the PER makes in structuring your portfolio. And later in this chapter you will observe how the PER approach acts to improve your portfolio's performance.

From Low P/E to Low PER

Now that you understand the PER concept, you can see how it overcomes the low-P/E defect of clustering stock selections into a few industries. The PER gives each industry equal stature. A low-PER portfolio provides you the safety of representation from many industry groups. Better yet, it enables you to identify and acquire high-profit-potential stocks that the low-P/E strategy would never consider. So the low-PER strategy affords you higher profit potential, but at lower risk because you diversify across many industries. You get the best of both worlds.

Just to illustrate how much difference the low-PER investment strategy can make, consider the sample low-P/E portfolio in Table 21. Now here's a portfolio of ten stocks constructed from nine highly diversified industries (two oil stocks) as of January 1, 1984. You'll recall that the average P/E ratio for the market at that time was 13.2. Observe that every stock in the portfolio has a P/E well below the market average. Moving to the last column of this table, you can see what a difference the PER makes. Every so-called low-P/E stock in this portfolio has a higher than average PER. What appeared to be an attractive low-P/E portfolio turns out to be a high-PER portfolio. In fact, on average, these stocks P/Es are 15 percent higher than their respective industry norms. So is this a high- or a low-P/E portfolio? Relative to all stocks it is low, but relative to similar stocks it is high. Which would you compare Phillips Petroleum to, a stock like American Brands or Exxon? Does Phillips produce oil and gas or does it manufacture cigarettes? It's as basic as that. Of course it makes more sense to compare Phillips to Exxon: they're both energy stocks.

Table 21

A Sample Low-P/E Portfolio

Company	P/E	PER
Bank America	9.3	1.24
COMSAT	10.9	1.21
Lincoln National Insurance	9.0	1.07

A. G. Edwards	8.6	1.23
Gulf Oil	8.1	1.04
Phillips Petroleum	8.4	1.08
Wesco Financial	10.9	1.27
American Brands	9.0	1.03
American Electric Power	8.0	1.25
Houston Natural Gas	<u>9.7</u>	<u>1.08</u>
Average	9.2	1.15

Now let's turn the tables. This time we construct a low-PER portfolio instead, as shown in Table 22. Now we have a portfolio representing 10 diverse industry groups. Each stock has a low PER, but look at the P/Es. Every single P/E is above the overall market average. Now can you see how dramatically different the low-PER strategy can be from the low-P/E strategy? The PER can make all the difference in the world because it allows you to participate in stocks with exceptionally low P/Es for their industries. These stocks would never find their way into a strictly low-P/E portfolio.

Table 22

A Sample Low-PER Portfolio

Company	PER	P/E
Owens Corning	.68	15.9
Matsushita Electric	.60	19.9
Federal Express	.66	19.4
Stanley Works	.44	17.7
General Defense	.63	14.6
Englehard Corp.	.61	14.8
Halliburton	.48	14.3
General Signal	.82	17.3

Company	PER	P/E
Resorts International	.65	14.8
Winnebago Industries	.58	18.7
Average	.62	16.7

The Bottom Line

You have now learned what the PER is and why it is an advancement over the simple P/E ratio. This is all well and good, but what's the bottom line? The all-important question is: Does it make money? If so, how much? Does it outperform the low-P/E strategy? These are the burning questions. In this section we demonstrate just how profit-productive a low-PER strategy can be for you. Using our research findings, we document why the PER deserves the stature of being the first pillar of Hyperprofits.

The reasoning and logic behind the low-PER strategy seem to make a lot of sense, but we wanted the ironclad evidence. So we undertook a study to determine whether portfolios comprised of low-PER stocks do indeed provide superior profit returns. We analyzed 42 stocks from each of the electronics (characteristically high P/Es), paper/container (average P/Es), and food (low P/Es) industries from the beginning of 1970 to midyear 1980. We calculated the P/E ratios and then converted them to PERs by dividing by the appropriate industry average P/E.

We arranged these stocks into five separate portfolios, called quintiles, ranked according to their PER magnitude. Quintile 1 contains the lowest fifth of PERs while Quintile 5 has the highest fifth. Both price appreciation and cash dividends were included when we calculated the profits for each quintile. We repeated the experiment three different times. First, the five PER-based portfolios were adjusted every three months, then every six months, and finally every year to reflect shifts in PER rankings. Thus, for example, if a stock's PER increased beyond the boundaries of its group, that stock would be "sold" at the end of the appropriate "switching" period and replaced with the lowest-PER issue from the next highest quintile. The "sold" stock would then advance to a higher-PER quintile and be "bought" for that portfolio. Table 23 presents the annual profit return and average PER for each quintile portfolio.[2]

[2] For further elaboration on the price–earnings relative criterion see John W. Peavy and David A. Goodman, "Industry-Relative Price–Earnings Ratios as Indicators of Investment Returns," *The Financial Analysts Journal,* July–August 1983.

Table 23

Rates of Return for PER Portfolios
January 1, 1970 – June 30, 1980

| | | Switching Portfolios After Each | | |
| | Three Months | Six Months | One Year | |
Quintile	Annual Profit	Annual Profit	Annual Profit	Average PER
Lowest PER	1	24.98%	23.17%	22.15%	.56
	2	17.88	17.31	17.05	.76
	3	11.87	11.09	11.18	.93
	4	5.02	5.16	5.62	1.13
Highest PER	5	1.65	2.15	3.69	1.69

Cruising the Right Route

A glance at Table 23 reveals some interesting insights. For one, the P/E ratio for the typical Quintile 1 stock is close to one half that of its respective industry norm—i.e., a PER of about 0.5. What does this suggest? A widely touted investment axiom contends that a P/E is no more than a barometer gauging collective investor expectations regarding a stock's outlook. The higher the multiple the more favorable the prospects. Then doesn't it follow that Quintile 1 stocks receive low relative multiples because investors envision less than desirable prospects for those issues? One would certainly think so.

But how perceptive are these investors? Another look at our table provides the answer. Clearly the low-PER quintiles provided superior profits as compared to the high-PER groups. For example, employing quarterly portfolio adjustments, Quintile 1 returned approximately 25 percent annually, substantially outdistancing Quintile 5's lethargic 1.65 percent yearly return. In fact, the portfolio returns declined consistently as the average PER increased—a strong testimony to the profit-generating capabilities of the low-PER approach.

We decreased the frequency of altering the portfolios to determine whether these same results occurred when portfolio changes were made less often. Table 23 shows what happens when semiannual and annual switching were used. Just as with quarterly switching, the lowest-PER quintile provided the largest return. Also, the portfolio returns generally declined as the PER increased. These results conform closely to those for the quarterly adjusted portfolios.

However, another pattern emerged. As portfolios were changed less often, the returns generated by the lowest quintile group declined while the returns of the highest decile increased. As a result, the difference between the returns for Quintile 1 and Quintile 5 narrowed as we altered the portfolios less often. Seemingly, more frequent updating of low-PER portfolios is beneficial in enhancing profits.

Next, let's see how the PER portfolios performed from year to year. Table 24 depicts the year-by-year comparison of the highest and lowest PER portfolios for both quarterly and yearly review.

You can see what a dramatic difference the PER makes. Looking at the yearly review, observe that the low-PER stocks jump off to an 11.69 percent gain, while the high PERs sustained a 25.38 percent loss in 1970. Note that all stocks, low PERs included, were devastated by the infamous bear market of 1973–74. But after that the progress of the low-PER portfolio was nothing

Table 24

Returns of Low-PER and High-PER Portfolios

Year	Quarterly Review		Yearly Review	
	Return of Low-PER Portfolio	Return of High-PER Portfolio	Return of Low-PER Portfolio	Return of High-PER Portfolio
1970	26.36%	-19.28%	11.69%	-25.38%
1971	20.90	3.41	24.14	9.55
1972	13.63	35.15	3.07	33.47
1973	-38.68	-16.05	-28.31	-9.00
1974	-7.34	-54.37	-25.16	-50.49
1975	69.96	49.23	76.22	48.50
1976	70.09	13.26	71.35	15.09
1977	25.72	-20.45	26.80	-22.47
1978	18.89	2.17	11.07	6.26
1979	46.77	23.41	53.02	31.40

short of phenomenal. Starting with 1975, the annual profits were 76 percent, 71 percent, 27 percent, 11 percent, and 53 percent, respectively—a spectacular average yearly return of nearly 48 percent. What a performance!

These findings may seem a sacrilege to those investment gurus who preach a strategy of accumulating the stocks of highly visible firms with superior earnings prospects. But often too many gurus worship too few stocks. The implication is obvious. Those sacrosanct issues may be driven to heavenly heights while the cast-outs languish in an investor purgatory.

Enter Ben Graham and his overreaction theory once again. His message, though far from glamorous, is strikingly appropriate. You must avoid the revered stocks. Their prices, already reflecting outstanding growth potential, are too vulnerable to any disappointment that may disillusion investors. To illustrate, look at Quintile 5 stocks. On average, a stock in this group has a P/E which is 69 percent higher than the typical P/E for its industry. If investor expectations regarding one of these stocks were to wane, causing the P/E to adjust to an average level, then the outcast issue's price would plunge dramatically. Or even worse, if its new unpopularity were coupled with an actual earnings collapse, the price deterioration could be far more staggering. Apparently enough of the once heralded stocks of the seventies fell from investor favor to cause the high-PER portfolios to consistently underperform both the market and the low-PER issues.

But consider the low-PER securities. What worse can happen? These stocks have already been exiled to an investor dungeon. Unlike with the glamour issues, bad news is expected. Such expectations have already depressed prices so bad news really doesn't have that much additional impact. In effect, these stocks don't have that much to lose. Just as the glamour issues are viewed with too much optimism, the outcasts are frequently regarded too negatively. Seemingly, enough pleasant surprises happened to produce superior investment returns for these outcasts.

2,600 Stocks Can't Be Wrong

The results of our first test were so promising that we decided to conduct a more comprehensive experiment. This time we gathered data for 2,600 companies dispersed over more than a hundred industries. Our test period spanned 1962–80. Using our trusty computer, we divided the stocks into PER-ranked portfolio quintiles which we reviewed and revised at the end of each year. Table 25 shows the profit performance results by PER group.

Table 25

Hyperprofits Pillar 1 Returns

PER Group	Annual Profit
Lowest quintile	23.61%
Next quintile	18.26
Next quintile	15.34
Next quintile	11.87
Highest quintile	5.42

These results provide confirmation of our first test. We observed the same phenomenon as before: as the PER gets smaller, profits get larger. The overall profit returns are a little higher here than in the first test. The reason for this improvement is that the market during the 1960s, included in this experiment, performed stronger than in the 1970s, the test period for the prior experiment. Once again the low-PER strategy shines with an average annual profit of 23.61 percent. Can the performance of 2,600 stocks over eighteen years be wrong? It's certainly not likely. The Pillar 1, low-PER strategy has produced exceptionally generous profits, considerably higher than the low-P/E strategy.

P/E Versus PER

Now let's see what this means to you in terms of cold hard cash. We'll pit the low-P/E strategy against the low-PER strategy, the first pillar of Hyperprofits. You will recall that over an extended period of time, the low-P/E strategy earned an average return of about 16 percent annually. According to our tests, the average annual profit return of the low-PER strategy is approximately 22 percent. So there's a 6 percent difference. How does this translate into dollars when you allow your profits to compound? Table 26 shows how a $10,000 investment grows over fifteen years when earning the historical rate of return of low PERs.

Table 26

Growth of $10,000
Low P/E Versus Low PER

Year	Low P/E	Low PER
1	$11,600	$ 12,200
2	13,456	14,884
3	15,609	18,158
4	18,106	22,153
5	21,003	27,027
6	24,364	32,973
7	28,262	40,227
8	32,784	49,077
9	38,030	59,874
10	44,114	73,046
11	51,172	89,116
12	59,360	108,722
13	68,857	132,640
14	79,875	161,822
15	92,654	197,423

You can see that by the end of ten years the PER is outdistancing the P/E by more than one and one half times. But look what happens at the end of fifteen years. The PER strategy has produced $197,423, more than double the P/E approach at $92,654. So that relatively modest-looking 6 percent difference turns out to make a hefty difference in the thickness of your wallet. The extra profits generated by Hyperprofits over other investment systems, when coupled with the use of compounding, can make you a big winner.

Good News

Here is a bit of more recent evidence. Recall that in Table 2 in Chapter 1 we showed you a portfolio which appeared in the August 30, 1982, edition of the Dallas *Times Herald*. Now that you have gained the understanding of Pillar 1, let's reexamine these data more closely in terms of the PER technique. The theme of the article was the low-PER investment strategy. The article was titled "New Wall Street Wisdom," and the tag line read "SMU study reveals some out-of-favor stocks are gainers." Table 27 appeared in the article showing the lowest and highest P/Es in each of seven key industries. Of course, the lowest and highest P/Es within a specific industry are, by definition, the lowest and highest PERs.

These seven low-P/E stocks constitute a typical well-diversified low-PER portfolio, one such as you or we might acquire. As you know, to see how well we would have fared, we tracked the performance of this portfolio for exactly one year. Table 28 shows a summary of the results including the PERs.

As you can well see, every low PER stock in the portfolio appreciated dramatically. Simmonds Precision led the way with a spectacular 190.9 percent gain, while the total portfolio was climbing 78.4 percent as a whole. You should bear in mind that this was an extremely hot year for the market, as evidenced by the fact that the average stock on the New York Stock Exchange gained 53.6 percent. Still, a 78 percent profit isn't too shabby, even in a banner year. This is an example of what a low-PER portfolio is capable of doing for you.

What Have You Done for Me Lately?

You have already seen that the low-PER investment strategy, otherwise known as Hyperprofits Pillar 1, generates high profits over a long period of time. But, you might ask, what Pillar 1 has done for me recently? How is it working now? Will it still make me big bucks?

Of course, it takes some time to set the type and print this book, so we can't tell you the answer right up to the moment you are reading this. But we can show you a recent test that you might find interesting. To see how well Pillar 1 has been performing recently, we took fifty-two major industry groups. From each group, we selected the single lowest-PER stock listed at the begin-

Table 27

Industry Price–Earnings Ratios*

Industry	Average P/E	Low-Multiple Company	P/E	High-Multiple Company	P/E
Computer	9.5	Honeywell	5.2	Tandem Computers	15.5
Drug	13	Schering-Plough	8.6	Marion Labs	32.7
Electronics	15.5	Applied Magnetic	7.5	Craig Corporation	25.2
Food	6.1	Borden	5.6	General Mills	9.5
Petroleum	5.3	Standard Oil—Ohio	3.9	Southland Royalty	23.5
Precision instruments	11.4	Simmonds Precision	6.0	Coherent, Inc.	34.9
Retail	7.6	Manhattan Industries	4.5	Wal-Mart Stores	14.7

* Appeared in the Dallas *Times Herald*, August 30, 1982.

Table 28
Low-PER Portfolio

Company	PER	Buy Price	Sell Price	Profit
Honeywell	.55	$74 1/8	$115 1/4	55.5%
Schering-Plough	.66	33 1/2	41 5/8	24.2
Applied Magnetic	.48	15 7/8	27	70.0
Borden	.92	34 1/4	52 1/4	52.6
Standard Oil—Ohio	.74	31 3/4	56 1/4	77.2
Simmonds Precision	.53	17 5/8	51 1/4	190.9
Manhattan Industries	.59	11 5/8	20 3/4	78.6
			Average	78.4%

ning of 1983 by *The Media General Financial Weekly*. So our portfolio contained fifty-two low-PER stocks, one from each industry.

To assess the profit performance of our portfolio, we compared the prices at the beginning and ending of 1983. Table 29 shows all fifty-two stocks in the portfolio, their respective industries, PERs, and, most important, price growth.

Table 29

Low-PER Portfolio, 1983

Company	Industry	PER	Profit
Rohr Industries	Aerospace	.52	157%
Aloha	Airlines	.04	−17
Standard Products	Auto	.09	189
Ameron	Building materials	.17	37
Todd Shipyards	Building contractors	.50	0
Storage Technology	Computers	.51	−36
Virco Manufacturing	Business equipment	.68	30
Hudson General	Business services	.34	85
Union Trust Bancorp	Banking	.69	65
W. R. Grace	Chemicals	.67	18
Philipp LD Telephone	Communication	.67	−29
MEM Company	Cosmetics	.78	33
First Conn. Savings	Credit	.48	−1
Genesee Brewers	Distilling	.47	61
Block Drugs	Drug	.54	32
Unimax	Electrical equipment	.58	−20
Scope, Inc.	Electronics	.10	0
Seaboard Corp.	Food	.21	46
Sea Company	Freight	.32	12

Anta Corp.	Health	.32	68
Florida Capital	Restaurant	.23	231
National Presto	Housewares	.47	36
Hanover	Insurance	.57	63
First Boston	Investments	.49	15
Penna Engine	Industry machines	.03	82
Cross & Trecker	Machine tools	.45	43
SIFCO Industries	Fabricated metal	.47	5
Great Northern Iron	Iron and steel	.04	10
De Beers Consolidated	Rare metals	.31	20
Rowan Companies	Oil service	.47	12
Tosco Corp.	Oil producers	.14	−55
Royal Dutch	Oil refining	.67	30
Park Ohio	Container	.60	4
Compudyne	Electronic instruments	.36	17
Grolier	Publishing	.25	75
CSX Corp.	Railroads	.73	45
American Realty	Real estate	.13	41
Elgin National	Recreation	.42	−19
Gross Telecast	Broadcasting	.62	61
Bowl American	Entertainment	.61	67
Volume Merchant	Apparel	.63	7
Crowley Milner	Department stores	.53	70
Three D Department	Variety stores	.35	233
Bormans, Inc.	Food chains	.35	−25
MacAndrews & Forbes	Wholesalers	.26	158
Great American Industries	Rubber and plastic	.38	112
Suave Shoe	Footwear	.42	−12

Company	Industry	PER	Profit
Bibb Company	Weaving	.43	15
BTK	Textile	.12	−48
BAT Industries	Tobacco	.25	6
Maine Public Service	Electric companies	.44	22
Unit Energy	Gas companies	.56	−8
Average			39.3%

In judging the results, bear in mind that the average NYSE stock appreciated 17.9 percent during 1983. Observe that the table reveals a number of winners and losers. But the overall average for the portfolio is a striking 39.3 percent profit—more than double the NYSE average in an impressive market year. This is the kind of performance of which fortunes are made.

One Step Beyond

As we noted, certainly not every stock in the low-PER portfolio was a big winner. Far from it. As a matter of fact, eleven of the stocks lost money and another twelve, although appreciating in price, underperformed the market. So you can see that while the average performance borders on sensational, a low PER alone is not a guarantee of a quick hit. But imagine how great it would be if there were some way to weed out the potential losers from the group. If there were only some way to do this, you could possibly increase your profits while lowering your risk.

You have now become acquainted with the first Hyperprofits pillar. But there's still much more. So far, we have focused on the profit-generating potential of Hyperprofits. Next, we add Pillar 2, which is largely designed to pare the risk in your stock portfolio. While no investment system can ever eliminate all risk, the method we introduce as Pillar 2 will enable your profits to climb while risk fades.

5

The Second Pillar:
Buying at
a Discount

In the previous chapter you learned about a different kind of P/E ratio called the Price–Earnings Relative. We demonstrated that by adhering to a low-PER investment strategy you can:

1. Identify high-profit-potential stocks that the low-P/E strategy over-looks.

2. Attain broad portfolio diversification to reduce your investment risk.

3. Achieve higher profits than the low-P/E strategy affords.

You saw how the PER concept allowed you to overcome one of the big deficiencies of the low-P/E strategy. That is, the low-PER strategy eliminates the problem of having your stock selections clustering in only a very few industries. Having presented this initial investment pillar, we now tackle the second major deficiency of the low-P/E strategy.

Bargain-Hunting

Remember back in Chapter 3, we brought up the idea that if a stock's P/E ratio is always low, it may not be a bargain. There may be some good reason that the P/E is low. To put it as Benjamin Graham would, overreaction may not be the reason for the low P/E. Rather, many low-P/E stocks are *always* low-P/E stocks. They're right where they belong. Hence, these issues may not be potential wealth builders at all. You will learn all about how Hyperprofits Pillar 2 overcomes this significant shortcoming. You will discover that by applying Pillar 2 to your low-PER stocks, you can eliminate a number of potential nonwinners. The result is that your overall profits escalate.

A Theory of Relativity

Let's now explore the second deficiency of the low-P/E strategy. Take a look at Table 30, which displays selected companies in the oil-refining and -marketing industry at March 1, 1984. This table shows each stock's current P/E ratio and, most important, its average P/E over the past five years.

Table 30

Oil-Refining and Marketing Industry P/Es

Company	P/E Ratio	Five-Year-Average P/E
Adam Resources	20.0	29.0
Amerada Hess	13.6	9.1
American Petrofina	12.0	7.8
Ashland Oil	13.1	10.9
Atlantic Richfield	7.3	7.5
British Petroleum	9.4	6.4
Crown Central Petroleum	43.2	17.8
Diamond Shamrock	NE	8.5
Exxon	6.8	5.9
Gulf Canada	NE	16.9
Gulf Corp.	13.5	6.2
Holly Corp.	19.5	12.5
Husky Oil	NE	20.6
Imperial Oil	NE	10.4
Kerr-McGee	15.1	10.3

Mobil Corp.	8.0	6.4
Murphy Oil	9.9	8.3
Pacific Resources	7.9	11.4
Pennzoil	12.7	9.7
Phillips Petroleum	9.1	7.5
Quaker State Oil	10.2	11.1
Royal Dutch	6.7	4.3
Shell Oil	11.0	7.9
Shell Transportation	7.9	6.1
Standard Oil—California	7.7	6.7
Standard Oil—Indiana	8.5	8.4
Standard Oil—Ohio	6.7	6.8
Sun Company	14.2	7.8
Texaco Canada	NE	10.2
Texaco	9.8	5.5
U.S. Industries	11.8	7.5
Unocal Corp.	10.6	8.2

NE = no earnings for the year; thus, no P/E can be calculated.

The average P/E ratio for the total stock market in March 1984 was 12.0. An inspection of the individual P/Es reveals that seventeen of these thirty-two energy stocks had multiples below the market average. In the traditional sense, these are low P/Es. Could it be that over half these stocks are attractive for purchase? That's what the traditional low-P/E strategy would suggest. Now scan the five-year-average P/E ratios. Of those seventeen whose P/Es are below the market average, fully thirteen have P/Es that are higher than their five-year averages. You can clearly see that this phenomenon of low-P/E stocks which are pervasively low is no figment of the imagination. It's a very substantial reality. So are these really low-P/E stocks or not? Before we attempt to answer this question, let's dig a little deeper into the characteristics of these energy stocks.

Are these solid companies? We're talking about the likes of Exxon, Mobil,

Standard Oil of California (Chevron), and Texaco. Is Gibraltar a rock? Here we have behemoth companies with low P/E ratios. But their P/Es have been low for a long time. According to the low-P/E strategy, these stocks are good buys. But are they really? Remember, there are two reasons why a stock may have a low P/E. One is that investors have overreacted to some news or event and thus driven down the price to a level that is low in relation to the company's earning power—the Ben Graham hypothesis. The second reason is that the stock's P/E simply deserves to be low. Why? Because the company's prospects aren't that inviting.

Now, if a stock's P/E ratio is low due to overreaction, then eventually investors should realize this inequity and a correction will take place, thrusting the price back up to its rightful level. Being in on this correction is how to make big money in the stock market.

But suppose a stock's P/E is low but it's been low for a long time. If the P/E became low through overreaction, doesn't it seem plausible that an upward correction should have already taken place? If no correction has occurred after a lengthy period of time, then isn't this an indication that the P/E is low not through overreaction but merely because it deserves to be low? After all, a bargain doesn't last forever. If there's good reason for a stock's P/E ratio being low, why should you consider it to be a hot investment prospect? The answer is, you shouldn't.

Proof Positive

This is our theory, and it seems to make sense. But a theory provides no more than empty promises until it's tested. So that's just what we set out to do. To verify our theory, we further analyzed our group of 2,600 companies over the period 1970 to 1980. At the beginning of each year, we sorted all stocks into rank order according to their respective P/E ratios. We retained the lowest one-fifth of the P/Es and eliminated the rest. Thus, we were only considering low-P/E stocks.

Remember, we already know that low P/Es do well. We want to know about low P/Es which have been low for some time already. To do this, we took each low-P/E stock and calculated its average P/E over the previous five years. Then we compared each stock's current P/E to this average. If our theory is right, then stocks whose current P/E is equal to or higher than the historical average should not perform particularly well. These are the stocks with persistently low P/Es, not the stocks with P/Es temporarily depressed as a result of investor overreaction.

We continued our experiment by sorting the low-P/E stocks by the ratio of their current P/E to their past average. We retained the top 40 percent, that is, the stocks whose past P/Es were relatively low. We then broke this group into two separate portfolios, one consisting of the top half and the other of the bottom half of these stocks. So what we had left was low-P/E stocks whose past P/Es were as low as or even lower than their current P/Es. We repeated the process for each year of our test period, accumulating the profits over time. Price growth and cash dividends both counted.

What did we find? Table 31 shows you the average annual profit percentage for the two groups.

Table 31

Profits of Low-P/E Stocks
with Historically Low P/Es

Historical Average P/E

Low Half	High Half
8.71%	12.49%

What does it all mean? Observe that when past average P/Es are in the lowest group, profits are relatively small, 8.71 percent per year. But as historical P/Es get higher relative to the present, so do profits, as proven by the 12.49 percent return for the second group. Remember, we are talking exclusively about stocks whose current P/Es are among the lowest one fifth of all stocks.

In order to put these profits in perspective, please recall from Chapter 4 that we found the average low-P/E stock to yield 16.24 percent annually. So both of these groups comprised of stocks whose historical P/E are low failed to produce profits up to par for low-P/E stocks. In fact, the lowest historical group mustered only a little more than half the profits typical of a low P/E stock portfolio.

Over this same period of time the Standard & Poor's 400 industrials earned right around 8 percent. Therefore, low-P/E stocks with very low P/E histories turn out to be quite typical stocks, earning little more than the average stock. This substantiates our theory. Stocks with long histories of low-P/E levels offer little or no advantage: they really don't do any better than the overall stock market.

Finding a Cure

So we have demonstrated a second deficiency of the low-P/E strategy. Low-P/E stocks which have low-P/E histories are no bargains. But what's the remedy? From what you have learned so far, you can probably construct Hyperprofits Pillar 2 for yourself. Doesn't it follow logically that if a P/E ratio which is high relative to its own history is bad, then a ratio which is low relative to its past should be good? Sounds reasonable, but certainly this idea will have to be tested before we can legitimately make such a claim. And we will do so shortly.

But first let's explore more precisely what Pillar 2 actually is. In order to overcome the second shortcoming of the low-P/E investment strategy, we introduce the *Discounted Price–Earnings Ratio* which we shall refer to as the DPE. The DPE measures the extent to which a stock's current P/E ratio is below its normal P/E. That's what you must know because the DPE indicates whether an overreaction has possibly occurred. The lower a stock's P/E compared to its historical norm the better.

Here's how to calculate the DPE. You start with a stock's current P/E ratio and then divide it by its average P/E ratio over the past. For example, you may desire to average a stock's P/E over the last five years to determine its historical norm. This ratio of current to past average is the DPE. As we said, the lower the DPE the better. Later, we will show you how to collect the information necessary to calculate the DPE. And please don't fret about the difficulty of implementing this important pillar. Fortunately, your task will be straightforward and simple. No complicated math or formulas are involved.

Now let's take another look at our oil industry table, only this time applying Pillar 2, the DPE (see Table 32). If a stock's P/E is equal to its past average, then its DPE is exactly equal to 1. So you can tell at a glance which stocks have a discount, those with DPEs below 1. Look how the DPE clears away the confusion. By looking at the simple P/E ratio, all you can tell is that there are a bunch of stocks with low P/Es. So what? It turns out that for a high percentage of these stocks, a low P/E is perfectly normal. So where's the bargain? Where's the opportunity to get in on the high profit potential of a correction to investor overreaction?

Table 32

Oil Industry Using Pillar 2

Company	P/E	DPE
Adams Resource and Energy	20.0	.69
Amerada Hess	13.6	1.49
Am Petrofina	12.0	1.54
Ashland Oil	13.1	1.20
Atlantic Richfield	7.3	.97
British Petroleum	9.4	1.47
Crown Central Petroleum	43.2	1.55
Diamond Shamrock	NE	NE
Exxon	6.8	1.15
Gulf Canada	NE	NE
Gulf Corp.	13.5	2.18
Holly Corp.	19.5	1.56
Husky Oil	NE	NE
Imperial Oil	NE	NE
Kerr-McGee	15.1	1.47
Mobil Corp.	8.0	1.25
Murphy Oil	9.9	1.19
Pacific Resources	7.9	.69
Pennzoil	12.7	1.31
Phillips Petroleum	9.1	1.21
Quaker State Oil	10.2	.92
Royal Dutch	6.7	1.56
Shell Oil	11.0	1.39

Company	P/E	DPE
Shell Transportation	7.9	1.30
Standard Oil—California	7.7	1.15
Standard Oil—Indiana	8.5	1.01
Standard Oil—Ohio	6.7	.99
Sun Company	14.2	1.82
Texaco Canada	NE	NE
Texaco	9.8	1.78
U.S. Industries	11.8	1.57
Unocal Corp.	10.6	1.29

NE = no earnings for the year; thus, no P/E can
be calculated.

But comparing the P/E column to the DPE column makes all the difference in the world. A quick glance reveals that most of the low-P/E stocks have DPEs above one. These are not discount P/Es at all. In fact, just the opposite is true. These stocks actually have inflated P/E ratios based on their historical norms. These are stocks you want to avoid.

Of the low P/Es in this group, only four stocks have DPEs less than one. Of these, three stocks—Atlantic Richfield, Quaker State, and Standard Oil of Ohio—have DPEs in the nineties, not a huge discount. This leaves only Pacific Resources as the only low-P/E stock highly rated in terms of Pillar 2. See how easy it is to spot potential winners using the DPE pillar.

What about a stock like Adams Resource, which has a high P/E but a low DPE? Don't touch it. Here's why. First of all, we already know that the percentages are stacked against high-P/E stocks. Previous research has substantiated this conclusion. Second, the fact that the DPE is less than 1 means that its P/E was even higher before. Hence, the low DPE probably indicates a correction to an overreaction all right, but one of a different kind. Most likely investors originally overreacted on the high side, driving up the price well beyond the stock's true value. So the correction in this case may well have been to bring the stock back to its rightful place.

Check and Double-Check

Now let's talk about the bottom line. Can we back up our theory and document that the DPE really works? Is it truly the remedy for the second deficiency of the low-P/E strategy? Let's check it out, and you will see for yourself.

To test Pillar 2, we conducted an experiment similar to the one we performed earlier in this chapter. You will recall that we showed that low-P/E stocks whose past P/E ratios had always been low did not fare particularly well. Now let's look at the opposite side of the equation. Let's examine the performance of low-P/E stocks whose P/Es were higher in the past (in other words, low-P/E stocks selling at a discount to their historical P/E averages). Of course, these are the low-DPE stocks. This experiment will show us whether the DPE does, in fact, overcome the second shortcoming of the low-P/E strategy, namely that many low-P/E stocks are persistently low and thus will probably stay low.

To uncover the truth we analyzed the same 2,600 companies utilized previously. Once again we took the lowest quintile of P/Es each year. Next we computed the DPE for each of these low-P/E stocks and then grouped these low-P/E stocks into subquintiles based on the stocks' respective DPEs. Remember, the lower the DPE the greater the discount. We kept the two lowest subquintiles (the lowest DPEs among the low-P/E quintile) for further analysis. This allows us to isolate the low-P/E stocks that have discounted price–earnings ratios. We accumulated profits over the 1970–80 observation period for these stocks. Table 33 shows what happened.

Table 33

Returns of Low-P/E Stocks with Low DPEs

Lowest DPE Quintile	Next Lowest DPE Quintile	Average Low P/E
24.12%	19.90%	16.24%

A glance at these figures shows the dramatic results. For the second lowest group of DPEs, annual profits averaged 19.90 percent, noticeably higher than the 16.24 percent average for all low-P/E stocks in the 2,600 company group. But for the lowest DPE quintile, profits soared to a resounding 24.12 percent annually, approximately one and a half times greater than that for the average low P/E. Quite a difference!

These results provide convincing support to the low-DPE approach. Yes, there is a relationship between low-P/E and low-DPE stocks. However, the two techniques are not one and the same. Bringing in the DPE adds a major impetus to the profit-generating capabilities of low-P/E stocks. And the best part is that this contribution displays itself in exactly the right place, your portfolio's profit picture.

Make Your Day

In order to illustrate for you the workings and profit potential of the DPE pillar, let's take a look at the gas utilities industry in 1983. Table 34 presents companies participating in this industry in 1983. By checking the P/E-ratio column, you can quickly see that this is a predominantly low-P/E industry. But check the DPEs in the next column and you will discover that about half of these stocks have discounted P/Es (DPEs under 1), while the remaining half do not.

Table 34

Gas Utilities Industry P/Es and DPEs, 1983

Company	P/E	DPE	Profit %
Alagasco, Inc.	4.8	.77	25
Arkla	9.4	1.01	26
Atlanta Gas Light	8.6	1.46	26
Bay State Gas	6.1	.88	−7
Brooklyn Union	6.5	1.10	8
Cascade Gas	11.9	1.45	1

City Gas Florida	5.4	.83	39
Columbia Gas	5.6	.73	22
Connecticut Energy	7.4	1.00	5
Connecticut Natural Gas	7.1	.92	5
Consolidated Natural Gas	6.7	.92	43
Diversified Energies	5.4	.86	45
Donovan	7.4	1.03	35
Enserch Corp.	6.3	.72	17
Entex, Inc.	7.7	1.17	10
Equitable Gas	5.6	.95	91
Houston Natural Gas	5.8	.76	20
Indiana Gas	8.3	1.36	17
Intermountain Gas	5.8	.39	26
Laclede Gas	5.8	1.02	25
Louisiana General	14.8	1.85	18
Michigan Energy	10.4	1.08	−14
Mississippi Valley Gas	7.2	1.47	36
Mobile Gas Service	7.0	1.11	−6
Mountain Fuel Supply	10.5	.85	50
National Fuel Gas	5.1	.78	18
National Gas Oil	6.6	1.08	22
New Jersey Resources	6.3	.89	57
NICOR, Inc.	7.5	1.04	−4
North Carolina Natural Gas	6.1	1.02	8
Northwest Natural Gas	7.4	.95	16
ONEOK	5.5	.85	15
Pacific Lighting	7.4	1.23	28
Pennsylvania Enterprises	5.3	.88	23

Company	P/E	DPE	Profit %
People Energy	6.4	.98	−1
Piedmont Natural Gas	7.5	1.01	51
Pioneer Corp.	7.8	.93	37
Providence Energy	4.6	.90	27
Public Service-N.C.	6.8	.91	20
Sonat, Inc.	5.2	.70	24
South Jersey Industries	11.2	1.60	12
Southeastern Public Service	6.5	1.41	39
Southern Union	8.6	1.16	38
Southwest Gas	9.6	1.02	29
Southwestern Energy	11.4	.83	56
UGI Corp.	6.3	.81	−12
Valley Resources	5.7	1.10	8
Washington Energy	7.1	.89	7
Washington Gas Light	7.0	.80	22
WICOR	7.7	1.08	8

Source: The Media General Financial Weekly.

Now what would happen if we broke these stocks up into two portfolios, those with DPEs below 1 versus those with DPEs above 1? Suppose you held both portfolios for the entire 1983 year. How would you have fared? The last column shows the percentage profit earned by each stock as measured by its price appreciation. You can see that in each group some stocks performed quite well while others didn't do so well. But we are interested in the overall profit from our investment. The high-DPE group yielded a profit return of 17.0 percent for the year. Not bad, but nonetheless considerably overshadowed by the 26.3 percent profit for the low-DPE group. The discounted P/Es outdistanced their rivals by a substantial margin. These results further reveal that not all low-P/E stocks are the same. In fact, the differences can be considerable. The DPE gives you a way to spot the important differences.

But has anyone ever heard of the DPE or taken note of it? Or is it just some newly devised mystical concept? Take a look at Table 35. Here we see a compilation of the stocks sporting the lowest DPEs as measured by their ten-year averages. But this time it's not our list. This list appears in *The Outlook*, a publication of Standard & Poor's—one of the largest and most reputable sources of stock data anywhere. So while the average person may not be familiar with the DPE, certainly some of the most knowledgeable investors are well aware of it.

Table 35

Discounted P/E Ratios

Company	Current P/E	P/E as a Percentage of 10-Year Average	2/24/84 Stock Price
SEDCO	6.22	42	37 1/2
Telex	8.45	48	19 5/8
Collins Foods	10.42	48	17
Mesa Petroleum	10.02	49	17 1/4
First Boston	5.63	50	37 3/8
Medtronic	9.20	51	33 1/8
Homestead Financial	2.95	54	15 3/8
Eastern Utilities	4.77	57	13 3/8
Kansas City Power & Light	4.03	57	16 3/4
Carter-Wallace	11.69	58	25 5/8
Illinois Power	4.73	58	18
BASIX Corp.	10.81	59	8 7/8
Procter & Gamble	8.74	61	46 5/8

Company	Current P/E	P/E as a Percentage of 10-Year Average	2/24/84 Stock Price
United Illuminating	3.72	63	21¹/8
Commonwealth Edison	5.12	63	22¹/2
Baxter Travenol Labs	11.68	63	18
Commonwealth Energy	3.99	64	18¹/2
Standard Oil—Ohio	7.65	64	47
Consolidated Foods	8.63	65	26¹/4
Ohio Edison	5.74	66	12³/4
NUI Corp.	6.83	66	25¹/2
Shaklee	5.96	66	15⁵/8
Citicorp	5.28	67	34¹/4
Lear Petroleum	11.29	67	22³/8
Eli Lilly	10.35	68	63¹/2

Source: The Outlook, Standard & Poor's Corporation, March 7, 1984.

One Plus One Equals Three

This all goes to show that (1) low-P/E stocks without attractive DPEs are at best only average investments and (2) low-P/E stocks with low DPEs are outstanding profit performers. The conclusion is undeniable. Pillar 2 is a highly effective technique for differentiating high- versus low-potential low-P/E stocks.

We have now uncovered and demonstrated to you two powerful investment techniques, namely the PER and the DPE. These two pillars have the power to convert an already profitable low-P/E strategy into a dynamite wealth builder for you. But one crucial question remains: How well do the two pillars work together? To answer this question, we will next show you the awesome impact of Pillars 1 and 2 when combined into one investment strategy.

Without a sound test, we really can't know how well the two pillars might mesh. We anticipated that there would be a synergy between the two, each one adding something to the other. But it was entirely possible that they would add little or nothing to each other profit-wise. Although we didn't think so, it was even possible that they might detract from one another.

Our curiosity was overwhelming. We simply had to know how these two pillars interacted. So we embarked upon a new experiment. We returned to our 2,600 companies once again, employing the years 1970–80 as our test period. We particularly like this test period. For one, it's fairly recent. Two, it provides a long enough time span to draw a valid conclusion. Third, these were not particularly great market years. The bear market of 1973–74 was one of the most devastating in history. Therefore, any profit estimates we might derive tend to be conservative. It's better to understate rather than overstate profit projections. Pleasant surprises are a lot better than unpleasant ones.

You'll recall that in our last chapter we showed you the profit results of portfolios at five different PER levels. Since we were interested in finding out whether Pillar 2 could supply any additional profits over Pillar 1, we started by sorting out the low quintile of PERs from our 2,600 companies. You have already seen that these stocks yielded an average of 22 percent profit per year over the test period. Is it possible that even more profits could be generating by applying Pillar 2?

In order to discover whether the DPE pillar could enhance our profits, we took these lowest-PER-quintile stocks and sorted them into five different DPE categories. The lowest fifth of the DPEs went into the first portfolio, the next fifth lowest into the second portfolio, and so on. In this way we could determine whether the DPE made any difference among strictly low PER stocks. We repeated this sorting procedure at the beginning of each year of our test period and kept track of accumulated profits. Table 36 shows how the experiment turned out.

Table 36

Pillar 1 Plus Pillar 2 Returns
(by DPE Categories)

DPE Group	Annual Return
Lowest quintile	28.2%
Second quintile	24.3
Third quintile	21.6
Fourth quintile	19.9
Highest quintile	16.7

As you can see, Pillar 2 does indeed make a big difference. Low-PER stocks which have a high DPE do not perform as well as the average low-PER stock. More important, however, is the observation that low-PER, low-DPE stocks perform extremely well. This very special portfolio of securities yielded 28.4 percent annually versus the 22 percent yearly average for all low-PER stocks. The table confirms the existence of a synergy between the two pillars. Pillar 2 does indeed give you incremental profit over and above that of Pillar 1. The additional profit yield is approximately 6 percent per year.

Although 6 percent does not seem like a lot, you will recall that relatively small percentage differences coupled with the magic of compounding produce big dollar differences in the long run. Table 37 reveals the dollar value of coupling Pillar 2 with Pillar 1. It's hard to believe, but true. Over the ten-year observation period Hyperprofits Pillar 2 would have provided you more than one and a half times that of Pillar 1 alone. And in fifteen years Pillar 2 would more than double your money over Pillar 1. Here you see the profit power of Hyperprofits coupled with the magic of compounding.

Table 37

Growth of $10,000 Using
Pillars 1 and 2

	10 years	15 years
Pillar 1	$ 73,046	$197,423
Pillars 1 + 2	$118,059	$405,648

A Star Is Born

By now you are well aware that the success of Hyperprofits is based on the overall performance of your portfolio. One stock in a portfolio may do extremely well while another stock may not do so well. No investing system ever devised, nor one that will ever be devised, can guarantee the success of a given stock. This is impossible. But what you really should emphasize is the performance of your entire portfolio, not the isolated performance of any single stock. What you want is to turn your $10,000 into a financial bonanza. So if your investment earns an average of 32 percent per year, for example, it makes little difference what each individual stock does. Hyperprofits works by putting the averages strongly in your favor.

While not every Hyperprofits stock is a winner, here is the illustration of what Hyperprofits stocks can do. We present the 1983 Pillars 1 and 2 all-stars in Table 38. The all-stars consist of fifteen stocks whose PERs and DPEs were both below 1 at the beginning of 1983. The profit percentage column shows the price growth which accrued by the end of the year. The all-stars averaged an awesome 156.7 percent profit in 1983. This does not prove the profit performance of any given stock or portfolio, but it does illustrate the profit potential of stocks coupling Pillars 1 and 2 together.

Table 38

Hyperprofits Pillars 1 and 2, 1983 Candidates

Company	Industry	PER	DPE	Profit
Rohr Industries	Aerospace	.52	.79	157%
Sparton Corp.	Auto	.41	.93	132
Espey Mfg. & Electronics	Electronics	.36	.81	149
Sun City Industries	Food	.65	.57	123
Golden Nuggett	Hotels	.72	.42	106
Carrols Corp.	Restaurant	.82	.60	179
Florida Capital	Restaurant	.23	.22	231
Yankee Oil & Gas	Oil	.67	.76	163
Great American Management	Real estate	.17	.40	123
Twin Fair	Real estate	.08	.37	213
Design Craft	Jewelry	.55	.70	153
S. E. Nichols	Retail	.64	.66	180
Action Industries	Wholesale	.44	.18	158
MacAndrews & Forbes	Wholesale	.26	.78	158
Caressa	Shoes	.61	.67	126

Average   156.7%

In this chapter, you have learned about the second investment technique of Hyperprofits, the Discounted Price–Earnings Ratio. You have seen that by combining Pillars 1 and 2 you can substantially increase your investment gains.

Now you are well along the way to understanding the Hyperprofits system and beginning your wealth-building program. But there's still more. In the next chapter we complete Hyperprofits by presenting Pillar 3. You will see how this final pillar interacts with the first two pillars to elevate your profits even higher. You will also learn how you can beat the pros at their own game even if you are a novice investor. Sound tempting? If so, come along as we put the final pillar into place to complete the Hyperprofits investment system.

The Final Pillar: Investing Small for Large Profits

In Chapter 4 we erected the first Hyperprofits pillar, the price–earnings relative. Using the PER strategy enables you to take your initial step down the path toward Hyperprofits. You learned that low-PER stocks, on average, yield substantially higher profits than the typical stock. You also discovered why the low-PER approach is superior to the low-P/E technique. Employing this first pillar alone, profits have averaged over 22 percent annually.

The addition of the discounted P/E (DPE) pillar creates a synergistic effect that increases profits considerably. Our research reveals that a combined low-PER, high-DPE approach has generated a 28 percent annual return over time. These two pillars, when combined, provide you with an easy method of identifying meaningful stock bargains.

In this chapter we raise the third and final Hyperprofits investment pillar. We call this the small-company pillar. By combining this pillar with the two previously introduced pillars, you can achieve even higher profits. You will soon realize that the full Hyperprofits investment potential brought about by the interaction of these three pillars is clearly within your grasp. And what's even better is that this strategy can enable you to earn even higher returns than the investment professionals do.

The three pillars synthesized into one investment strategy comprise the Hyperprofits system of wealth-building. By reading this chapter you will learn why the small-firm pillar is so crucial to your financial success. In the following chapters you will learn the easy-to-use instructions for putting the Hyperprofits system to work for you.

The Small-Company Pillar

Most investors believe that the well-established corporate giants such as General Motors and du Pont are the soundest investments. If you examined the portfolio holdings of your own pension fund or those of most mutual funds, you would find many of those "blue chips." But, as you will soon see, these are not the most profitable investments. Our own findings and those of other researchers reveal that historically the profits from investing in small companies have been, in fact, much higher than those from acquiring large firms. Shortly, we will explain how you can benefit from this discovery.

First of all, what do we mean by a small company? There are several different ways we could view the size of a company. For example, we could look at the number of employees, the dollar volume of sales, the net profits, or the amount of assets the company has. Each of these provides a different measure of a company's size. What we need is a common measure and, more important, to know that this measure assists us in our search for stock market profits.

The measure of size we use for the small company pillar is called market value, or MV. MV tells you the size of a firm in terms of the total market value of its common stock. It is calculated by taking the total number of outstanding shares and multiplying by the current price per share of the firm's stock.[1] The resulting figure is the total market worth of the company's stock. The MV measure of firm size is important because all major studies which detect high profits for small companies use MV as a gauge for size.

Small Is Beautiful

Now let's see what this third profit pillar means to your wealth-building program. In which of the companies presented in Table 39 do you think most people prefer to invest their hard-earned money? The large or the small companies? Do they stake their future well-being on IBM, Texas Instruments, and Exxon? Or do they prefer Kapok and Presidio? If you answered IBM, Texas Instruments, and Exxon, you're absolutely right. And why not? These are the

---

[1] The number of shares outstanding for a particular company can be obtained from a number of sources including the company's annual report, Standard & Poor's *Stock Guide, The Media General Financial Weekly* and *The Value Line Investment Survey*. A stock's current market price is available in *The Wall Street Journal.*

corporate elite. They are well known, large and successful. How could you possibly go wrong with these investment giants? Well, the following paragraphs will dramatically illustrate why these blue chips are not as infallible as you think they are.

Table 39

Large and Small Companies

Industry	Large	MV*	Small	MV*
Banking	Citicorp	4,393	Equimark	24
Computer	IBM	72,511	Audiotronics	8
Electronics	Texas Instruments	2,736	Cognitronics	10
Insurance	Aetna	3,681	American Plan	11
Petroleum	Exxon	32,478	Presidio	23
Restaurant	McDonald's	3,637	Kapok	11

* Market value in millions of dollars.

Obviously, the size of companies varies enormously. As an investor, you have the opportunity to go with either large or small companies in almost every industry. Generally speaking, when we refer to small firms, we mean those whose stock has less than $75 million of total market value.

Now for the exciting part. We investigated the performance of a diverse group of five hundred different common stocks. Companies of all sizes were included in this group. Some firms were very small; others were extremely large. We observed the stock of these companies from 1970 to 1980 to determine whether small stocks really did outperform large stocks. Our findings, shown in Table 40, were most revealing.

Table 40

Stock Returns of Different-Sized Firms

Portfolio	Average Size (MV)*	Annual Profit
20% smallest firms	25.1	20.4%
Next 20%	85.3	14.1
Next 20%	225.8	10.4
Next 20%	562.5	6.3
20% largest firms	968.4	3.6

* In millions of dollars.

These results illustrate the startling impact of company size on your investment profits. The smallest 20 percent of firms, such as Equimark and Audiotronics, averaged a very healthy 20.4 percent annual profit. As company size grows, stock profits decline consistently. The corporate giants, such as IBM and Exxon, averaged an unrespectable 3.6 percent annual profit over this period.

Shatter one myth. The blue chips are not your route to riches. On the contrary, the small, unheard-of companies hold the key to your financial future. But let's be absolutely sure of this most critical conclusion.

Winning During the Bad Times

We have shown that if you confined your investments to the common stocks of small companies, you would have prospered during the 1970–80 period. The 20.4 percent average annual return provided by a small-stock portfolio easily outpaced the 7.8 percent average yearly inflation rate over that same period. But is this really a surprising result? After all, we know that stocks in general provided very high returns during most of the post–World War II period. From the end of 1945 to the beginning of 1969, the Dow Jones Industrial Average soared from 152.48 to 943.75—a gain of some 519 percent. This gain translates to an average yearly return of 21.6 percent. Over the same

the annual rate of inflation in this country averaged only 3.0 percent. So not unusual to experience high returns from common stocks, especially compared to the rate of inflation. It's no wonder that stocks were labeled inflation hedges. By investing in a diversified portfolio of stocks, you have increased your purchasing power dramatically.

But twenty-five years of a generally increasing market does not mean that prices are destined to soar forever. In fact, these "perfect inflation es" were anything but perfect during the next decade. Investors were in the teeth of a very expensive dilemma: Common stock prices reed while the rate of inflation accelerated. The Dow Jones's close at the end decade was lower than its high as far back as 1965. And in the mean-, inflation rates began to rise. Remember, the price of a market basket of and services in the U.S. increased an average of 7.8 percent per year ng the seventies. The net result was that common stock portfolios lost hasing power.

As you can clearly see, common stocks turned in dismal performances this decade. After a quarter century of prosperity, stock investors found holdings to be losing ground to inflation as well as every other major estment group. Who would ever have imagined that a portfolio comprised Chinese ceramics, Persian rugs, and Grecian urns would outdistance stocks he battle to beat inflation? But that is exactly what happened. The notion of mmon stocks being the perfect inflation hedge seemed to go the way of the el and the nickel candy bar. The cover of a major business magazine claiming "The Death of Equities" captured the sentiments of many frustted investors.

There is no doubt that the seventies were very trying times for the average ck investor. But any successful stock market strategy must weather the bad es: a blindfolded monkey throwing darts at *The Wall Street Journal*'s finanal pages might select "winners" during a bull market. And that is exactly hat makes our findings even more exciting. Even though the stock market red miserably in the seventies, small stocks continued to generate superior rofits.

What Others Find

You have seen that our research indicates that a portfolio invested in small rms would have provided handsome profits over the 1970–80 period. But maybe you're not yet convinced about the attractiveness of investing small. After all, we may have selected a time period that doesn't fairly represent the

profit differences between small and large stocks. Or maybe we just got lucky and selected a lot of better-than-average small stocks. In the back of your mind you're thinking that this is a very risky investment approach. Don't some small companies go broke during bad economic times? If so, how can you afford to take a chance by investing in companies that may fail? Before answering these important questions, let's take an even closer look at investing in small stocks.

Other researchers have also discovered the attractiveness of investing small. We readily admit that our research was not the first to document that small stocks provide superior profits. Nor do we claim that our study is the most comprehensive. What is most important is that our findings closely coincide with the results obtained by other stock market researchers.

The first formal evidence offering that small stocks provide superior profits appeared in the March 1981 edition of *The Journal of Financial Economics*. In that issue, two University of Chicago researchers, Rolf Banz and Marc Reinganum, independently observed that small firms consistently provided very high rates of return over long periods of time. Neither was able to provide a solid reason for the existence of the small-firm superiority. However, the magnitude of the returns generated by the small stocks indicated that something very interesting was occurring among the universe of small-company stocks.

If this sounds interesting, then please read on. The more you learn about this investment inequity, the more excited you'll get. Although simple in concept, the small-firm investment strategy definitely merits your undivided attention.

It may seem unusual that documentation of the superior performance of small firms' stocks did not appear in published form until 1981. But you must consider that this type of research requires the analysis of many hundred thousand stock prices and dividends. To accomplish such analyses, two resources must be available: an extensive, easy-to-access record of historical financial information and a very large computer.

The emergence of the Center for Research in Security Prices (CRISP) at the University of Chicago (jointly sponsored by Merrill Lynch, Pierce, Fenner & Smith) made available a massive source of such financial data. Now, comprehensive price and dividend information on all New York– and American Stock Exchange–listed stocks dating all the way back to 1926 can be retrieved in an instant. This information base, coupled with today's high-powered computers, makes possible studies of stock price performance that were previously beyond researchers' wildest dreams.

The Banz study was one of the pioneering efforts in investigating the performance of small-firms stocks. Using the CRISP files, Banz (now a finance professor at Northwestern University) pored over stock prices from 1926 to

1979. His conclusion: the stocks of small firms consistently outperform the large companies' stocks. He discovered that stocks with a market value under $50 million achieved an 11.6 percent annual rate of return compared to 8.8 percent for large stocks. While this difference may seem trivial, the 2.8 percentage point spread means that $100 invested in the small stocks in 1926 would have snowballed to approximately $37,000 by the end of 1979 versus only $9,600 for the large stocks.

But what may be even more noteworthy is the fact that Banz considered only securities listed on the New York Stock Exchange. And we all know that the NYSE contains only large firms; that's why it's commonly called "the Big Board." Even the smallest firms on this exchange are large. So if the smallest Big Board stocks yield abnormally high returns, think what might happen if we observed even smaller stocks, such as those listed on the smaller American Stock Exchange or the even smaller over-the-counter market. The performance results of these truly small firms could be even more breathtaking.

Enter Marc Reinganum. Also working with the CRISP files at the University of Chicago, Reinganum (currently a U.S.C. finance professor) looked at both New York and American Stock Exchange stocks. As you might expect, his findings were even more dramatic than those of Banz. He arranged all listed companies in order according to the size (MV) of the firm and then grouped these stocks into ten portfolios, called deciles. Each decile contained exactly one tenth of the stocks. Decile 1 held only the smallest MV companies, Decile 2 the next smallest, and so forth. Of course, Decile 10 contained the largest MV firms. An "excess" return was calculated for each decile from 1926 to 1975.[2] The portfolio of smallest firms (Decile 1) produced an annual profit (excess return) of 12.5 percent greater than that of the average stock over this period. On the other hand, the portfolio consisting of the largest firms (Decile 10) did over 8.5 percent worse than the average security. This performance gap between small and large stock portfolios vividly portrays the beauty of investing small. And remember, Reinganum did not consider over-the-counter stocks where many of the really small firms dwell.

Table 41 presents a more complete picture of Reinganum's results. You may note that his "small firms" had a median (midpoint) market value of only $8.3 million dollars, whereas Banz used a considerably higher $50-million cutoff for classifying a firm as small. Also, Reinganum's small-firm portfolio was almost entirely comprised (82.6 percent) of the smaller American Stock

---

[2] An "excess" return is defined as the rate of return observed for a given decile *minus* the rate of return generated by the entire group of stocks observed. An excess return, therefore, measures how much a given decile's return differs from the overall portfolio return.

Exchange securities. Very few Big Board stocks were included in his smallest decile. It becomes plain to see why Reinganum showed more powerful documentation for the superiority of small stocks: his small stocks really were small.

Table 41

Performance of Stocks Ranked by Firm Size
1926–1975

Portfolio[1]	Excess Return (Profit Compared to Average)	Median Market Value (Millions of Dollars)	Percent A.S.E. Listed[2]
Decile 1	12.5%	8.3	82.6
Decile 2	4.8	20.0	48.3
Decile 3	−0.8	34.1	23.8
Decile 4	−1.3	54.5	11.2
Decile 5	−2.9	86.1	8.6
Decile 6	−4.8	138.3	4.4
Decile 7	−4.7	233.5	4.3
Decile 8	−5.4	414.0	2.7
Decile 9	−7.3	705.3	2.5
Decile 10	−8.6	1759.9	1.6

[1] Decile 1 consists of the smallest MV firms, whereas Decile 10 contains the largest MV companies.

[2] This column reveals that most small exchange-traded stocks reside on the American Stock Exchange (A.S.E.), in contrast to most large exchange-traded stocks, which trade on the New York Stock Exchange.

Source: Marc Reinganum, "Misspecification of Capital Asset Pricing: Empirical Anomalies Based on Earnings Yield and Market Values," *The Journal of Financial Economics,* March 1981.

Further Results

The pioneering studies by Banz and Reinganum caused quite a stir among investment professionals and academics alike. But many investment pros were very suspicious of the results. After all, these investors were accustomed to buying the stocks of "sacred," large growth companies like IBM, Eastman Kodak, and Johnson & Johnson. In the early 1970s, these companies were known as "one-decision stocks"—meaning the only decision to make is when to buy them. They're presumably so good that you never have to sell them.

You can see why the pros questioned the evidence showing that small firms in the long run provided superior profits when compared to the large growth companies. Probably the most frequent criticism of the Banz and Reinganum studies was that the results were computed based on an investment strategy that required daily purchases and sales in the portfolio. As a stock rose in price, its market value increased, and it would eventually be sold out of the small-firm portfolio and be replaced by a stock whose price and market value had declined. Of course, this type of "churning" can incur substantial administrative and transactions costs. Many pros argued that these costs would be so high as to negate the superior profits of the small stocks.

To counter this argument, Reinganum conducted a new study. This time he made portfolio adjustments only once a year. Again his findings confirmed that buying small stocks would have produced handsome profits. Analyzing all New York and American Stock Exchange common stocks over the 1963–80 period, Reinganum discovered that an annually changed or rebalanced portfolio of small stocks outperformed the large stock portfolio by over 20 percent annually. Also, the small stocks were consistent winners. They "won" in the battle for high returns against large stocks in fourteen of the eighteen years observed. The results of this study are shown in Table 42. Truly, small is beautiful.

The 32.8 percent average annual return of the small stock portfolio confirms the glamour of this investment approach. But what does this mean in hard dollars? If, for example, you were fortunate enough to invest $10,000 in this strategy in 1963, your portfolio would have grown to the staggering sum of $462,800 by the end of 1980. That's almost half a million dollars! Over the same period, $10,000 invested in the stocks of the largest firms would have grown to only $44,120. Now can you see why the small-stock investment strategy merits your attention?

Table 42

Firm-Size Portfolio Returns Using Annual Rebalancing
1963–1980

Portfolio[1]	Annual Profit	Median Market Value	Median Share Price
Decile 1	32.8%	$ 4.6	$ 5.24
Decile 2	23.5	10.8	9.52
Decile 3	23.0	19.3	12.89
Decile 4	20.2	30.7	16.19
Decile 5	19.1	47.2	19.22
Decile 6	18.3	74.2	22.59
Decile 7	15.6	119.1	26.44
Decile 8	14.2	209.7	30.83
Decile 9	13.0	434.6	34.43
Decile 10	9.5	1102.6	44.94

[1] Decile 1 contains the smallest MV companies, whereas Decile 10 consists of the largest MV firms.

Source: Marc Reinganum, "Portfolio Strategies Based on Market Capitalization," *The Journal of Portfolio Management,* Winter 1983.

Small Wins Again

You may recall that in Chapter 2 we showed the comprehensive Ibbotson and Sinquefield performance results for various types of securities over the 1926–81 era. We noted that common stocks provided superior returns when compared to bonds, short-term bills, and inflation. What we didn't show was that these two researchers were so intrigued with the performance of small-firm stocks that they separately computed another performance index. This time they observed the smallest 20 percent of the companies in their original common stock group.

You guessed it. The small stocks outpaced the overall stock market by earning a compound annual return of 12.1 percent as compared to 9.1 percent for all stocks over the same 1926–81 period. That means that small stocks more than quadrupled the period's 3.0 percent average yearly inflation rate. Stated another way, $100 invested in a portfolio of these small stocks at the beginning of 1926 would have snowballed to the almost unbelievable total of $59,710 by the end of 1981. On the other hand, a $100 portfolio of all stocks would have grown to $13,362—a creditable performance, but less than one fourth the wealth accumulated with small stocks. Figure 1 vividly portrays the dramatic performance contrast between small stocks and the overall market over the post-World War II period ended 1975.

You may wonder if the small-stock effect has already run its course. After all, 1926 (when this study began) was a long time ago. Maybe most or all of the extraordinary small-stock returns occurred long ago, thus opening the possibility that small stocks are no longer banner performers. Look again at Figure 1. You can't help but notice that small stocks have acted extremely well in those most recent years. And furthermore, the period beyond 1975 produced even greater small-stock returns. From 1975 to 1981, the small-stock portfolio appreciated an awesome 35.8 percent annually. Over the same period all stocks recorded a less inspiring 14.0 percent yearly return. Yes, it's plain to see that the small-stock phenomenon is still alive.

These results should cause even the most skeptical investor to take note. Yes, we realize that these findings are almost too astonishing to believe. In fact, we were highly suspicious of the small-firm performance results until our own research along with that of many others confirmed that small stocks really do perform admirably.

Figure 1
Small Stocks and the Market
1945–1975

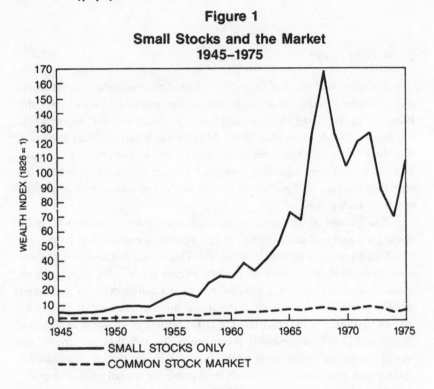

SMALL STOCKS ONLY

COMMON STOCK MARKET

Buy Low, Sell High

One other point of interest emerges from these recent studies. The stocks of small firms are usually low-priced. The Reinganum small-stock portfolio, to cite an example, had a midpoint, or median, share price of only $5.24. Thus 100 shares (an amount known as a round lot) of a typical small-firm stock would cost you only $524 plus commission. On the other hand, 100 shares of a representative large firm stock would set you back $4,494, excluding commission. As you can see, it is much easier to diversify your portfolio by purchasing the shares of small companies. You could easily acquire five or six different small stocks in round lots for a sum as modest as $5,000. Small stocks not only promise higher returns, they also offer considerably greater investment flexibility.

We have seen that small-company stocks usually sell at low share prices. We have also noted that studies of the performance of small stocks have emerged only recently. But what we have not yet mentioned is that the performance record of low-priced (typically small-firm) stocks has been available for many years. Let's take a closer look. Standard & Poor's Corporation, a major financial publications firm, regularly provides performance figures on the overall market and on many market subgroups. The S&P 500 is probably their most recognized performance index. This index is made up of the stocks of five hundred corporations, most of which are large. By tracing the S&P 500 over time, you can get a feel for the movement of the overall market.[3]

In addition to this market indicator, S&P also releases figures on the performance of representative "low-priced" stocks. This low-priced index provides an excellent opportunity to compare the performance of these "cheap" stocks to that of the overall market as gauged by the S&P 500. Figure 2 shows the results. Both indices began at an arbitrarily established level of 10 (1941–43 base period). But by the end of 1983, the low-priced index had exploded to 536.8—over fifty-three times its original level! However, the S&P 500 had grown to only 164.9. Since 1941, stocks with low prices have achieved significantly higher profits than the average security.

But don't be misled. We're not advocating that you venture out and accumulate a bunch of penny stocks. Why? The answer is elementary. Although many Hyperprofits stocks are low-priced, the reverse is not true. That is, most low-priced stocks are not Hyperprofits stocks. Even though low-priced stocks have performed well, you can still do better—particularly in the dreaded bear markets. A quick glance at Figure 2 tells all. Look what happened to low-priced stocks during the bear crash ending in 1974. This index tumbled to a mere one third of its earlier year-end 1968 reading—a far inferior performance than the overall market. Largely due to the risk-reducing character of Pillars 1 and 2, Hyperprofits moderates your exposure to such bear market disasters. Just because Hyperprofits selects many low-priced stocks, don't be lulled into believing that any cheapie will do.

Small in Action

Do these results seem too good to be true? Any investor who has fought a losing battle against the stock market may certainly think so. You may be asking yourself, "If the small stock strategy is so attractive, then why isn't someone actually using it?" The answer to your query is: Someone is using it, and quite successfully we might add. The Over-the-Counter Securities Fund,

[3] The S&P 500 is discussed in greater detail in Chapter 9.

Figure 2
Low-Price Stocks and the Market
1965–1983

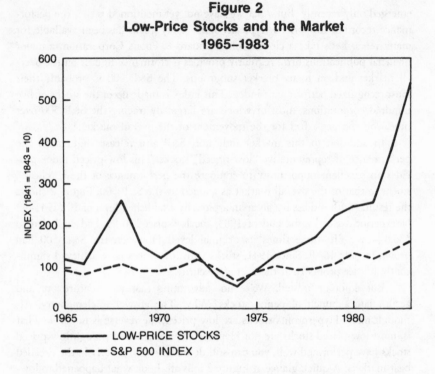

LOW-PRICE STOCKS
S&P 500 INDEX

Inc., hereafter called the O-T-C Fund, is a specialized mutual fund which concentrates its investments in the stocks of small companies traded in the over-the-counter market.

The O-T-C Fund does not acquire any of the larger New York or American Stock Exchange stocks—only nonexchange-listed, over-the-counter issues. The fund's objective, of course, is to capitalize on the performance of attractive small stocks. For example, at year's end 1983, the O-T-C Fund's five largest individual stock investments were Woodward Governor, Wister Oil, New Yorker Magazine, Rochester and Pittsburgh Coal, and William Carter—not exactly your typical corporate giants.

The fund has not been highly publicized and its $79 million total portfolio is not particularly large as mutual funds go (the average stock mutual fund has more than $150 million in assets). But the O-T-C Fund's track record is impressive. If you had invested $10,000 in this fund at the beginning of 1974, your portfolio would have grown to a tidy $77,713 by year's end 1983 (assuming you reinvested all dividends and capital gains). This represents a total gain of 677 percent during a time when overall stock prices increased much less, as evidenced by the Dow Jones Industrial's more modest 154 percent increase over this ten-year period. Small stocks, but certainly not small profits.[4]

How do they do it? Not by buying the large institutional favorites. Rather, the O-T-C Fund reaps the benefits of investing in small, undiscovered stocks. In the fund's 1983 annual report portfolio manager Binkley Shorts reveals the secret of this impressive performance record.

> We invest in pre-institutional holdings. We have found over the years that our most successful investments come in undiscovered situations where there are few if any other institutional holdings and little or no coverage from the brokerage community. If a broker is recommending a stock to his clients it's frequently too late for us.

Why can't you earn the same magnitude of profit with your own portfolio? Of course you can! Possibly you may be able to make an even greater profit. Remember, the O-T-C Fund has a portfolio of $79 million. That's a lot of small-firm stock. At year's end 1983, the fund's portfolio contained more than three hundred different issues. But you don't have to select that many. By purchasing from five to ten of the *best* stocks, you have the chance to achieve even loftier profits.

So you see, investing in the stocks of small companies really works. And what's more important is that it can work for you. When combined with the low-price–earnings-relative strategy (Chapter 4) and the discounted P/E approach (Chapter 5), the small-firm investment strategy will enable you to fulfill your quest for Hyperprofits.

You Can Beat the Pros!

You may feel that it's futile to try to beat the large financial institutions at their own game of picking attractive stocks. The major banks, pension funds, insurance companies, and mutual funds, to name a few, all have tremendous amounts of investable funds. Many highly educated and experienced invest-

---

[4] A study of mutual fund performance over the twenty-five-year period ended March 31, 1982, by Johnson's Investment Company revealed that the O-T-C Fund's 14.7 percent average annual return exceeded that of any other fund. Over this period, a $10,000 investment in the O-T-C Fund would have grown to $311,035—more than thirty-one times the original outlay in only twenty-five years.

ment professionals spend sixty, seventy, or even more hours every week to invest these funds in attractive situations. How can you possibly survive financially against such intense competition?

Well, you can't if you compete in the institutions' own arena. It's highly unlikely that you will ever make a find among the stocks that are closely followed by the Wall Street pros. Highly paid securities analysts so closely monitor the performance of these companies that anytime any new information appears, it is almost instantaneously observed and acted on by the pros. As a result, securities prices of these institutional favorites rapidly adjust to new information releases. The diligent efforts of securities analysts ensure that such immediate price reactions occur. Chances are, by the time you, an ordinary investor, receive the information, it's already been acted on and thus fully reflected in the stock's price. If you try to beat ·he pros at their own game, you're in for a very frustrating (and probably expensive) investment experience.

But do you really have to compete head-on with the pros? Definitely not! And furthermore, if you desire to be a successful investor, you had better plan on not competing against these financial experts.

You ask: "How can I avoid competing with these investment wizards? Aren't they everywhere, combing every nook and cranny of the marketplace to discover stock bargains?" The answer to your inquiry provides the key to your future success in stock market investing. No, the institutions do *not* scour every corner of the market. Far from it! Rather, the institutional investors tend to concentrate their resources in the stocks of the very largest corporations. Table 43 convincingly documents this institutional tendency. Every single one of the top twenty-five institutional favorites is a corporate Goliath. The *smallest* of these stocks has institutional holdings alone totaling over $3 billion. What's important is that you concentrate on those stocks which are not singled out by the pros—those "pre-institutional," issues as the O-T-C Fund appropriately labels them.

Table 43

Stocks Heavily Owned by Institutions
June 1984

Stock	Number of Institutions	Percentage of Total Shares	*Market Value of Institutional Holdings
IBM	1569	49	31.9
General Electric	1041	49	12.0
Exxon	947	31	10.7
General Motors	957	37	7.7
Standard Oil—Indiana	773	37	6.3
Atlantic Richfield	883	51	6.1
Schlumberger	871	42	6.0
Standard Oil—California	695	44	5.6
Eastman Kodak	858	50	5.5
Minnesota Mining	696	60	5.4
Philip Morris	686	63	5.2
Sears, Roebuck	588	47	5.1
Hewlett-Packard	600	48	4.4
American Home Products	694	51	4.4
Mobil	689	37	4.1
Ford Motor	421	57	4.0
Digital Equipment	547	76	4.0
Du Pont	597	34	3.9
Merck & Co.	661	58	3.8
Coca-Cola	567	51	3.8
Procter & Gamble	564	41	3.6

Stock	Number of Institutions	Percentage of Total Shares	*Market Value of Institutional Holdings
Bristol-Myers	595	56	3.6
Johnson & Johnson	623	55	3.4
R. J. Reynolds	520	48	3.2
Pfizer	666	59	3.1

Source: *The Outlook,* Standard & Poor's Corporation, June 13, 1984.

* In billions of dollars.

A few facts will reveal why the institutions ignore certain segments of the market. Back in the 1950s, for example, individuals were the dominant factor in the market, accounting for as much as 80 percent of all trading activity in some years. The institutions, on the other hand, were meager participants. But things changed. The institutions experienced meteoric growth in the post-1950s era. Today, institutional trading comprises approximately two thirds of the market's activity. Without a doubt the institutions have replaced individuals as the dominant market force.

This rapid escalation in institutional activity was accompanied by a growth in the amount of money a typical institution invested in a given stock. In 1965, an average of only nine "block" trades (transactions of 10,000 shares or more) occurred each day on the New York Stock Exchange. By 1983, an average of over 1,000 block trades transacted daily on the Big Board. Obviously, this explosion in big transactions points to the growing stock appetite of the institutions.

You may think that this concentration of investment power in the hands of the institutions will keep you from earning large profits. But that's not so. In fact, it is this very power concentration that so severely handicaps the institutions. Sound confusing? Let's look a little closer so that you can see exactly what we mean.

A survey of institutional investors reported in the article, "Thinking Small," in the April 1983 issue of the *Institutional Investor* indicated that over 95 percent of all responding institutions had less than 20 percent of their stock funds invested in the common stocks of companies with a market value of $100 million or less. Not a single institution reported having more than 60 percent of its stock money invested in small firms. The same institutions, however, when asked, "Which of the following do you think will provide the greatest return over the next five years?" responded as follows:

Stock Category	Percentage of Institutions Selecting
Large capitalization (over $500 million)	21.9
Intermediate capitalization ($100 million–$500 million)	34.3
Small capitalization (under $100 million)	43.8

The contradiction is apparent. Many institutions believe small stocks will provide high returns, but still do not invest heavily in these issues. Why? The example in the next section will help explain.

The Institution's Plight

The College Retirement Equities Fund (CREF) is a pension fund designed to provide retirement benefits to the employees of some 3,600 educational and research institutions. Currently CREF has approximately $15 billion invested in over 1,000 different common stocks. That's right, $15 billion in over 1,000 stocks! With that massive of a portfolio, does CREF have a chance to beat the market? Not likely. Owing to its huge size and large number of holdings, in fact, CREF has basically become the market. After deducting the costs of management fees and other expenses, the CREF portfolio is doing well to keep up with the market.

CREF is merely one example of the investment inflexibility confronting the large institutional stock managers. On account of their enormous size, many institutions find it almost impossible to beat the market because, when grouped together, they are the market. Performance records seem to verify this conclusion. SEI Funds Evaluation Services, an institutional investment consultant, reports that for the ten-year period ending in 1982 the S&P 500 outperformed two thirds of the institutional stock managers.

It's not surprising that portions of several giant investment funds such as the pension portfolios of AT&T, General Motors, and Exxon have been "indexed" as stock market clones. If you buy the same 500 stocks (in the same proportions) that comprise the S&P 500 market index, you officially become the market. When Harvard University recently indexed about one third of its $1.6 billion in stocks, fund manager Walter Cabot commented, "If you can't beat 'em, join 'em."

This brings us to the most important point: the reason you have a substantial investment advantage over the large institutions. Can you imagine an institution like CREF devoting much effort to the research of small companies? When you consider that the fund usually invests over $1 million in a single stock, you can answer that question with ease. No matter how attractive a small company's stock may be, CREF, with its huge amount of assets, could not benefit because there's just not enough of the stock to cause even a ripple in the portfolio's profitability. And furthermore, the fact that size constraints discourage the selection of small-firm stocks means that CREF analysts cannot afford to waste much time and effort researching these stocks.

Now can you get a feel for the implications of the large institutions ignoring the small stocks? If so, you have realized that by concentrating your investments in the stocks of small companies, you don't have to compete with the pros. As an individual, you are spared the problem of having so much money that you can only invest in the largest stocks. To the contrary, you can use your funds to buy the stocks of attractive small companies that have not been overanalyzed by the institutions. An attractive small company may not ever make a ripple in an institution's portfolio, but it could create a tidal wave in yours.

A study by Frank Reilly (now dean of the College of Business at Notre Dame) points out the predicament of the institutions. He maintains that the stock market consists of three levels, or tiers:

Top tier: The stocks of companies that are large enough for the investments of all institutions. An estimated 400 firms meet the assumed minimum market value of $400 million.

Middle tier: The stocks of firms that are large enough to accommodate the investments of all except the 25–30 largest institutions. An additional 300 or so firms satisfy the $200-million minimum cutoff for this tier.

Bottom tier: The stocks of all remaining firms not large enough to be considered by institutions. Although no one knows for sure, the total number of companies in this tier is at least 5,000 (and could be considerably more).

Source: Frank K. Reilly, "A Three Tier Stock Market and Corporate Finance," *Financial Management,* 1975, pp. 7–15.

As you can plainly see, there are thousands of stocks that are ignored by the professionals. The absence of these pros in the small-stock ranks spells opportunity for you. Since these small-company stocks are basically ignored by the big investors, you can step in and earn profits beyond your wildest expectations. But you must be selective. Not all small stocks are destined to provide high returns. Indeed, you must be careful to construct a portfolio that contains only those small stocks that have outstanding profit potential.

A Pro in Action

Just how do the professionals really invest? Does a typical money manager use his on-the-job expertise to reap superior profits for his or her own portfolio? To answer these questions, let's observe the activities of a real-life institutional money manager. Because this manager desires to remain anonymous, we will simply call him Peter R. Outlook, or P.R.O. for short.

For the past decade P.R.O. has been very successful in his money management activities. He has consistently been able to "beat the market" by some two to three percentage points each year. His performance credentials have earned him great respect among his peers.

P.R.O.'s employer also recognizes his capabilities and, as a result, has basically given him free rein to select and buy stocks for the institution's equity portfolio. But there is one big exception: P.R.O. is not allowed to purchase any individual stock with a total market value of less than $200 million. The reason: the big institutions usually invest millions of dollars in a single company's stock. Given the size of the small companies, there isn't enough stock available to make it worthwhile for a big institution to search out these situations. In addition, a small stock, even if discovered by the institution, is very difficult to buy and sell in the large dollar amounts to which this institution has grown accustomed. The attempt to buy too many shares could immediately push the stock's price too high to be desirable.

P.R.O. readily agrees that small stocks are not appropriate for big institutions and thus has no problem in accepting this size restriction. On the other hand, for his personal account P.R.O. virtually never buys the same stocks that he acquires for his employer's portfolio. Why? Even though he believes that he can slightly outperform the market with his big-stock selections, he realizes that he can perform even better by purchasing the stocks of smaller, less analyzed companies.

His assertion that "small stocks are not as intensely analyzed as are the big stocks and therefore not as efficiently priced" is the very foundation for his personal investment strategy. P.R.O. sums up his personal investment experience with the following statement:

> There's a considerably higher probability that I can find undiscovered bargains among the very small companies, but these kinds of bargains simply don't exist with the large companies. By applying my analytical techniques to small stocks, I know that I can consistently make high profits. And because I don't have the liquidity problems like an institution does, I can buy and sell those small stocks without the fear of 'moving the market.'

So you see, even a highly regarded pro realizes the secret to stock market profits. By confining his personal investments to the stocks of small firms, P.R.O. has been able to earn personal profits at an extremely high rate—considerably outdistancing the performance of his employer's professionally managed portfolio. And the only reason for his superior performance: the ability to acquire attractive small stocks.

But Small Is Not Enough

Indeed small is beautiful. Our computer research verifies this belief, as do the research findings of other students of the stock market. But as attractive as the small-stock investment approach is, it's just not enough. After all, we have already shown that other investment strategies produce handsome profits. So why not benefit from all strategies combined? You may think that a 20 percent or so annual profit is highly satisfactory. Maybe you haven't been able to earn that much before. But why stop at 20 percent when you can earn 30 percent or more from our combined investment strategy? If this sounds attractive, then keep reading.

Now let's look at the overall structure. Built upon a foundation of profit-compounding, the three crucial investment pillars have been individually constructed. Each pillar on its own provides the structure for substantial financial rewards. But when combined, the pillars yield an even more profitable financial palace.

We previously showed you how the profits of low-price–earnings-relative stocks were greater than their high-PER counterparts. So that you can see that not all small firms are the same, let's observe what happens when we combine the PER method with the small size strategy. Table 44 reveals that your profits substantially improve when you buy small-firm stocks with low PERs.

Table 44

Small-Firm Stock Profits by PER Groups

PER Group	Annual Return
Lowest quintile	27.8%
Next quintile	24.7
Next quintile	21.4
Next quintile	16.6
Highest quintile	11.5

Remember, all these stocks are those of small firms. The performance results are most gratifying. The lowest-PER group earned an average of 27.8 percent annually, compared to only 11.5 percent per year for the highest-PER category. This means that if you were to buy a portfolio of small-firm stocks with very high PERs, you would have earned less than the average low-P/E stock over the 1970–80 period. That is, you probably could have selected a better portfolio merely by throwing darts at a random list of low-P/E stocks. And we have already exposed the shortcomings of the low-P/E approach. Clearly, investing small is not enough. You must be careful to select only the most attractive small-firm stocks.

And for the next step we add to this the second pillar. We are now looking at stocks of small firms, with low PERs and P/Es below past norms. This melds the three pillars together into the full forces of the Hyperprofits investment plan. What is the impact of this force? To find out, we asked the computer to select only low-PER, low-DPE stocks of small firms ($75 million of market value or less). Our computer research confirms that over the years Hyperprofits stocks have averaged 32.3 percent profit annually.

But there's more to the story. There's a second reason that random selection of small stocks alone may be an expensive proposition. The reason is risk. Small stocks, on average, are riskier than the stocks of large companies. The most recent Reinganum study exposed small stocks to be an average of 58 percent riskier than the typical common stock. Risk measures the extent to which your stock will decline when the overall stock market falls. So if the market declines, say, 10 percent, your typical small-company stock will fall 15.8 percent—a 58 percent greater decline than experienced by the market. That's a lot of risk—maybe enough to discourage you from investing in the stocks of small companies. The results speak out clearly: investing small is not enough.

Turning Small Stocks into Large Profits

Fortunately there's more to the small-stock saga. The three pillars of Hyperprofits transform small-stock investments into huge profits without exposing your funds to excessive risks. Here's how:

Fact #1: In Chapter 4 you found that low-PER stocks yield high rates of return. This is the first pillar toward achieving Hyperprofits.

Fact #2: In Chapter 5 you learned that you will be rewarded financially if you purchase stocks that are selling at P/Es that are lower than their historical norms. This is the second pillar.

Fact #3: In this chapter you observed that small stocks, on average, produce high profits. This is the final pillar toward your quest for Hyperprofits.

Fact #4: While the use of the final pillar by itself entails significant risks, the application of each of the first two pillars can be accomplished at a relatively low risk level.

Fact #5: The combination of these three investment pillars into one integrated financial strategy will allow you to pursue Hyperprofits without being exposed to excessive risks.

The upshot of these five facts is this: by applying the Hyperprofits investment strategy you can transform small stocks into large profit potential without being exposed to extreme risks. The first two pillars are the real keys to moderating your risk. They enable you to select the superprofit opportunities from the small-stock group and at the same time ensure that your risk is not excessive. Now you can see why we use all three pillars in the Hyperprofits wealth-building strategy.

7

How to Achieve Hyperprofits

You now have the complete picture. You have seen what Hyperprofits can do for you and how it does it. Now comes the most important part of all, putting the system into action. This is the bottom line, the payoff. You already have the theory, and this chapter will give you the practice. You will learn the step-by-step procedure for putting the Hyperprofits system to work for you. The implementation of this system will enable you to reap the high rewards which we have shown that Hyperprofits produces.

Traveling the Easy Road

You're probably thinking, "I've heard the good news, now here comes the bad. Any system shown to yield that much profit is bound to cost plenty in terms of time and effort. Sure, I want to build that kind of wealth, but I don't have the time to dedicate my life to it. There's got to be more to life than calculating pillars for thousands of stocks."

Yes, we've seen the ads, "No pain, no gain." Well, let us set your mind at rest right here and now. Hyperprofits isn't like that. Not at all. With the right information in hand and our step-by-step procedure to follow, you'll be amazed to discover how easy it is to put your wealth-building program into full swing. Even if you've never invested in stocks before, there should be no hesitancy on your part. The road to Hyperprofits is already all mapped out for you.

Actually, there is more than one way that you can derive the benefits of Hyperprofits. There are three ways to capture the rewards in ascending order of automation: (1) managing the system yourself, (2) utilizing Hyperprofits computer software, and (3) having a professional manage it for you. If you choose method (1), first and foremost, you must follow the instructions given in this chapter. This approach will afford you the pleasure and self-satisfaction of the do-it-yourself method. Most of the chapter is devoted to this purpose.

But there is another way to implement the Hyperprofits system. If you own or have access to a personal or professional computer, you can let your computer do the walking for you by using Hyperprofits software. The Hyperprofits software includes all the stock data and is programmed to follow the same basic procedure that is provided in this chapter.[1]

Probably the easiest way of all to get started on your own is to let us assist you. In Chapter 10, we provide a list of ten top Hyperprofits stock prospects. These selections will give you an idea of what Hyperprofits stocks look like and will steer you in the proper direction for making your own choices.

Hyperprofits in Action

While our top-prospects list may be a splendid way to get out of the blocks quickly, there will come the day when you decide to sell some of your initial stocks and reinvest the proceeds in some new prospects. That's when the Hyperprofits procedure will be invaluable to you. So let's look at the Hyperprofits system one step at a time.

You already know that at the heart of the Hyperprofits system lie the three pillars. Firmly resting on the foundation of the magic of compounding, these three pillars enable you to select outstanding common stocks for your portfolio. So the first and most important step is to find out which stocks promise the best profit potential in terms of these pillars. To uncover these, you must have the right data available. Also, you need this data in a form which allows you to locate the top prospects speedily and easily.

To this end, there are several data sources available. Two that you will find helpful are *The Value Line Investment Survey*, published by:

Value Line, Inc.
711 Third Avenue
New York, NY 10017

---

[1] If you would like to know more details about the Hyperprofits software or the use of professional management write:

Hyperprofits
P.O. Box 821292
Dallas, Texas 75382-1292

and *Moody's Handbook of Common Stocks,* published by:

> Moody's Investors Service
> 90 Church Street
> New York, NY 10007

Both of these sources offer the advantage of being available at many public libraries. We will come back to these later in the chapter.

From our own investigations, we have found that the most serviceable source of data for Hyperprofits is *The Media General Financial Weekly* (annual subscription is $108[2]), published by:

> Media General, Inc.
> P.O. Box C-32333
> Richmond, Virginia 23293

The *Financial Weekly* contains comprehensive financial data on more than 4,300 stocks presented in a fashion which makes it easy for you to exploit the benefits of Hyperprofits. Take a look for a moment at the Media General reprint on the following page which shows stocks grouped by industry.

As the Media General reprint shows, the companies are arranged into industry segments. This grouping will be useful to you both in terms of selecting attractive Pillar 1 stocks and in achieving proper diversification. The column headings reveal several pieces of information about each stock, such as closing share price for the week, most recent annual earnings per share, and the stock's dividend yield.

All right, which of these information pieces is going to be helpful to you in determining the three pillars of Hyperprofits? Yep, it's our old friend the P/E ratio. By now you've probably gotten the idea that the current P/E is the single most important piece of stock data ever conceived by the mind of man. And you're not far from correct. The P/E is the basis for the first two Hyperprofits pillars.

In particular, let's consider Pillar 1, the price–earnings relative. You'll recall that the PER is determined by dividing a stock's current P/E by the average P/E for the related industry segment. Now what do we do? We could, for example, add up all the P/Es for a particular group, such as the aerospace components segment, and average them. Are we trapped into pulling out the old calculator and making some computations? No, thank goodness. Fortunately, the *Financial Weekly* spares us from such a tedious fate.

---

[2] A ten-week trial subscription is available for $21.00.

Company-Page-Market		Close $	Price Chg. Yr. to Date %	Curr. P/E Ratio -	EPS 12 Mth. Chg. %	Div. Yld. %	Ret. on Com. Eqty. %
011 Aerospace Industries							
Boeing Co	12-N	43.75	.0	12.4	7	3.2	11.7
Curtiss-Wright	19-N	34.75	- 27.6	11.4	- 23	3.5	8.7
Fairchild Ind	23-N	17.13	- 7.4	9.4	20	4.7	11.6
Gen Dynamics	26-N	52.50	- 9.7	9.9	82	1.9	22.7
Grumman Corp	27-N	26.00	7.2	6.7	15	3.5	24.5
Lockheed Corp	34-N	39.25	- 1.9	9.1	16	.4	31.8
McDonnel Doug	36-N	56.00	- 5.5	7.9	24	2.9	13.3
Northrop Corp	40-N	93.00	7.8	11.4	252	1.9	17.5
Rockwell Intl	47-N	27.13	- 17.8	10.5	19	3.7	16.5
Utd Technol	56-N	32.50	- 10.3	8.3	18	4.3	15.7
012 Aerospace Components							
AAR Corp	6-N	20.38	18.1	21.0	45	2.2	6.5
Aeroflex Labs	6-N	12.25	- 25.8	12.1	9	.0	18.7
Aeronca Inc	6-A	5.13	- 6.8	6.7	27	.0	37.0
Anadite Inc	8-M	7.25	- 37.0	NE	-100	1.4	NE
Atlantic Research	10-M	29.75	1.7	15.3	31	.0	18.1
Cdn Marconi	13-A	17.88	- 14.4	NA	36	NA	18.9
Gull Inc	28-M	7.75	- 16.2	12.3	NC	.0	14.2
Hexcel Corp	29-N	22.75	8.3	20.1	14	2.6	7.9
Intl Controls	31-A	16.00	- 8.6	10.7	- 16	1.6	18.6
Kaman Corp A	32-M	19.00	- 16.5	10.4	36	2.5	14.4
Lundy Elec	35-A	7.75	- 31.1	29.8	- 75	.0	6.4
Matec	36-A	6.13	16.7	34.0	157	.0	2.6
Moog Inc	38-A	14.38	- 17.9	15.0	7	1.9	10.3
OEA Inc	41-A	21.25	- 12.4	13.6	21	.0	17.4
Raytheon Co	46-N	38.00	- 11.9	10.5	- 2	3.7	15.9
Rockcor Inc	47-M	11.38	- 11.7	15.8	1	.0	9.6
Rohr Industries	47-N	34.25	- 6.5	8.3	46	.0	16.2
Sargent Indus	48-A	8.38	3.1	10.5	196	.0	14.1
Sierracin Corp	49-A	12.38	- 13.2	10.5	258	3.2	22.9
Sundstrand Cp	52-N	40.50	- 16.9	13.5	- 3	4.4	10.3
TransTechnol	54-A	14.25	- 14.3	9.4	11	3.9	16.8
TRE Corp	54-N	19.25	- 36.4	9.2	- 36	5.2	7.8
Utd Aircraft	55-A	14.50	- 14.7	9.4	- 1	3.7	19.9
Van Dusen Air	57-M	13.63	- 7.6	20.1	392	2.9	1.2
Walbar	57-A	19.63	.6	12.7	22	1.6	16.2
Watkins Jhnsn	58-N	24.75	- 10.4	15.5	38	1.3	15.0
013 Aircraft Manuf., Serv.							
Advance Ross	6-O	5.13	- 22.6	17.7	26	.0	5.9
Aero Svc	6-O	1.88	- 25.0	31.3	- 25	.0	5.3
Aero Systems	6-O	2.13	- 43.3	16.3	- 38	.0	23.2

Observe the *Financial Weekly* reprint shown on the next page. Here you see a summary of statistics broken down by industry group. The particular statistic that you need most is the "last close" column under the P/E headline. This column provides the average P/E ratio for each of the respective industry segments. For example, if you observe industry number 012 (aerospace components), you will note an 11.7 average P/E ratio (the circled figure on the next page).

By turning back to the individual company listings on the previous page you can mentally compare each company's current P/E to the 11.7 industry norm. Remember, you are looking for the lowest PERs. It only takes a moment to uncover every Pillar 1 candidate. You can identify the top Pillar 1 prospects in a matter of seconds. But actually it's even easier. Isn't it true, by definition, that the lowest P/E in an industry is also the lowest PER? Of course it is. So all you have to do is scan down the P/E column for the lowest P/Es, and presto you've got the lowest PERs. For instance, in the aerospace components group, you can tell at a glance that Aeronca, Inc., at a 6.7 P/E is the lowest PER in the group. The ability to select low PERs sends you off to a flying start at identifying the top Hyperprofits prospects.

Now, what about the other two pillars? Take a look on the next page, which reproduces data from the *Financial Weekly*. These stock tables, which list all companies alphabetically, provide more comprehensive information. Let's take Pillar 3 first. You've learned that extensive Pillar 3 research demonstrates that over the long run small-company stocks outperform large-firm stocks. We measure this company-size factor by multiplying the stock's current market price by the number of shares outstanding to arrive at the company's market value. Now check the rightmost column of the data. Behold, there it is. Market value is already computed for each stock. Two down, one to go.

Pillar 2 is slightly tougher to compute, but not much! Recall that this pillar is the discounted P/E ratio, or DPE, calculated by taking a stock's current P/E and dividing by its historical average P/E. Well, let's see what the *Financial Weekly* provides here. Scanning the column headings under the P/E caption, you can find both a current and a five-year-average P/E.

How lucky can you get? There are the two pieces of data you need lined up right next to each other. The current P/E divided by its five-year-average provides you with Pillar 2. But wait a minute. Does this mean that some 4,300-odd Pillar 2's need to be calculated? Certainly not. Remember that the DPE is favorable when it is less than one. In fact, the smaller the DPE, the better.

So by just visually comparing the number in the current column with the number in the average column, you can tell instantly which stocks are attractive Pillar 2 candidates. Moreover, this same comparison even tells you which

No.	Name	Number in Grp	Total Market Value ($Mil)	Week's Trading Dollar Volume ($Mil)	Pct of Market Value (%)	Latest 12 Months Total ($Mil)	Latest 12 Months Change (%)	5-Year Annual Growth Rate (%)	Price Change Last 52 Weeks (%)	Last 13 Weeks (%)	Last Week (%)	P/E 52 Weeks Ago	P/E 13 Weeks Ago	P/E Last Close	Profit Margin (%)	Dvd Yield (%)	Return on Stock Equity (%)
—	Composite	4,331	1,722,750	16,827	.98	144,853	+ 19	+ 2	−13.2	− 4.6	− .7	14.4	12.0	11.3	4.7	4.4	10.8
—	NYSE	1,505	1,458,680	14,437	.99	129,969	+ 19	+ 2	−11.1	− 4.3	− .7	13.8	11.6	10.6	4.8	4.8	11.1
—	AMEX	754	73,382	329	.45	2,630	0	−11	−19.5	− 6.1	−1.0	27.1	21.3	26.9	3.0	2.5	5.8
—	O−T−C	2,072	190,688	2,060	1.08	12,264	+ 23	+ 3	−24.8	− 6.0	− .5	18.1	13.7	15.4	4.9	2.0	10.1
01	Aerospace	50	30,047	338	1.12	2,896	+ 20	+ 7	−13.1	+ 7.1	+ .1	14.2	9.9	10.3	3.9	2.9	14.9
011	Aerospace Industries	10	22,512	277	1.23	2,335	+ 26	+ 9	− 9.3	+11.3	+ .8	13.4	8.9	9.6	3.7	2.9	15.6
012	Aerospace Components	26	6,223	51	.82	528	+ 6	+ 5	−21.2	− 2.0	−2.5	15.7	12.2	11.7	5.0	3.0	14.1
013	Aircraft Manuf, Serv	14	1,312	10	.76	33	− 53	−25	−30.3	−11.2	+1.6	26.3	40.6	39.5	2.1	1.0	5.8
02	Airlines	38	9,927	172	1.73	−151	NE	+27	−27.9	− 9.2	−2.6	NE	NE	NE	−1.2	.6	NE
021	Trunk Airlines	16	7,247	142	1.96	−214	NE	+15	−24.3	− 8.9	−3.2	NE	NE	NE	−1.3	.7	NE
022	Regional Airlines	22	2,680	30	1.12	64	NE	+47	−36.5	−10.0	−1.0	NE	NE	42.1	− .6	.6	NE
03	Automotive	43	43,457	420	.97	8,376	+749	+73	− 8.2	− 2.2	+ .3	27.8	6.6	5.1	3.9	4.4	10.4
031	Auto Manufacturers	7	36,173	370	1.02	7,690	+890	+64	− 6.7	− .5	+ .5	25.7	5.9	4.7	4.0	4.7	10.7
032	Auto Parts, Access	36	7,284	50	.69	687	+240	+ 6	−14.7	− 9.8	− .9	46.7	14.3	10.6	3.2	3.2	8.8
04	Banking	249	63,676	548	.86	8,583	− 9	− 2	−11.5	− 9.2	− .8	7.3	7.6	7.3	5.7	5.9	11.6
041	New England Banks	25	3,375	29	.86	504	+ 3	+ 7	− 9.8	− 6.7	−2.2	6.5	6.1	6.6	6.5	5.5	12.9
042	Middle Atlantic Banks	42	18,921	250	1.32	3,652	+ 12	+11	−16.4	−10.1	−1.9	6.4	5.6	5.1	6.0	7.0	13.4

A L -Ala

Company and Market		Symbol	Ind. Grp.	Price					Relative Price			Earnings Per Share			Dividend		Other	
				Close	Price Change		52-Week		Price to Equity	P/E Ratio		Latest 12 Months		5-Year Growth Rate	Amount	Yield	Debt Equity Ratio	Market Value
					Last Week	Year To Date	High	Low		Current	5-Year Average	Amount	Change					
				$	%	%	$	$	%	·	·	$	%	%	$	%	%	$Mil
A L Labs	A	BMD	151	10.00	-1.2	NC	15.75	9.75	1053	12.7	NC	.79q	NC	56	.00	.0	532	41
A&M Food Svcs	O	AMFD	243	5.75	-8.0	-20.7	8.75	.00	263	13.1	17.5	.44q	NC	10	.00	.0	55	20
AA Importing	O	ANTQ	529	4.00	.0	-23.8	6.00	4.00	176	8.7	11.2	.46q	NC	14	.00	.0	16	11
AAR Corp	N	AIR	012	20.38	1.9	18.1	20.38	13.25	185	21.0	13.2	.97n	45	-6	.44	2.2	54	121
Aaron Rents	O	ARON	094	15.50	-4.6	-15.1	24.50	14.00	371	16.1	20.6	.96n	28	38	.00	.0	5	83
★ Abbott Labs	N	ABT	151	43.63	-2.5	-3.6	53.38	38.25	373	14.7	13.9	2.97q	20	27	1.20	2.8	34	5,283
Abrams Ind	O	ABRI	061	9.25	.0	7.2	9.25	7.44	84	7.5	6.3	1.23f	48	30	.32	3.5b	135	11
Academy Ins Grp	M	ACIG	261	8.50	-5.6	-40.4	17.88	8.50	145	7.7	12.6	1.11q	31	67	.20	2.4	15	132
Acapulco Rest	O	ALAR	243	5.00	2.6	-13.0	7.25	3.88	495	NE	38.5	-1.81s	-100	-75	.00	.0a	632	12
Acceleration Cp	M	ACLE	261	11.00	4.8	-6.4	13.00	8.50	163	18.6	7.8	.59q	13	-11	.05	.5	0	51
AccoWorld	N	ACO	084	28.13	3.7	2.3	30.25	23.75	517	17.6	16.8	1.81f	28	29	.60	2.1	32	258
AccuRay Cp	M	ACRA	403	17.88	-2.1	-29.6	26.63	15.13	185	13.1	13.0	1.30q	20	86	.16	.9	53	74
Aceto – Chem	O	ACET	101	19.00	4.1	.0	22.22	16.97	120	9.2	6.6	2.07n	16	10	.00	.0a	20	33
★ ACF Industries	N	ACF	284	53.88	2.1	7.8	54.00	31.50	118	NM	NM	.08f	-98	-13	1.40	2.6	107	451
ACMAT Corp	O	ACMT	062	10.00	2.6	-21.6	17.00	9.50	333	6.6	7.8	1.52q	83	104	.00	.0	50	11
★ Acme-CleveInd	N	AMT	291	17.38	2.2	-31.2	27.25	16.50	90	NE	6.2	-2.19q	-100	-29	.32	1.8b	30	102
Acme Elec	N	ACE	161	8.88	.0	-10.1	12.28	8.38	168	26.1	35.0	.34n	10	-13	.28	3.2b	38	32
Acme Genl	O	ACME	058	13.25	.0	20.5	15.25	9.50	146	8.8	16.8	1.50s	56	2	.25	1.9	3	26
Acme Precision	A	ACL	294	2.75	.0	-50.0	8.63	2.50	69	NE	20.6	-.13s	NE	40	.00	.0	136	2
Acme United	A	ACU	231	12.75	-4.7	-20.9	19.50	12.25	205	(12.6)	(14.2)	1.01q	20	13	.32	2.5	9	41
Acro Energy	O	ACRO	059	5.00	.0	-44.4	11.25	4.75	243	(6.5)	(83.4)	.77n	NC	43	.00	.0	39	10
ACS Indus	O	ACSC	341	2.38	.0	5.6	2.75	1.75	40	(.9)	.3	.53q	51	93	.00	.0	28	3

are the best candidates. You're interested only in those stocks with low DPEs. For example, you can see at just a glance that while Acme United has a favorable (low) DPE, Acro Energy actually has a much better DPE. So without actually calculating a thing, you can quickly identify the Hyperprofits qualifiers.

From our discussion so far, you can see how easy it is to uncover the three pillars. Now for a dress rehearsal. Let's analyze the Aerospace Components industry as of July 2, 1984, to see if there are any Hyperprofits candidates among this group. As shown on the *Financial Weekly* page reproduced on page 123, we know that Aeronca has the lowest PER. But it's possible that it may not qualify under Pillars 2 and 3. So let's begin by including a few more of the lowest PERs in our Hyperprofits candidates group. Observe that only three other stocks (Rohr Industries, Trans Technology, and United Aircraft) have P/Es below 10.

We'll start with this group of the lowest four PERs. Notice that to the immediate left of the company name appears the page number of the stock tables where the other two pillars can be found. Now we have enough information to construct each stock's complete pillar structure (Table 45).

Table 45

Potential Aerospace Hyperprofits Prospects

Company	Pillar 1	Pillar 2	Pillar 3
Aeronca, Inc.	.57	.08	15
Rohr Industries	.71	1.05	264
Trans Technology	.80	.85	70
United Aircraft	.80	.70	31

Let's see what we've got. For Aeronca, Pillars 1 and 2 are clearly very low and thus quite favorable, while Pillar 3, market value, stands at $15 million. We know that small is beautiful. But how small is small? Our research indicates that companies under $75 million of market value are the best bets. So Aeronca easily qualifies on all counts.

How about the other three? Rohr Industries has a DPE above 1 and an MV above $75 million, disqualifying it on both counts. However, Trans Technology and United Aircraft qualify on all three pillars. How do we distinguish among these three finalists? First of all, it is not particularly important that Aeronca is a somewhat smaller firm. However, it is critical that Aeronca has substantially lower Pillars 1 and 2. This fact means that its chances of blooming into a superwinner are somewhat higher than those of the other two. Therefore, you would rank Aeronca as the top Hyperprofits prospect in the aerospace components industry. That's just how easy it is to apply the three Hyperprofits pillars.

Does this mean that Trans Technology and United Aircraft will not perform as well as Aeronca? If only life were this simple. Of course not. There are no guarantees. But what it does mean is that based on the accumulated research of the Hyperprofits system, Aeronca has the best odds of being a top performing stock in this industry.

Actually, there isn't any need to even jot down all four companies. As soon as you see that any one pillar is not favorable, you can forget the stock. What if there are no stocks within an industry which qualify under all three pillars? No problem. Just select another industry which is to your liking. That's the beauty of having more than 100 industry segments and 4,300 companies at your disposal. Okay, but what if there are some qualifiers, but their PERs or DPEs are close to one? Forget them. Choose another industry. You want only superprospects, not mediocre ones, in your portfolio. You're in the driver's seat. You can afford to shop around for the best.

One additional word of advice that we have found helpful. We showed you earlier that on the average the smaller the firm, the higher the profit return for the stock. At the same time, the smaller the company, the more volatile is the performance of its stock. For this reason, we suggest that for smaller portfolios, those with fewer than eight stocks, you might want to limit your selections to companies of $15 million or more in market value. You may sacrifice a small amount of profit potential, but in return you will receive the benefit of better diversification and greater stability for your portfolio.

Diversify, Diversify, Diversify

Now where do you go from here? At this point, let's review the rules of diversification you learned in Chapter 2. We can summarize these as follows:

1. Maintain several stocks in your portfolio.

2. Make sure your stocks are selected from widely differing industries so that the risks are as unrelated as possible.

3. Do not overdiversify by buying too many stocks.

Remember that diversification gives you security. Not every stock in your portfolio will be a big winner. Yes, you'll even have some losers. It's the net result of your whole portfolio you are looking for. Then how should you apply the first rule? How many stocks do you need?

Suppose, like many of us, you are beginning with only $5,000 to $10,000 of investable funds. In that event we suggest that you should select a minimum of five stocks. Why five? Because studies demonstrate that by holding five widely differing stocks, you can achieve 79 percent of the total diversification benefit possible. What does this mean? If you were to hold a portfolio consisting of all stocks in the market, literally tens of thousands of stocks, you obviously would procure 100 percent of the diversification benefit. But with merely five, you've got nearly four fifths of this protection. Think of it. It seems amazing, but it's true.

You might say, If five is good, why isn't 20 or 30 even better? The obvious answer is that $5,000 won't buy 20 stocks, let alone 30. But the important point is that you don't need 30 stocks in order to achieve most of the comforts of diversification. Moreover, when you dip down to that 30th stock, its pillars are not as likely to be as attractive as those for your number one pick. Therefore, you might be sacrificing investment potential which could translate into a lower profit outlook.

So you are looking to achieve the best possible balance between financial security and profit potential. With minimum working capital, five stocks is a minimum starting point while eight or ten, if possible, is preferable. But what if you are fortunate enough to be able to start with more than the minimum investment? Then what would be the best balance? What is the maximum number of stocks you should own?

Remember you want as much safety and upside potential as you can get. If you are in a position to be able to purchase 20 stocks, then you will achieve nearly all of the diversification benefit that is possible while making almost no sacrifice in terms of quality. Therefore, 20 stocks is an ideal maximum. This doesn't mean that 22 or 23 stocks isn't any good. In fact, if you're really wealthy you might want to spread your wealth among even more stocks. But remember, by holding 20 properly selected stocks, you obtain virtually all of the benefits of diversification. By so doing, you will satisfy Rule 3 of proper diversification while obtaining excellent upside profit potential.

So far, we have talked about Rules 1 and 3 of proper diversification. What about Rule 2, concerning differing industry groups? Consider our aerospace group list. We have already identified the top Hyperprofits candidates. According to Rule 2, if you are to achieve the maximum diversification benefit, how many stocks can you afford to include from a given industry? That's right, only one. So after selecting the top prospect from the first industry, you should move on to an entirely different kind of group. Here Hyperprofits gives you some investment flexibility. If you particularly favor a certain industry, select a Hyperprofits stock from that industry and then move on to your next favorite industry, and so forth. In this manner you can purchase attractive stocks in attractive industries.

Let's briefly recap what you have learned so far about putting Hyperprofits into action. For one thing, you know how to scan the data to quickly identify the Hyperprofits candidates. For another, you know how to select the top prospects from a group of candidates within an industry group. You have also learned that ideally you want to hold a minimum of five stocks in your portfolio. The maximum number of stocks to own depends on how much capital you have to invest. Unless you are very wealthy, we suggest that 20 stocks is a reasonable maximum.

Now suppose you have one stock selected, say, from the aerospace components group. Where do you go from here? You want at least five Hyperprofits stocks to complete a diversified portfolio. Does this mean that you'll have to scan all 4,300-plus stocks in the data list just to arrive at your final five?

Well, if you wanted to, you could. And using the methods we have given you thus far, you could do it in a reasonably short period of time. But there is an easier way. Recollect that the second diversification rule tells you that you want each of your stocks to come from a different industry. Therefore, instead of checking through all 4,300 stocks in the universe list, just select another industry group which is unlike the one from which you have already picked a stock.

The first one on our reprint page is the aerospace industry. We sure don't want that one because it's much too closely related to aerospace components. Fortunately, the *Financial Weekly* offers sixty major industry groups plus many more subgroups. With this varied assortment, you can't possibly fail to achieve the maximum diversification benefit.

So, for example, you might next choose to take a look at the chemical industry. Although there are some small Pillar 3 firms in this group, most of these companies tend to be large. What if it turns out that none of the companies in an industry are satisfactory in terms of all three pillars? Then forget that industry. Move right along to another industry. You want only *top* Hyperprofits prospects in your portfolio. Since you have a wealth of groups from which to choose, you can afford to be very fussy. And you should be.

Now let's observe one more industry and see what happens. How about computers? That should be an interesting one. The thing you want to ensure is that the industry you choose is unrelated to any of the other industries you have already chosen. You already know why—to achieve the maximum diversification benefit. The computer group listings reproduced from the *Financial Weekly* are shown on the next four pages.

Observe how many computer companies appear. We bet that there are more than you ever dreamed existed. This is to your advantage because you can be highly selective. Let's check out the five lowest PERs and see if we come up with any qualifiers. This industry's P/E average is 13.6. Five Hyperprofits candidates emerge: Alpha Micro, Anderson Jacob, Control Data, Information Displays, and Raymond Engine. All have very low PERs. We omitted Control Data from further consideration because its market value exceeds $1.5 billion —thus being disqualified on Pillar 3. Checking the alphabetical stock tables as we did earlier for the aerospace companies, we are able to construct Table 46.

Table 46

Computer-Industry Hyperprofits Qualifiers

Company	Pillar 1	Pillar 2	Pillar 3
Alpha Microsystems	.55	.52	35
Anderson Jacob	.41	.22	23
Information Displays	.13	.05	2
Raymond Engine	.63	.83	28

Four pretty good-looking prospects appear. Information Displays clearly shows the top pillar ratings, while Anderson Jacob also looks strong. As we suggested, for smaller portfolios Anderson Jacob is a good choice since it is over $15 million of market value. The very small market value of Information Displays makes it a very risky selection for a small portfolio but acceptable for a larger, more diversified portfolio. If you were to select one of these, for example, to go along with Aeronca, you would be well on your way to constructing an attractive Hyperprofits portfolio. Your next step is to move on to an entirely different industry, such as broadcasting, food, or textiles, and identify the top Hyperprofits picks. See how easy it is?

Adhering to this procedure you will achieve two objectives:

Company-Page-Market		Close $	Price Chg. Yr. to Date %	Curr. P/E Ratio	EPS 12 Mth. Chg. %	Div. Yld. %	Ret. on Com. Eqty %
Alpha Microsysts	7-M	11.00	- 26.7	7.5	132	0	10.4
Amdahl Corp	7-A	11.25	- 38.8	12.1	417	1.8	11.6
Analogic Corp	8-M	12.75	- 45.2	13.1	20	0	13.3
Andersn Jacob	9-A	8.63	- 15.9	5.6	206	0	11.1
Apollo Cptr	9-M	24.25	11.8	55.1	120	0	14.6
Apple Compt	9-M	26.50	8.7	37.9	- 49	0	20.3
Applied Magnet	9-N	11.88	- 54.2	11.4	- 12	0	7.3
Archive Cp	9-O	6.13	- 37.2	43.8	NC	0	NS
Astrocom Cp	9-O	3.00	100.0	27.3	NE	0	11.8
Audiotronics Cp	10-A	7.00	3.7	NE	-100	2.3	NE
BancTec Inc	10-M	7.50	- 47.4	NE	NE	0	NE
Barry Wright	11-N	27.00	- 10.0	16.1	29	1.8	15.4
Beehive Intl	11-A	2.75	- 62.1	NE	NC	0	.6
Burroughs Cp	13-N	53.25	5.7	11.5	105	4.9	8.6
C COR Electronics	13-O	8.75	- 14.6	14.6	- 53	0	13.5
C 3 Inc	13-N	10.38	- 33.1	22.1	- 55	0	18.6
Cadec Sys	13-O	1.00	- 42.9	NE	NC	0	NE
Cambex Corp	13-O	1.13	- 18.2	NE	NC	0	NE
Centronics Data	14-N	11.63	- 22.5	NE	NE	0	NE
Check Tech	15-M	6.25	0	NE	NE	0	NE
Cipher Data	15-M	21.75	- 10.1	29.0	70	0	5.6
Ciprico Inc	15-O	11.00	18.9	20.0	NC	0	8.2
Columbia Data	16-O	5.63	NC	9.9	NC	0	88.1
Compaq Cptr	16-N	6.50	- 48.0	50.0	NC	0	5.2
Compucorp	17-M	3.88	- 49.2	NE	-100	0	12.0
Compuscan Inc	17-M	3.88	3.3	20.4	0	0	8.3

Company-Page-Market		Close $	Price Chg. Yr. to Date %	Curr. P/E Ratio	EPS 12 Mth. Chg. %	Div. Yld. %	Ret. on Com. Eqty %
Comp & Commun	17-M	14.50	- 10.8	NE	-100	0	NE
Comp Automation	17-M	6.00	- 11.1	NE	-100	0	NE
Comp Consoles	17-A	18.50	- 9.8	15.8	225	0	18.0
Comp Dev	17-O	.50	0	NE	NE	0	NE
Comp Entry	17-O	5.25	- 12.5	26.3	122	0	9.8
Comp Memories	17-M	6.50	- 42.2	46.4	17	0	2.7
Comp Network	17-O	5.13	- 22.6	NE	-100	0	3.6
Comp Prods	17-M	15.25	- 14.1	19.8	51	0	15.7
Comp Resources	17-M	4.75	- 35.6	79.2	NC	.2	0
Comp Transceiver	17-O	2.13	- 46.9	14.2	- 21	0	5.0
Computervision	17-N	38.75	- 10.7	28.9	22	0	16.0
Control Data	18-N	30.88	- 31.8	7.5	4	2.1	8.9
Convergent Tech	18-M	13.50	- 43.2	38.6	- 27	0	6.7
Corvus Systs	18-M	3.88	- 53.0	NC	-100	0	10.5
Cray Research	18-N	45.00	- 19.1	25.4	28	0	15.1
CSP Inc	19-M	7.25	- 39.6	14.8	- 29	0	14.2
Data General	19-N	47.00	26.2	32.2	175	0	4.9
Data Switch Cp	19-M	15.00	- 50.0	20.8	53	0	21.2
Datacopy	19-O	4.38	- 41.7	NE	NC	0	NE
Datapoint Cp	19-N	19.00	- 30.9	14.8	266	0	2.5
Dataproducts	19-A	16.88	- 40.8	13.4	80	.9	8.2
Dataram Cp	19-A	7.88	- 18.2	14.3	NE	0	11.1
Datasouth Cmptr	19-M	5.25	- 46.8	11.9	NC	0	18.8
Dataspeed Inc	19-O	9.25	- 35.1	NE	NC	0	NE
Datum Inc	19-M	5.75	- 31.3	14.0	NE	0	8.3

Company-Page-Market		Close $	Price Chg. Yr. to Date %	Curr. P/E Ratio	EPS 12 Mth. Chg. %	Div. Yld. %	Ret. on Com. Eqty. %
Decision Data	19-M	9.75	-11.4	13.2	57	.0	11.9
Delta Data	20-O	2.75	15.8	91.7	-63	.0	25.0
Denelcor Inc	20-M	7.25	-14.7	NE	NE	.0	NE
Digital Equip	20-N	84.00	16.7	18.3	-26	.0	8.0
Distributed Log	20-M	9.00	-34.5	13.8	NC	.0	18.3
Dysan Corp	21-M	8.75	-63.5	NE	-100	.0	4.3
Educational Cmptr	21-M	7.00	-37.8	12.7	20	.7	16.2
Electron Assoc	22-N	4.88	-27.8	NE	-100	.0	NE
Electron Mem	22-N	6.38	-20.3	14.2	246	.0	8.0
Electron Modules	22-M	11.50	-4.2	NE	-100	.0	NE
Enron Electronic	22-M	8.50	-33.3	21.8	-86	.0	37.9
Emulex Cp	22-M	18.25	-15.1	22.5	108	.0	19.3
Esprit Syst	23-A	5.50	-32.3	45.8	NC	.0	33.3
Fingermatrix	23-M	6.63	-20.9	NE	NC	.0	NE
Float Pt Sys	24-N	16.50	-54.2	9.7	36	.0	15.1
Fortune Systs	25-M	4.13	-41.1	NE	NE	.0	NE
Gandalf Tech	26-O	11.00	18.9	NA	-31	NA	9.3
Gen Automation	26-M	10.25	-6.8	NE	NE	.0	NE
Gen Datacomm	26-N	15.63	-2.3	27.4	1040	.0	9.1
Genisco Tech	26-A	6.50	-21.2	15.9	-43	.0	6.1
Grt SW Inds	27-O	.63	-16.7	NE	-100	.0	NE
Honeywell Inc	29-N	52.88	-18.7	9.8	16	3.6	10.0
Info Displays	30-O	.63	-91.9	1.7	NC	.0	14.1
Info International	30-O	11.25	-10.0	13.4	-13	1.8	10.9

Company-Page-Market		Close $	Price Chg. Yr. to Date %	Curr. P/E Ratio	EPS 12 Mth. Chg. %	Div. Yld. %	Ret. on Com. Eqty. %
Infotron Systs	30-M	28.50	-23.5	20.2	74	.0	12.6
Intecom Inc	31-M	10.88	-40.0	33.0	83	.0	7.9
Intelligent Sys	31-M	13.75	-27.6	16.4	95	.0	19.4
Intergraph Cp	31-M	43.50	13.0	43.1	146	.0	19.9
Intermec Cp	31-M	16.75	-4.3	25.4	38	.0	18.6
Int Bus Mach	31-N	105.75	-13.3	11.3	22	3.6	23.6
Int Totalizator Sys	31-M	3.13	-30.6	39.1	-76	.0	21.6
Intertec Data	31-A	3.50	-52.5		-100	.0	4.0
Iomega Cp	31-O	5.13	-4.7	39.4	NC	.0	NE
IPL Sytems	31-M	2.75	-50.0	NE	-100	.0	NE
ISC Systems	32-M	15.25	-23.2	26.8	78	.0	8.3
Kaypro Cp	32-O	4.50	-35.7	10.7	NC	.0	96.0
Key Tronic	33-O	12.00	-48.4	9.8	NC	.0	10.5
Lee Data	34-M	10.38	-43.2	8.3	36	.0	21.5
Lexicon Cp	34-M	4.13	6.5	NE	NE	.0	NE
Lexidata Cp	34-M	6.25	-9.1	69.4	-53	.0	NE
LTX	35-M	16.25	-9.7	25.8	80	.0	6.9
Mgmnt Assist	35-N	26.13	46.2	NE	-100	.0	.0
Masstor Sys	36-M	4.25	-48.5	NE	NC	.0	NS
Micom Syst	37-M	38.75	-9.9	28.9	46	.0	22.9
Micropolis Cp	37-M	6.50	-37.3	15.1	4200	.0	.6
Miniscribe Cp	37-O	5.25	-51.7	23.9	NC	.0	6.7
Modular Comp	38-N	7.75	.0	NE	NC	.0	NE
Mohawk Data	39-N	13.25	-11.7	20.1	-27	.0	6.9
Monolithic Mem	39-M	18.38	-35.2	17.5	338	.0	8.2

Company-Page-Market		Close $	Price Chg. Yr. to Date %	Curr. P/E Ratio	EPS 12 Mth. Chg. %	Div. Yld. %	Ret. on Com. Eqty. %
Natl Micronetics	39-M	8.25	- 48.0	16.8	4	.0	8.7
NBI Inc	39-N	21.25	- 20.6	19.5	54	.0	5.3
Netwk Systems	39-M	23.25	12.7	46.5	61	.0	11.6
New World Cmptr	39-O	.63	- 78.7	NE	NE	.0	NE
Object Recogn	41-M	4.63	- 35.1	NE	NC	.0	NE
Onyx IMI Inc	41-M	3.88	- 59.2	NM	- 98	.0	11.6
Par Tech Cp	42-O	17.00	21.4	20.5	41	.0	22.7
Priam Cp	44-M	8.00	- 25.6	12.9	NC	.0	3.5
Primages	44-O	6.25	- 26.5	NE	NC	.0	NE
Prime Computer	44-N	13.38	- 24.1	19.7	- 31	.0	12.1
Printronix	44-M	19.00	- 29.6	11.2	12	.0	12.3
Prodigy Sys	44-O	2.50	- 33.3	41.7	- 33	.0	8.0
Protocol Cptr	45-M	5.75	- 28.1	17.4	NC	.0	NC
Recog Equip	46-N	11.38	- 7.1	20.3	NE	.0	5.3
Remington Rand	46-O	.88	- 56.3	NE	NE	.0	NE
Rexon Inc	46-M	5.50	- 53.2	NE	NE	.0	NE
Rodime Plc	47-O	11.75	- 43.4	11.8	300	.0	12.3
Rolm Corp	47-N	39.75	- 21.1	28.0	- 23	.0	9.3
Scan Optics	48-M	9.13	- 8.8	14.5	21	.0	15.3
Scan Tron Cp	48-M	12.50	- 26.5	18.1	21	.0	11.7
SCI Systs	48-M	13.88	- 38.3	19.8	59	.0	15.0
Seagate Tech	48-M	10.25	- 26.1	11.8	295	.0	10.9
Selecterm Inc	49-O	13.50	- 25.0	13.8	61	.0	16.7
Sperry Corp	51-N	37.13	- 21.2	10.6	10	5.2	4.5
Storage Technl	51-N	9.75	- 28.4	NE	- 100	.0	11.7
Stratus Cptr	51-M	9.75	- 15.2	97.5	NC	.0	3.9
Sykes Data	52-M	3.00	- 29.4	NE	NC	.0	NE
Symbol Tech	52-M	7.50	- 24.1	NE	NC	.0	NE
Syntech Intl	52-M	9.00	- 4.0	17.0	NE	.0	2.4
System Indus	52-M	7.00	- 54.8	18.4	NC	.0	2.6
Systems Integ	52-A	10.25	.0	13.9	NC	.0	33.9
Tab Products	52-A	14.13	- 11.7	10.2	66	.8	14.0
Tandem Cpt	52-M	23.50	- 33.1	33.1	- 4	.0	9.9
Tandon Cp	52-M	7.13	- 64.4	12.3	16	.0	11.2
TEC Inc	53-A	10.13	- 2.4	NE	27	.0	NE
Televideo Syst	53-A	6.00	- 62.2	10.7	27	.0	16.1
Telex Corp	53-N	26.75	3.4	10.8	42	.0	24.5
Telxon Cp	53-M	11.00	2.3	14.7	NC	.1	20.2
Terminal Data	53-M	11.00	- 16.6	22.9	- 17	.0	11.3
Timeplex Inc	54-N	14.25	- 26.9	23.8	62	.0	6.9
Trilogy Ltd	55-O	1.94	- 79.3	NE	NC	.0	NE
TRW Inc	55-N	64.25	- 19.3	11.2	38	4.4	12.4
Ultimate Cp	55-A	19.63	20.8	18.9	108	.0	23.2
Ungermann Bass	55-M	13.25	1.9	94.6	600	.0	3.0
US Design	56-M	6.50	8.3	NE	NE	.0	NE
Valid Logic	57-M	11.88	- 5.9	NM	NE	.0	NE
Vector Graphic	57-M	.63	- 88.8	NE	NC	.0	16.6
Verbatim Cp	57-A	10.13	- 40.4	16.9	3	.0	22.6
Verdix Corp	57-O	2.19	75.0	NE	NC	.0	NE
Vermont Resch	57-A	6.13	- 30.0	NE	- 100	.0	NE

Company-Page-Market		Close $	Price Chg. Yr. to Date %	Curr. P/E Ratio	EPS 12 Mth. Chg. %	Div. Yld. %	Ret on Com. Eqty. %
Vernitron Corp	57-A	13.13	- 22.8	12.9	- 4	1.2	10.0
Visual Tech	57-M	10.00	- 42.0	11.5	12	.0	10.2
Wang Labs	58-A	28.25	- 20.7	20.3	29	.4	16.2
Wang Labs C	58-A	28.00	- 21.4	NA	69	.3	NA
Wespercorp	58-A	4.50	- 47.1	NE	-100	.0	NE
Wicat Systs	59-M	2.50	- 50.0	NE	NC	.0	NE
Widcom Inc	59-M	10.25	- 6.8	13.2	103	.0	NE
Xebec	59-M	9.13	- 48.6	NE	-100	.0	5.3
Zentec	60-M	4.50	- 50.0	NE	-100	.0	NE
Ziyad Inc	60-M	11.25	- 6.3	22.5	NC	.0	20.8

1. Your portfolio will contain the top Hyperprofits candidate in each of your selected industries.

2. You will enjoy the advantage of proper diversification.

Setting Hyperprofits into Motion

You should now recognize that you will be able to construct a top-notch Hyperprofits portfolio with minimal time and effort. Once you have selected the individual stocks, the next step is to decide on the number of shares of each to buy. Let's consider the least flexible case. That is, where a minimum of $5,000 capital is to be invested. Let's take a concrete example. Consider the Hyperprofits portfolio in Table 47.

Table 47

Sample Hyperprofits Stocks

Company	Industry	Price
Anderson Jacob	Computer	$ 8.38
Cognitionics	Electronics	5.63
Naugles, Inc.	Restaurant	7.75
Barnwell Industries	Oil	10.00
Movie Star, Inc.	Textile	16.88

In buying your portfolio, there are two rules you should bear in mind. First, if possible, buy in 100-share lots. Why? Because broker commissions are cheapest this way. You will have to pay expensive premiums if you buy in odd lots, other than 100 shares.

Second, you want, as close as possible, to invest equal dollar amounts in each of your stocks. The reason for this is to achieve maximum diversification benefit. Suppose you have a high percentage of your funds in one or two stocks and a very low percentage in another. Then whatever the performance of the low-percentage stock, the impact on the portfolio profit could be negligible.

The effect would be like having too few stocks in the portfolio—a blatant violation of the rules of diversification.

Applying these two rules to your $5,000, if you bought 100 shares of five stocks at $10 a piece, your capital would be fully utilized, without allowance for commissions. So when you are dealing with minimum working capital, it is helpful to stick with low-priced stocks. Conveniently, most Pillar 3 small-firm stocks are, in fact, low-priced. Taking this into account, you might want to replace Movie Star with a lower-priced candidate. Eagle Clothes in the same industry at $3.63 would be a likely choice. Applying these rules, your new portfolio would resemble that shown in Table 48.

Table 48

Sample Hyperprofits Portfolio

Company	Shares	Total
Anderson Jacob	100	$ 838
Cognitionics	200	1126
Naugles, Inc.	100	775
Barnwell Industries	100	1000
Eagle Clothes	300	1089
		$4828

That's it! That's all there is to constructing your Hyperprofits portfolio and getting started in the program. In forming our hypothetical portfolio, we have relied upon the *Financial Weekly* data source. And it turned out to be very convenient for our purposes.

Using Other Sources

Earlier we cited two other sources of Hyperprofits data. On the following page, you will see material excerpted from a single page of *The Value Line Investment Survey*. Each page of *Value Line* covers one company. In this case we propose to examine BankAmerica. The needed information appears on this page.[3]

Let's see how we would use *Value Line* to select Hyperprofits stocks. We'll start with Pillar 1, the PER. At the top center of the page, you will find the designation P/E ratio 8.0. Note, however, that we have circled the adjacent figure, 9.8, called the trailing P/E. This is the actual P/E ratio, the one you want to use. Conveniently, *Value Line* has already grouped their pages by industry. So, for example, to review the bank industry, all you need to do is turn the consecutive pages and observe the trailing P/Es. By noting the lowest ones, you have already honed in on the top PER candidates.

To check out these finalists, the remaining needed data are also on the page. In the lower part of the right-hand column, you will find the number 9.0 circled. This is the average annual P/E ratio. The trailing 9.8 divided by this 9.0 is our Pillar 2, the DPE. By inspection, we see that the DPE is greater than one, therefore, not favorable for our purposes.

This leaves only Pillar 3, the MV. Recall that this is market price times shares outstanding. As you can well imagine, BankAmerica is not the smallest company around. Let's confirm this. At the top, we see the data, recent price 18 and at the lower left common stock 150 million shares outstanding. Indeed, this is a giant because of its enormous $2.7-billion market value, and it is well out of the Hyperprofits range. We'll leave this one to the big boys.

Now that you see how to use *Value Line,* let's turn to *Moody's Handbook of Common Stocks.* On the next page, you will find a portion of a page reproduced from *Moody's.* The company is Pepsico, Inc. The current P/E ratio is not given, but we can easily calculate it. The recent market price is $43. Under interim earnings, we have circled the most recent four quarters' earnings per share, so the P/E ratio is:

$$P/E = \frac{43}{1.00 + .82 + .50 + .98} = 13.0.$$

In *Moody's,* the companies are not arranged by industry. However, they do provide a listing of the names of all companies grouped by industry. So you can still start by selecting a given industry and then checking the P/Es of the companies in it. Once again, the lowest of these are the top PER candidates.

The DPE can be determined from the circled P/E ratio column. These

[3] The reproduced *Value Line* information on BankAmerica represents only a portion of the total data given by *Value Line* about this company. All data needed to calculate the pillars appear here.

AMERICA NYSE-BAC

RECENT PRICE	P/E RATIO	(Trailing: 9.8) (Median: 8.5)	RELATIVE P/E RATIO	DIV'D YLD
30.6	⑱ 8.0		0.78	8.4%

	1986	1987	1988	1989	2003

December 21, 1984 Value Line

Target Price Range — 60 50 40 32 24

13.0 × Earnings p sh

'Target Price Range

Relative Price Strength

Options Trade On CBO

2-for-1 split
2-for-1 split

Percent 6.0
shares 4.0
traded 2.0

	16.6	17.8	25.4	25.0	23.8	23.5
	12.2	15.2	17.5	20.1	11.9	15.6

Decisions

	4Q'83	1Q'84	2Q'84	3Q'84
ions	65	64	53	56
	83	77	85	75
	50544	52559	52161	50649

N D J F M A M J J A S O
0 0 0 0 0 0 0 0 1 1 0
0 0 0 0 0 0 0 0 1 1 0

TIMELINESS 3 Average
(Relative Price Performance Next 12 Mos.)

SAFETY 3 Average
(Scale: 1 Highest to 5 Lowest)

BETA .95 (1.00 = Market)

1987-89 PROJECTIONS

	Price	Gain	Ann'l Total Return
High	45	(+150%)	31%
Low	30	(+ 65%)	20%

© Value Line, Inc.

	1976	1977	1978	1979	1980	1981	1982	1983	1984	1985		87-89E
Earnings per sh	2.40	2.71	3.53	4.10	4.39	3.02	2.60	2.18	2.20	2.80	(A)	4.00
Div'ds Decl'd per sh	.79	.87	1.02	1.27	1.41	1.52	1.52	1.52	1.52	1.52	(B)	1.65
Book Value per sh	16.63	18.46	20.81	23.58	26.55	27.72	28.43	29.43	30.10	31.35		37.00
Common Shs Outst'g	145.61	145.78	146.01	146.82	147.23	147.57	150.42	150.42	150.85	150.60	(C)	153.00
Avg Ann'l P/E Ratio	10.8	9.1	7.0	6.4	5.7	8.2	7.3	9.8	Bold figures are			9.0
Relative P/E Ratio	1.38	1.19	.95	.93	.76	1.00	.80	.83	Value Line estimates			.75
Avg Ann'l Div'd Yield	3.1%	3.5%	4.2%	4.8%	5.6%	6.0%	8.0%	7.1%				4.6%
Total Assets ($mill)	73913	81989	94902	08389	11617	11215	12221	121176	122000	125000		140000
Loans ($mill)	35448	41531	49313	57096	62482	71236	73921	81327	83000	90000		105000
Net Interest Inc ($mill)	1537.0	1838.9	2287.8	2589.2	2780.8	2776.5	3006.8	3483.3	4000	4200		4800
Loan Loss Prov'n ($mill)	147.1	146.7	176.7	226.2	241.5	322.3	501.8	657.9	750	650		500
Noninterest Inc ($mill)	475.9	445.9	517.0	586.0	798.3	859.9	1024.7	1216.8	1300	1450		1850

CAPITAL STRUCTURE as of 9/30/84

LT Debt $4048.0 mill.
Due in 5 Yrs $1500 mill. LT Interest $392.0 mill.
Leases, Uncapitalized Annual rentals $123.9 mill.
Pension Liability None in '83 vs. None in '82
Pfd Stock $794.0 mill. Pfd Div'd $76.0 mill.
6 mill. $50 par. cumulative adjustable-rate Series A pfd. shs., 4 mill. $100 stated value cumulative adjustable-rate Series B pfd., 4.6 mill. Series C pfd. $2.87½ div. until '88, declining to $2.25, redeemable 9-1-90 at stated value (minimum $2.00, maximum $25.00, depending on loan losses from Seafirst acquisition).
Common Stock 150,805,727 shs.

Copyright © 1984 Value Line, Inc. Reprinted by permission.

PEPSICO, INC.

LISTED	SYM.	LTPS•	STPS•	IND. DIV.	REC. PRICE	RANGE (52-WKS.)	YLD.
NYSE	PEP	90.6	118.1	$1.68*	43	44 - 33	3.9%

INVESTMENT GRADE. DIVERSIFICATION THROUGH ACQUISITIONS AND NEW PRODUCT DEVELOPMENT ENHANCES THE LONG-TERM OUTLOOK.

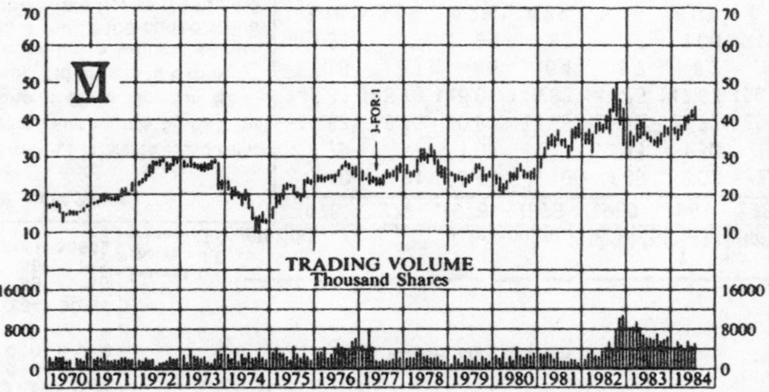

70
60
50
40
30
20
10
M
3-FOR-1
TRADING VOLUME
Thousand Shares
16000
8000
0
1970 1971 1972 1973 1974 1975 1976 1977 1978 1979 1980 1981 1982 1983 1984

CAPITALIZATION: (12/25/83)

		(000)	(%)
Long-Term Debt	a$	671,480	22.2
Cap. Lease Oblig.		147,710	4.9
Defer. Inc. Tax		416,900	13.7
Com. & Surp.		1,794,158	59.2
Total		$3,030,248	100.0

Shs.($0.05) 93,560,642

INTERIM EARNINGS:

Qtr.	Mar.	June	Sept.	Dec.
1981	0.58	0.95	1.09	0.99
1982	0.69	0.97	1.16	d0.42
1983	0.40	0.79	1.00	0.82
1984	0.50	c0.98	...	...

INTERIM DIVIDENDS:

Amt.	Dec.	Ex.	Rec.	Pay.
0.405Q	5/4/83	6/6/83	6/10/83	6/30/83
0.405Q	7/28	9/2	9/9	9/30
0.405Q	11/17	12/5	12/9	12/31
0.405Q	2/23/84	3/5/84	3/9/84	3/31/84
0.42Q	5/2	6/4	6/8	6/30

YEAR	GROSS REVS ($mill.)	OPER PROFIT MARGIN %	RET. ON EQUITY %	NET INCOME ($mill.)	WORK CAP ($mill.)	SENIOR CAPITAL ($mill.)	SHARES (000)	EARN PER SH.$	DIV PER SH.$	DIV PAY %	PRICE RANGE	P/E RATIO	AVG YIELD %
74	2,080.8	8.3	15.7	87.4	287.0	349.0	71,169	1.13	0.43	38	23⅞ - 9¾	14.9	2.6
75	2,321.2	8.7	16.7	104.6	311.0	282.3	71,253	1.38	0.50	36	24¾ - 13⅝	13.9	2.6
76	2,360.2	7.3	18.1	136.0	400.9	278.6	73,602	1.79	0.63	35	29⅛ - 23⅛	14.6	2.4
77	3,545.7	10.0	19.3	187.3	415.9	427.9	86,859	2.14	0.83	39	28⅝ - 22¼	11.9	3.3
78	4,300.0	10.0	19.3	225.8	358.7	479.1	93,075	2.43	0.98	40	33⅞ - 24⅜	12.0	3.4
79	5,090.6	9.4	21.0	264.9	357.5	619.0	90,954	2.85	1.11	39	28½ - 21⅞	8.8	4.4
80	5,975.2	9.6	20.4	b291.8	352.4	781.7	91,277	b3.20	1.26	39	28½ - 20	8.1	5.2
81	7,027.4	9.2	20.3	333.5	405.6	816.1	91,605	3.61	1.42	39	39¼ - 27	9.2	4.3
82	7,499.0	8.6	13.6	224.3	245.0	864.1	93,374	2.40	1.58	66	50 - 31⅛	16.9	3.9
83	**7,895.9**	**6.9**	**15.8**	**284.1**	**443.9**	**819.2**	**93,561**	**3.01**	**1.62**	**54**	**40¼ - 32⅝**	**12.1**	**4.4**

Taken from *Moody's Handbook of Common Stocks*, Fall 1984 Edition. Reprinted by permission of Moody's Investors Service, 99 Church St., N.Y., NY 10007.

are the historical values. It is a sound procedure to use the average of the last five years. So we would have

$$DPE = \frac{13.0}{(12.1 + 16.9 + 9.2 + 8.1 + 8.8)/5} = 1.18.$$

Finally, for the MV, under the capitalization section, we find 93 million shares which we would multiply by the market price per share of $43. In assessing data sources such as *Value Line* and *Moody's* we see that their advantage lies in the fact that they are freely available. On the other hand, they present the disadvantage of requiring more time and effort than does the *Financial Weekly*.

Taking Stock of Your Investments

Once you have bought your Hyperprofits portfolio, you are in business. Now, what about staying in business profitably? This is what you'll learn next. To do this, we'll draw upon some principles you learned in Chapter 2 about profitable investing. There, you'll recall, we pointed out that the most successful investment programs adhere to three basic principles. These can be summarized as:

1. maintaining proper diversification,

2. avoiding too frequent trading, and

3. investing for long-term profits.

Thus far in this chapter, you have already seen how to incorporate diversification into Hyperprofits. Now we will show you how to successfully merge investment Principles 2 and 3 into the system. In applying these principles, we will tackle some important questions. For instance, how often should you revise or rebalance your portfolio? What signals tell you when it's the right time to sell a stock? What should you do with the proceeds from the sale of a stock?

Okay, let's start with the first question. How often should you consider changes in your portfolio? Here is a very important fact we have derived from our research: the more often you revise your Hyperprofits portfolio, the higher your gross profits are likely to be. For example, suppose you were to change your revision policy from yearly to semiannually. Then, according to our computer research, on the average you could expect to increase your gross return by some 4 percent each year. While 4 percent doesn't sound like much, when coupled with the magic of compounding, it can make a noticeable difference in how fast your wealth increases. Further, if you rebalance your portfolio more often, then you should increase your gross profits by an even greater margin.

This sounds great. Then why not revise the portfolio each month or even once an hour for that matter? Well, by now you probably know our answer to this: if only life were that simple. But what's the catch? Notice that we keep using the term "gross" profits. "Gross" means before brokerage commission and income taxes. The painful truth is that you can't afford to trade stocks too frequently because the commissions would eat you alive.

What about taxes? In Chapter 8, you will learn much more about taxes and investing. But right now we want you to be aware, if you are not already, of a dramatic development which recently occurred. The Congress of the United States enacted into law a provision which reduces the holding time to qualify for the capital gains tax rate from one year to six months (effective June 22, 1984). What this means to you is that if you hold a stock over six months, then the profit you make from the sale is taxed at a lower rate—much lower! On first blush, this may not sound so startling, but consider this. The attractive profit returns of Hyperprofits which we have reported to you are based on holding stocks for one year. But we also know that more frequent review can produce higher profits. This new rule enables you to capture these higher profits while retaining the most favorable tax treatment. Quite a bonus.

The important fact to bear in mind is that profits on stocks held for more than six months are taxed at the long-term capital gains rate, which is vastly lower than the short-term capital gains tax rate. So both commissions and taxes militate against frequent trading. On the one hand, we have profits growing with frequency of trading, but on the other hand expenses are also increasing. What should you do? Not to worry. We have thoroughly researched this question for the Hyperprofits system on the computer. The ideal is to strike the very best balance among all these factors. That is, we want the highest possible *net* profits.

The computer's answer is quite clear and logical. Barring unusual circumstances, the highest net profits are obtained by revising your portfolio only twice each year. In this way, you will achieve the best balance possible. You will be able to maintain top Hyperprofits prospects in your portfolio at all times. You will hold your commission costs down and most important, you will qualify for the preferential long-term capital gains tax rate.

We said "barring unusual circumstances." "Unusual" means, for example, that you have good reason to believe a company whose stock you own is going to face some special problem in the near future. Or let's say that two months after you've bought a stock it's made a tremendous run up and you have reason to believe that it cannot hold these gains for several months. Then by all means, you are justified in making a more frequent trade. But these are the exceptions. The profit returns we have shown you on the Hyperprofits system were achieved without the benefit of taking into account *any* unusual circumstances at all. So if you are able to exploit some special case, you should do even better.

In order to receive the benefit of the long-term capital gains treatment, you must hold your stock for at least six months plus one day. There is, however, one notable exception to our six-month holding rule. Suppose, for instance, that you purchase a stock in September and by December of that same year the stock has depreciated in value. Naturally, you can hold on to the stock as long as you like and wait for it to rebound. This is fine.

But you also have another alternative. You might want to consider the possibility of selling the stock at a loss. Why? Well, for two possible reasons. First, you might conclude that this stock is no longer a top Hyperprofits prospect. If so, you might prefer to replace it with another stock which *is* a top prospect. This brings us to the second reason. Selling the stock in December provides you with a tax write-off in that year. This could help offset gains accrued earlier in the year, easing your tax burden. In the next chapter we present several tax strategies which can be used in concert with Hyperprofits to make your portfolio's value grow.

This is a good place to step back for a moment and recap what you've learned so far about reviewing and trading your Hyperprofits portfolio. The key rule is that you want to review your stocks every six months. You may optionally choose additional review periods but only alter your portfolio if (1) a stock is no longer a good prospect and/or (2) the sale provides a needed tax write-off. Otherwise, hold for the six-month review.

Taking the Plunge

All right. You are making good progress in activating the Hyperprofits system. Two crucial questions still remain. First, when you review the portfolio how do you know whether or not it's the right time to sell? Second, what should be done with the proceeds if a sale occurs? Let's plunge into the first question.

Six months has rolled around, and it's time to review your portfolio. You want to determine which stocks, if any, should be sold. To answer this question, think about why you selected these stocks in the first place. Wasn't it because they were top Hyperprofits prospects? Of course. Then what should determine whether or not you want to continue holding a particular stock? That's right, the same thing. So the key question becomes, Is the stock still a top prospect after the end of six months?

How do you know? By observing the three Hyperprofits pillars, of course. Since Pillar 3, the MV, seldom changes substantially, you can usually focus your attention on Pillars 1 and 2. Remember, you want both of these pillars to be favorable. That means both the PER and DPE should be significantly below one, the smaller the better. So the crucial principle for you to apply is: If the PER and DPE are both significantly below 1, then continue to hold the stock; otherwise, sell and replace with a more attractive stock.

Let's see if we can reason why this makes sense. You originally selected the stock because the pillars suggested strong upside potential. This potential derives from the likelihood of overreaction, causing the stock to be temporarily underpriced. Now let's suppose that this proves to be the case, much to your delight, and the price takes off. By the end of your review period, what will have happened to the PER and the DPE?

If the price appreciates and earnings fail to keep pace, then the P/E ratio will grow. Since the P/E ratio is the numerator for both the PER and the DPE, both of these pillars will increase toward the average. So when you review the stock, these pillars may not be highly favorable any longer. This means that the stock's potential has materialized in the form of profits for you. If the profit potential is largely manifested, then it's time for you to sell the stock and reap your reward.

If, on the other hand, earnings do accelerate and move along with the price growth, then the P/E ratio, the PER, and the DPE will all remain low. Hence, when your review time comes, you may have a nice gain in the stock. But the three pillars may indicate there's still more potential left in the stock. Therefore, you should continue to hold it. It makes sense, doesn't it? So we have a simple and logical rule. If Pillars 1 and 2 remain highly favorable, hold. If not, then sell.

There is no particular magic number when it comes to the PER and DPE. It's a matter of degree. Lower is better. Certainly a figure like .95 does not show a great strength. That's much too close to the reading for an average stock. And, of course, you want to do much better than average. A sound rule is that a rating below .90 is the beginning of true strength for these pillars. Hopefully, however, you will be able to identify plenty of sub-.90-rating stocks to adorn your portfolio.

The last question is the easiest: What should you do with the proceeds from your sales? The answer: Reinvest them in Hyperprofits! What else? Remember that the wealth-building power of Hyperprofits is predicated upon the high profit return from the system coupled with the magic of compounding. Here's where the magic comes in.

When you reach your six-month review, if you find that the system dictates that it is wise to sell one or more stocks, then at the same time consult your data source. Select the top Hyperprofits prospects that are available at that moment in time. Then when you sell an old holding, plow your capital plus the profits you have accrued right back into your new selections. This is precisely how you put the magic of compounding to work for you.

Bear in mind two important points when you revise or rebalance your Hyperprofits portfolio. First, be sure that your new stocks coupled with the stocks you continue to hold still represent widely divergent industries. This maintains your maximum diversification benefit. Second, make sure that you still have at least five stocks at a minimum and that you don't become "over-diversified" by accumulating too many stocks.

If you are like us, you'll probably start with five stocks. Since twenty stocks provide greater diversification benefit than do five, you should gradually increase the number of your holdings to twenty. How can you accomplish this most effectively? Let's take an example. Suppose at your six-month review, the system indicates selling two stocks, both at a profit. This is your opportunity to increase the size of your portfolio by replacing them with three stocks. The profits you've earned can allow you to do this. Little by little, you will eventually reach the twenty-stock goal.

There you have it. It's easy and it's fun. The most fun is watching your estate grow. But remember, our research shows that not every individual stock can be a winner. It also shows that there are periods when the value of your portfolio may decline. These are the fortunes of the real world. Hyperprofits is a long-term wealth-building program. If you will follow the system and stick with it over time, it will make you a winner.

Now that you know the system, let's take a real example of a selection that you might make and follow it through to the review period. Suppose that you wish to investigate the trucking industry. At midyear 1984, the trucking group appeared as shown on the next page. Scanning the P/Es, we see that the lowest P/E, hence the lowest PER, belonged to National City Line.

Checking the other pages, you compile the following: PER = .27, DPE = .14, MV = 35. There you have it, an absolutely ideal Hyperprofits pick. So you buy the stock at the current price of 13½.

At the beginning of 1985, it's now review time, so you first check the price. To your delight, the price has appreciated to 20⅜, a 51 percent gain in

221 Trucking						
Am Carriers	7-M	9.00 - 53.8	4.9	39	.0	16.9
Arkan Best	9-N	15.50 - 41.5	7.0	NE	.3	10.1
Atlas Van Lines	10-A	17.38 37.6	11.3	- 1	1.2	18.2
Banner Inds	10-N	9.25 - 14.0	13.4	NE	.3	NE
Branch Indus	12-A	1.25 - 44.4	NE	NE	.0	NE
Builders Transpt	13-O	15.25 - 23.8	6.9	NC	.0	18.6
Burnham Svc	13-M	15.50 - 7.5	16.1	25	1.0	18.8
Carolina Freight	14-N	17.25 - 42.5	8.5	24	2.1	19.7
Chem Leaman	15-O	15.75 - 4.5	NE	NE	.0	NE
Consol Frtways	17-N	46.13 - 23.4	9.4	17	4.3	12.1
Detsco Inc	20-O	1.75 NC	6.3	NC	5.7	18.8
Flexi-Van	24-N	24.88 - 13.5	NE	-100	3.2	2.8
Frozen Food Exp	25-O	12.25 - 31.0	6.2	81	2.3	9.8
Hunt JB Transport	30-O	17.00 - 10.5	19.8	NC	.0	24.1
Interstate Mtr Fr	31-O	.56 - 83.3	NE	NE	.0	NE
Lynden Inc	35-M	18.50 - 20.4	5.6	- 26	.0	16.1
Mayflower Cp	36-A	22.00 20.5	7.4	56	3.2	14.3
MidAmer Lines	37-O	1.75 40.0	5.1	NE	.0	33.3
MRFY Cp	38-O	3.38 - 51.8	NE	NE	9.5	NE
Natl City Line	39-O	13.50 - 3.6	3.6	573	7.4	16.1
Overland Express	41-O	13.25 - 41.1	7.2	- 5	.0	14.3
Overnite Trans	42-N	19.75 - 34.7	9.2	32	2.8	18.4
Preston Cp	44-O	14.00 - 34.1	10.4	18	3.6	7.1
Roadway Svc	47-M	25.75 - 25.1	10.1	23	3.9	18.8
RTC Transport	47-A	4.88 - 42.6	NE	-100	.0	NE
TIME D C	54-O	.25 .0	NE	NE	.0	NE
Transcon Inc	54-N	8.88 - 36.6	6.3	NE	.0	7.8
Tri-State Mot	55-A	9.50 - 29.6	6.8	NE	4.2	9.8
US Truck Lines	56-O	10.88 - 9.4	54.4	100	11.0	2.2
Viking Frght	57-M	11.00 - 22.8	50.0	- 80	.0	2.1
Yellow Freight Sys	59-M	23.63 - 45.1	6.5	NC	3.9	19.7

six months! Great, but now what to do? Should you reap your reward or hold for even greater reward? Well, let's check the pillars. They now stand at: PER = .32, DPE = .14, MV = 52.

Here is a case where all three pillars are still strong. The total picture indicates that there remains considerable potential in this stock. So you would be well justified in holding until the next review period. The odds are definitely in your favor.

But what if you want to play it safe and secure your gain? No problem. You're on solid ground here too because you can realize your profit and reinvest it in other Hyperprofits stocks whose futures are just as bright. The choice is yours.

Getting Your Money's Worth

Now let's turn our attention to another topic which affects your success. Even if you've never bought a stock before, you know that you must make your purchase through a broker. Unfortunately, the broker does not offer his services out of brotherly love. He has to earn a living too.

So it will be necessary to pay brokerage fees. But does it make any difference to which broker you pay the fees? You'd better believe it does—a lot of difference. There are two basic kinds of brokers. One kind is called full-service, and the other is called discount. It's sort of like the full-service and self-service islands at your corner gas station. Only in this case, the price differential is far more eye-popping.

How much differential is there? Discount brokers charge up to 70 percent less than the top full-service fees. Both types of brokers will buy and sell stocks for you. Then what does the full-service broker give you for the extra 70 percent? Why, his or her expert advice and counsel on what to buy and sell. The broker acts as your investment guru. So we might say that you pay roughly 30 percent to trade your stock and 70 percent for expertise and services.

The catch is that after reading this book, *you* are the expert. Now you're your own investment guru. So why pay for a service that you yourself are providing? There's no reason to, because this cuts too heavily into your profits. You only want to pay for trading, not advice. But shop around, because even among discount brokers the fee schedule varies.[4]

Double Your Pleasure

The most successful business people know that you can make much more money by investing other people's money on your own behalf. This is called applying financial leverage. The idea is to earn profits on money that you didn't have to invest from your own pocket. Hence, the return on the portion of money you did invest can be much greater.

There is a way to apply the concept of financial leverage to Hyperprofits. Although we don't recommend this method to most people, we do acknowledge the fact that some investors have a more speculative nature. For those of you with this temperament, leveraging might be appealing.

[4] An abbreviated list of discount brokers appears in the appendix to Chapter 8.

The method we are referring to is called buying on margin. Here's how it works. Let's say that you have $5,000 to invest. If you buy your stocks on margin, your broker will loan you another $5,000. Now you can invest $10,000. Suppose that by the end of one year you have earned a 30 percent profit return on your $10,000 investment. This translates into an actual 60 percent return on the $5,000 that you invested. So by buying on margin you double your profit potential. This can certainly be dramatic when your profit potential is high to begin with, as in the case of Hyperprofits. That's the good news.

Now for the bad news. There are three disadvantages of buying on margin. First, you have to pay interest on the money you borrow. This interest rate varies from broker to broker, so if you plan to open a margin account it pays to do some shopping. Second, you are exposed to the risk of receiving a margin call. What's a margin call? At the time you make your investment you must put up at least half of the money, and your broker puts up the rest. Thereafter, you are required to maintain a minimum equity amount in your margin account.

If it should happen that the price of your stocks declines, such that the market value of your portfolio is no longer equal to this minimum equity, you are then required to make up the difference. This is the margin call. So you could be exposed to having to come up with additional cash at an untimely moment. Or even worse, you might have to sell off some of your portfolio at a most inopportune time.

Last, but not least, is the fact that leveraging works both ways. While you may gain the benefit of doubling your profit, at the same time you could be saddled with the curse of also doubling any losses. Since over the long run Hyperprofits is highly effective, leveraging could substantially enhance your wealth-building program. However, over the short run, there could be some larger losses and the possibility of margin calls. So we advise definite caution here. You should not use leverage without very careful consideration of these factors. Quite frankly, we believe that Hyperprofits does just fine on its own without having to introduce the additional risks brought about by leverage. But if you really want to invest in the "fast lane," then a margin account may be just the vehicle for you.

Boiling It All Down

In this chapter, we have shown in considerable detail how to put Hyperprofits into action. But now that you have gained this understanding, the steps that you want to follow can be greatly simplified. In this section, we will lay out for you our quick five step reference summary for managing the Hyperprofits system. Here it is:

1. From the data source, choose an industry and scan for the lowest PERs. For each qualifier check Pillars 2 and 3 to see if they are Hyperprofits stocks.

2. Construct a list of qualifiers with their pillars. Then select the strongest Hyperprofits prospect. If there are no qualifiers or top prospects, go on to another industry.

3. Repeat steps (1) and (2) for at least five widely divergent industries to construct your Hyperprofits portfolio. It's to be hoped that you will observe far more industries in order to identify the truly exceptional Hyperprofits stocks.

4. Review your Hyperprofits portfolio every six months. Sell those stocks whose Pillars 1 and 2 are no longer favorable.

5. Reinvest your capital plus any profits back into new Hyperprofits selections.

That's all there is to it. Again let us emphasize that you should find managing the Hyperprofits system exciting and fun as well as financially rewarding. Now that you know how to reap the rewards, in the next chapter we explain how to avoid sharing so much of your financial success with the tax collector.

Protecting Hyperprofits from the Tax Collector

You have observed the profit-generating potential of the Hyperprofits investment strategy. Coupled with the magic of compounding, Hyperprofits enables you to achieve your goal of financial independence. However, one serious roadblock still stands between you and your ultimate financial destination. As you may have already guessed, that obstacle is the bite of income taxes.

Without a doubt, just the mention of taxes evokes an adverse reaction from most Americans. Do you really know anyone who pays taxes graciously? Of course you don't. But taxes are here to stay. And furthermore, taxes are as high as they have ever been. The highly publicized tax cut of 1981 merely enabled the average taxpayer to recover a small portion of the ground lost during previous years. That's why the popular "Wall Street Week" host, Louis Ruykeyser, aptly referred to it as the "amazing invisible tax cut." With federal deficits soaring to unprecedented heights, the prospects of additional tax cuts appear remote.[1]

You may think that taxes are just another necessary evil. You don't like them, but you still must pay your share. The real question is, What is your share? Does everyone carry an equal tax burden? If you believe that everyone shares alike in the payment of taxes, then you are very mistaken. The tax laws have become so complex and cumbersome that virtually any taxpayer with a little know-how can uncover some loophole that will lead to a tax reduction. We have all heard stories of how the wealthy often pay little or no taxes. Well, now it's your turn. In this chapter we present several legitimate tax strategies

[1] Already the Tax Equity and Fiscal Responsibility Act of 1982 has increased income taxes by an estimated $98 billion over three years, thus qualifying as one of the largest tax increases in history. In addition, the Deficit Reduction Act of 1984 hiked income taxes approximately $50 billion more.

that will enable you to advance toward your goal of financial independence without having to share such a large portion of your financial success with Uncle Sam. And remember, if you don't take advantage of these tax strategies, then you will probably shoulder more than your fair share of the tax burden. Such a heavy tax exposure can severely interrupt the compounding process that otherwise allows your Hyperprofits to accumulate rapidly.

What Is Your Tax Obligation?

You probably agree that the payment of taxes is an unpleasant, even torturous duty. But, after all, the law requires that taxes be paid. Not wanting to violate the law and suffer the consequences, you most likely have resigned to the fact that you will continue to pay taxes for the rest of your life. Taxes are like the weather: everyone talks about them, but you really can't do anything about them. Here is where you are mistaken. You can do something about your tax bill. That's right, with proper planning you can substantially reduce your tax liability each year. And you can do it legally.

Judge Learned Hand, the noted New York jurist, aptly described the tax obligation of the American citizen: "Anyone may so arrange his affairs that his taxes shall be as low as possible: He is not bound to choose that pattern which best pays the Treasury . . . nobody owes any public duty to pay more than the law demands." You have no patriotic duty to pay high taxes. You are only responsible for the payment of the minimum legal amount for which you are liable. It is your job to make sure that you do not pay more than that minimum obligation. Or, as Senator Harrison, the former chair of the Senate Finance Committee, once remarked about the payment of taxes: "There's nothing that says a man has to take a toll bridge across a river when there is a free bridge nearby."

Still, many Americans continue to pay more taxes than necessary. The same person that diligently shops to save a few dollars when purchasing food, clothing, and other necessities may be forfeiting thousands of dollars as a result of poor tax planning. While this chapter is much too brief to serve as a complete personal tax guide, it will enable you to utilize several meaningful tax strategies in your quest for financial independence. These tactics can save you thousands of dollars and, more important, can enable you to achieve your financial target in a much shorter time.

Taxing the Magic out
of Compounding

You recall that the three Hyperprofits pillars stand firmly on a foundation of compounding. The magic of compounding enables your modest investment to expand to a meaningful sum. Even the Hyperprofits investment strategy would be neutralized to a large extent if it were not for this magic of compounding. As an example, assume that you begin with $5,000 and are able to earn a 32 percent annual return on that investment (the historical rate of return for the Hyperprofits investment strategy). If you reinvest all profits, at the end of ten years your $5,000 will have grown to the handsome amount of $80,299—but only if you pay no taxes. Now you ask: "But I do pay taxes, so how much will I have left?" You're probably thinking that all except $5,000 of that final amount represents a gain and, of course, most gains are taxed. But don't panic now! We haven't led you through nine chapters only to dash your financial hopes by showing the Hyperprofits strategy is merely a quick way to increase your tax bill.

To answer your query, we must first ask you an important question: What is your tax bracket? You may not even be aware that you have one. But, chances are, if you don't know your tax bracket, then you are paying too much tax. You can be assured that the wealthy are cognizant of their tax brackets. Every financial decision affects that bracket and for that reason the most prosperous individuals rarely engage in a transaction without first determining the tax repercussions.

Simply stated, your tax bracket (or your marginal tax rate, as the accountants call it) is that percentage that you pay on your very last dollar of earnings for a particular year. One additional dollar of earnings would be taxed at that rate. Because we have a progressive income tax in this country, a person's tax bracket increases as taxable income grows. The more money you make, the less of it you get to keep. Table 49 illustrates how your tax bracket swells as your taxable income increases. By consulting this table you can get an approximate idea of your current tax bracket.

Table 49

Individual Income Tax Brackets

Taxable Income	Tax on Next $1,000 Single	Married	Tax Bracket Single*	Married
$15,000	$240	$171	24%	17%
20,000	280	223	28	22
25,000	320	260	32	26
30,000	360	300	36	30
35,000	360	300	36	30
40,000	400	350	40	35
45,000	450	361	45	36
50,000	450	400	45	40
55,000	485	400	48	40
60,000	500	440	50	44
. . .	. . .	. . .	. . .	. . .
75,000	500	440	50	44
. . .	. . .	. . .	. . .	. . .
100,000	500	480	50	48

* The maximum (50 percent) tax bracket for individuals begins at $55,300 and for marrieds (filing jointly) at $109,400.

Now we can answer your question. You already know that you would have $80,299 if you earn a Hyperprofits rate of return over the next ten years and you pay no taxes. Now assume the worst: your tax bracket is 50 percent—the highest possible. In other words, if all your gains are recognized and taxed at 50 percent, you would earn only 16 percent (not 32 percent). Half of your return would go to the U.S. Treasury, your equal investment partner. So it appears that since your rate of return is cut in half, your profits will be likewise halved. Wrong! Your ending portfolio value will be only $22,057 if you pay a 50 percent tax rate. That's only slightly more than one fourth of the $80,299 amount you would have if you paid no taxes. In effect, the bite of taxes has interrupted the compounding process and taken much of the magic out of your investment gains.

Surely you see the importance of managing your taxes. The payment of taxes not only reduces your rate of return, it also lessens the amount of funds you can reinvest. It is the loss of the use of these funds that so severely handicaps the compounding process. Table 50 illustrates how much your $5,000 will be worth at the end of ten years if you earn a Hyperprofits rate of return and pay taxes at various rates. Even if you are only in a 30 percent tax bracket, you will accumulate less than half the amount that an untaxed investor would.

Table 50

Value of $5,000 Hyperprofits Portfolio in Ten Years*

Tax Rate	Market Value
0%	$80,299
20	48,850
30	37,738
40	28,956
50	22,057

* Assuming Hyperprofits historical rate of return.

So much for the bad news. Now for the good. There are ways to reduce your taxes and thus allow the Hyperprofits strategy gains to accumulate in a more uninterrupted manner. And best of all, these tax strategies are legal, easy to implement, and very effective. In the following paragraphs we identify and describe the most important tax-reduction techniques that can be employed in concert along with the Hyperprofits investment strategy. These strategies include the use of retirement plans, income-shifting techniques, preferential capital gains treatment, and tax-deferral methods. Only in this way can you reap the full advantages of the Hyperprofits investment strategy.

Individual Retirement Accounts

By now, you have probably heard more than you want to hear about Individual Retirement Accounts, or IRAs. Thanks to 1981 tax legislation, the IRA is now available to almost every working person in the United States. As long as you earn at least $2,000 in a year, you can set aside that amount in an IRA, thus sheltering your earnings from income taxes. If your spouse also earns $2,000, then another IRA can be established. The IRA has been extolled as the "working person's tax shelter" and, as such, has been widely publicized. A recent *Wall Street Journal* article entitled "At This Train Station, You Can Buy the Paper and a Merrill Lynch IRA" attests to the popularity of the IRA. Merrill Lynch, which had sold 870,000 IRA accounts by the beginning of 1984, now even offers IRAs at a makeshift booth next to a New York newsstand.

Is an IRA beneficial to you? We certainly think so. But not just any IRA account will do. In fact, in order to derive the benefits of Hyperprofits you must be very selective in setting up your IRA. We will show you how best to establish an IRA, but first let us review the merits of this tax-advantaged plan.

IRAs offer two primary tax advantages:

1. The amount contributed to an IRA is fully deductible for federal income tax purposes.

2. The earnings on your IRA funds are not taxed until you eventually (at retirement) withdraw those funds.

Combined, these two advantages mean that you can use a portion of your earnings each year to set aside in a tax-deferred investment fund. By avoiding current taxes, you are able to use all of your earnings to build a substantial investment portfolio by the time you retire. Only at retirement do you have to pay any taxes, and even then, if you use the proper strategy your tax bite will not be too severe. It's like receiving a long-term, interest-free loan from Uncle Sam. How can you resist?

The only requirement for establishing an IRA is that you must have some earned income. You can set aside any amount up to $2,000, as long as you have earned that amount. If both spouses earn $2,000, then two IRAs can be opened

—a total of $4,000 in a year. And, if only one spouse has earnings, then a spousal IRA can be opened for the nonearning person, subject to the restriction that no more than $2,250 can be placed in the combined employed spouse's IRA and the spousal IRA. Also, a minimum of $250 must be invested in each account.

IRA contributions can be made each year. In fact, you have until April 15 of the following year to make your IRA contribution. For example, your 1985 IRA contribution can be made as late as April 15, 1986, and still be eligible for a 1985 income tax deduction. Yes, you can even file your tax return in January and claim an IRA deduction even though you have not yet made your IRA contribution. If you're in the top tax bracket, this deduction will generate $1,000 in cash (the $2,000 deduction times your tax rate of 50 percent). Then, you can use the cash tax savings to partially fund your IRA, as long as you fund by April 15.

Even though $2,000 does not seem like much, this amount when set aside each year will grow to a very healthy sum, especially when invested using Hyperprofits and relying on the magic of compounding (tax-free in this case). Let's assume, for instance, that you set aside $2,000 for each of the next ten years—a total sum of $20,000. How much would your portfolio be worth if you used an IRA as compared to investing that same amount without benefit of an IRA? The differences are noticeable. If, for example, you earned only 10 percent, your IRA tax-sheltered portfolio would total $31,874, compared to only $25,154 if you used after-tax dollars. But what if you were able to achieve a higher rate of return, say, the historical rate earned using Hyperprofits? Now the difference becomes truly staggering. Your Hyperprofits IRA plan would explode to $94,122 in ten years—far in excess of the $42,642 you would accumulate earning Hyperprofits outside the tax-sheltered confines of an IRA.

Calling the Shots

Now you have seen that IRAs offer tremendous tax advantages, so let's next see how to set up one of these accounts. There are two main points to consider before you open an IRA:

1. Most IRA plans are very easy to open: no complicated paperwork or tax filings are necessary.

2. Most IRAs do not offer sufficient investment flexibility to enable you to reap the maximum return from your funds.

Let's consider each point. First, you should not be hesitant to open an IRA. Yet recent statistics reveal that only 12 percent of eligible Americans take advantage of this attractive plan. And, furthermore, many citizens are bypassing this opportunity simply because they fear the paper work and tax filings will be too cumbersome. But that is not the case at all. Banks, insurance companies, mutual funds, credit unions, and brokerage firms offer IRA investment plans and will provide all of the necessary forms and instructions for setting up your IRA. It's no more difficult than opening a checking account. In addition, you do not have to file a tax form when you set up or make contributions to your IRA. All you do is claim your tax deduction each year; there is a special line on your Form 1040 tax return for this purpose (Line 25).

The second point is extremely crucial to your financial future. Not all IRAs are the same—far from it. These plans differ considerably from one financial institution to another. Banks tend to encourage (or even require) that you invest your funds in a bank (typically their own) certificate of deposit. Life insurance companies push annuity contracts and credit unions and savings and loan associations often push their own investment products. While most of these investment vehicles are satisfactory, you are looking for something more: an IRA investment plan that offers you the potential to earn very high rates of return. And the best way for you to accomplish this goal is to be able to call your own shots. You want an IRA plan that will allow you to make the investment decisions, not a plan that requires that you invest only in a limited number of mediocre investment products.

You may ask, "How do I find a financial institution which will handle my IRA and still allow me to freely buy and sell securities within that account?" The answer: house your account with an institution which offers a "self-directed" IRA. With a self-directed IRA, you can buy or sell any security within your IRA; the only costs are a small annual fee and a minimum charge per transaction. That means that you can even buy Hyperprofits-selected stocks and place them in a self-directed IRA and thus avoid current income taxes.

Self-directed IRAs are not offered by most institutions because they require more servicing and effort. However, there are usually several banks, brokers, or S&Ls in every major metropolitan area offering this specialized plan. The *ABCs of IRAs* by William J. Grace (available in paperback) devotes an entire chapter to self-directed IRAs and includes a list of firms offering this service. The appendix to this chapter provides a partial list of firms which currently offer self-directed IRA accounts.

The most important advantage of your self-directed IRA is that it allows you the investment flexibility to employ the Hyperprofits strategy on a tax-advantaged basis. You can reap the benefits from the magic of compounding without having the ravages of taxes interrupt your compounding process. Don't hesitate; this is an opportunity you shouldn't pass up. Uncle Sam doesn't offer many tax breaks of this magnitude.

Answering IRA Questions

We hope you are convinced that an IRA offers tremendous investment potential. But you still may have some unanswered questions. We shall now attempt to provide answers to the most frequently asked IRA questions.

Q: What if I need the funds in my IRA account to pay for an unexpected emergency?

A: Payments from an IRA are treated as ordinary (taxable) income in the year received. If you withdraw funds before age fifty-nine and a half, you will also have to pay a penalty tax equal to 10 percent of the amount withdrawn.

Q: If I already have an IRA at an institution which does not offer a self-directed plan, can I transfer my account to another institution without creating a tax liability?

A: You can withdraw assets from one IRA and, as long as you transfer the assets to another IRA within sixty days, avoid any tax liability. However, a tax-free transfer may occur only once in a one-year period (unless you are shifting your account from one bank to another; in this case the one-year restriction does not apply).

Q: Do I ever have to withdraw funds from my IRA or can I allow them to continue to compound tax-free indefinitely?

A: You must begin receiving distributions from your account by age seventy and a half, but you do not have to withdraw all of your funds. For example, if you are an unmarried male in the year you reach age 70 and a half, you must withdraw a minimum of 6²/₃ percent of your account's balance that year (8.27 percent for an unmarried woman). But, remember, your assets should be growing at a rate considerably faster than that. Therefore, even with required distributions, your IRA account can continue to grow if you withdraw only the minimum requirement.

Q: What if I neglect to make mandatory withdrawals at age seventy and a half or after?

A: A penalty tax of 50 percent applies to the difference between the minimum amount you should have received and the amount you did receive (if any).

Q: What happens to the funds in my IRA if I die?

A: You can select a beneficiary when you set up your IRA. If you die, your IRA funds go to your beneficiary. Further, these funds pass directly to the beneficiary without having to pass through a lengthy probate process.

Q: When I retire, I have the option to receive a lump-sum distribution of the amount that has accumulated in my pension and/or profit-sharing account. Is there any way to continue to tax-shelter these funds?

A: You may "roll over" the distributed funds from these plans into an IRA Rollover Account as long as you do so within sixty days of receiving the funds. You cannot, however, make additional contributions to an IRA Rollover, nor can you combine these funds with those in your ordinary IRA. Minimum distributions must still begin at age seventy and a half.

Q: When is the best time to open an IRA?

A: Now! Don't delay.

Now let's move on to other tax savings strategies.

Keogh Plans

A Keogh, or HR-10, plan offers self-employment individuals a way to tax-shelter a portion of their self-employment earnings. The specific tax advantages are the same as those for an IRA, namely, the ability to deduct qualifying contributions from taxable income and to allow the earnings on these funds to compound tax-free. Not as many individuals are eligible for Keoghs as for IRAs, but those who do qualify can benefit from a very substantial tax break. A self-employed person can contribute up to $30,000 (but limited to no more than 25 percent of self-employment earnings) each year into a tax-advantaged Keogh plan. Say, for example, that you earn $40,000 working for yourself in 1985. Then you are allowed to contribute up to $10,000 in a Keogh plan (25 percent of your earnings), thus providing you with a $10,000 tax deduction (or a $5,000 cash savings if your tax bracket is 50 percent). In addition, you can still contribute $2,000 to an IRA.

The mechanics of opening a Keogh plan are similar to those for an IRA, but typically more complex. You can arrange for a self-directed Keogh through the same institutions which offer self-directed IRAs. But, unlike an IRA, you can act as custodian for your own account and, therefore, invest the funds without having to go through a financial intermediary. In effect, a self-managed Keogh offers even greater financial flexibility than does a self-directed IRA. This, of course, means that you can buy Hyperprofits stocks for your Keogh, often in an amount considerably larger than for an IRA. And furthermore, you don't have to pay fees for managing the account. If you decide to establish a self-managed Keogh, be absolutely sure that the arrangement satisfies IRS regulations. This can be done by sending the details of your plan in a determination letter to the IRS district director and asking for advance approval of your plan. You may desire to consult with a tax accountant or attorney before submitting this determination letter.

Everything else about a Keogh closely resembles an IRA. You cannot withdraw funds until age fifty-nine and a half without invoking a penalty, and you must begin to receive distributions by age seventy and a half. In addition, you can designate a beneficiary to receive your Keogh funds in the event of your death. Although fewer people qualify for the use of a Keogh plan, those who do should seriously consider the attractiveness of this tax-advantaged vehicle. By investing your Keogh funds according to the Hyperprofits strategy, you can begin your trip down the road toward financial independence.

Income-Shifting

Most of us realize how easy it is to be thrust into a high tax bracket. It seems that the more financial success you have, the less you get to keep. With our progressive tax system, your last dollar of earnings in a year is taxed at a substantially higher rate than is your first dollar. For many would-be investors this tax structure is a real disincentive. Why bother to try to earn more when those extra earnings will catapult you into an even higher tax bracket? We share your concern about higher earnings being taxed at progressively higher rates and, therefore, in the following paragraphs we illustrate several attractive strategies that will permit you to earn additional returns without thrusting you into an even higher tax bracket. All of these strategies use the concept of income-shifting to minimize your tax bill.

But first, what do we mean by income-shifting? Income-shifting involves the transfer of earning assets from one family member to another so that the income or gain from those assets will be taxed at the marginal tax rate of the recipient. An illustration may help to explain this concept. Assume, for instance, that both you and your spouse are gainfully employed and earn a combined income of $50,000. Your tax bracket is 40 percent (refer back to

Table 49). If you earn another $1,000 from your investments, you will be able to keep only $600 after taxes. On the other hand, what if your dependent child (regardless of age) earned that same $1,000 from investments? The answer: no tax liability! The child, having no other source of income, is in a much lower tax bracket than you are. In this case the child has a zero tax bracket and thus owes no taxes. The result is astonishing: your child can retain all $1,000 of the investment earnings whereas you can retain only $600. As long as you view the family as an economic unit, you can generate significant tax savings by using the income-shifting technique. In this illustration alone, the family's net worth was increased by $400 by utilizing this tax strategy.

There is, however, one primary caveat. You cannot merely assign income to your child and, as a result, have that income taxed at your child's tax rate. Rather, the IRS requires that the child must actually earn the income; in this instance, the child's assets (not yours) must generate the return. "That's all well and good," you say, "but my children don't have any assets." Don't stop reading yet. The following sections of this chapter contain two specific ways that your child can receive assets so as to reap the advantages of income-shifting.

1. *Gifts*

The easiest way to transfer assets to a child is through an outright gift. You can give each child $10,000 yearly without incurring a gift tax (amounts above that are subject to this special gift tax—not to be confused with an income tax). Your spouse can also give the child $10,000—a total of $20,000 per year. If you have three children each spouse can give a tax-free total of $30,000 to be split evenly among the children. But keep in mind that a gift is irrevocable. You can never take that money back. Once the child attains majority age, he or she is free to use the funds in any way (of course, you can still try to use a little "friendly persuasion" to encourage your child to use the funds in a prudent manner).

Now let's see just what dramatic results this tax-saving strategy can produce. To do so, we shall assume that you are planning to provide for your child's college education and decide to set aside $500 of your salary each year specifically for that purpose. Two major problems emerge. First, the $500 of your earnings is subject to income taxes so that really leaves only $300 after taxes annually to contribute to the college fund (assuming, of course, that you remain in the 40 percent tax bracket). Second, as long as you hold these contributions in your name, the investment income and gains from this portfolio will be subject to your individual tax rate. As you can clearly see, income taxes dramatically reduce the magic of compounding and thus reduce your ability to accumulate college funds for your children. After ten years this college fund will have grown to $6,286 if you earn the historical Hyperprofits return of 32 percent yearly on the funds you invest (Table 51).

Table 51

A Hyperprofits College Portfolio
(After-Tax Value of Portfolio)

Year	Using Parents' Income	Using Gift*
1	$ 250	$ 500
2	548	1,160
3	903	2,031
4	1,326	3,181
5	1,831	4,699
6	2,433	6,702
7	3,151	9,347
8	4,007	12,839
9	5,028	17,447
10	6,286	23,531

* Does not include the gift amount and assumes the child pays no income taxes.

Surely, you can see that your child's college portfolio would grow considerably faster if the bite of taxes was reduced or eliminated. But is there a way to pare taxes? Consider now that instead of earmarking $500 of your salary each year, you give your child a $5,000 U.S. Treasury bond which pays 10 percent annual interest and matures in ten years. That bond will pay the $500 annually —the same as the $500 of your salary. However, this time the $500 income is taxed to the child, not you. This same stream of $500 annual income can be invested in a college fund. The big difference is that this time the income is taxed at the child's tax rate because the child owns the bond and therefore is taxed on the bond's interest. You pay no taxes. If the child has no other sources of income he or she will be in the zero tax bracket and thus pay no taxes on this income.[2] The net result is that the college fund will appreciate to $23,531 at the end of ten years if the historical rate of return earned by Hyperprofits can be achieved. Yes, that's right: $23,531 compared to only $6,286 if the funds are accumulated in the parents' account. And, furthermore, that $23,531 amount does not include the original $5,000 gift amount; it never has to be touched.

2. Short-Term Trusts

Maybe you are concerned about giving such a large amount to your child. Rather, you would prefer to maintain control of your assets. On the other hand, you would like to give the child the income generated by some of your assets to provide for college or just to give the child a financial head start in life. Then a short-term trust, also known as a Clifford Trust, may be just the thing for you. Under this arrangement, you can place assets, preferably Hyper-profits stocks, in a trust with the stipulation that the assets will return directly to you after the expiration of some specified time period (must be at least ten years and a day). Thus you are losing the use of your assets for only the stated time. The gains produced by the assets, however, are paid to the beneficiary of the trust—in this instance your child—and thus taxed to the child. In effect, you are able to transfer the gains from the assets to your child without giving away the assets.

The short-term trust effectively shifts gains from a high-bracket taxpayer to a low-bracket taxpayer and in so doing lowers the family's overall tax burden. And, all this is accomplished without giving away your property. But most taxpayers are not aware of the advantages of short-term trusts and even those that do know about the trust often fail to use them because of their complexity. Our advice: If a short-term trust seems suitable to your situation, proceed with vigor. Any competent tax attorney can set up one of these trusts for a relatively small fee. When properly structured and used, the favorable results of this type of trust far overshadow the complexities.

You have now observed two attractive ways to shift income from one taxpayer to another. Each planning technique offers a slightly different way to accomplish this objective and you will probably favor one technique over the others. But the important thing to keep in mind: Everyone has a tax bracket. In

---

[2] Any individual reporting $1,000 (the amount of the statutory personal exemption) or less income in a given year is exempt from payment of income taxes. Beginning in 1985, this exemption amount is indexed to the inflation rate and thus may increase.

fact, a tax bracket is thrust upon a newborn babe at the exact moment of worldly arrival. By shifting income to lower brackets you can permanently reduce your family's tax burden and, therefore, allow Hyperprofits and the magic of compounding to work more effectively for you. Now, let's move on to another important tax consideration, capital gains and losses.

Capital Transactions:
The Long and Short of It

Anytime you sell a stock or any other investment asset, for that matter, you must report the resulting capital gain or loss on your annual tax report. A special form, Schedule D (available free upon request from any IRS office), is provided for you to record such transactions.

You already know that you are liable for taxes on any recognized gains, but if you're like millions of other Americans, you're not really sure exactly how the special capital gains tax treatment works. Let's take a look. First, keep in mind that the IRS categorized capital gains into two groups: short-term and long-term. Courtesy of the Deficit Reduction Act of 1984, a long-term holding is now defined as being over six months for most assets; therefore, anything held for six months or less is short-term.[3]

Second, remember that there are different effective tax rates on short-term and long-term transactions. The primary difference between the two results from the preferential tax treatment afforded long-term gains. The IRS allows 60 percent of long-term gains to be excluded from taxation. That's correct, 60 percent of your gain is tax-free. In our opinion this is one of the most generous tax breaks available today so it really behooves you to be fully aware of its existence.

On the other hand, a short-term gain is fully taxed as ordinary income. No special tax exclusion exists. The tax implications are as obvious as the answer to the following question: Would you rather be taxed on all your gains or only on 40 percent of your gains?

Simple, isn't it? Just to show the dramatic difference between short-term versus the long-term tax treatment, we offer the following example. Suppose that you sell some shares of stock for a $10,000 gain and you are in a 40

[3] For capital transactions prior to June 23, 1984, an asset must be held longer than one year to qualify as long-term. The current six-month long-term qualification period is scheduled to revert back to one year starting in 1987.

percent tax bracket. Can you calculate the savings in taxes you would achieve if the gain were long-term instead of short-term? Table 52 provides the answer.

Table 52

Short-Term Versus Long-Term Capital Gains

	Short-Term	Long-Term
Amount of gain	$10,000	$10,000
Capital gains exclusion	—0—	6,000
Taxable gain	$10,000	$ 4,000
Tax rate	40%	40%
Tax	4,000	$ 1,600
Effective tax rate	40%	16%

What a difference! A $10,000 short-term gain creates a $4,000 tax liability, but a $10,000 long-term gain produces only a $1,600 tax bill—a considerable $2,400 tax difference. The effective tax rate for the long-term gain is a modest 16 percent versus a full 40 percent rate for the short-term alternative. Need we say more?

Now let's turn the table and look at losses. Admittedly, we sincerely hope that you never see another loss, but the truth is that, sooner or later, every active investor will get nicked. So when a loss occurs, make sure that you make the most of it.

In the event of a loss, you benefit more by recognizing the loss before it becomes long-term. Here's why. A short-term loss, standing alone, can be deducted from ordinary income—up to $3,000 per year.[4] Any loss exceeding $3,000 can be "carried forward" indefinitely to be used to offset future years' gains and/or ordinary income. For example, if you incur a $10,000 short-term loss this year, you can deduct $3,000 now (thus reducing your current taxes) and carry forward the $7,000 difference into years beyond.

If you have a long-term loss, however, you are allowed to use only half to offset ordinary income. Yes, half the loss is wasted. Therefore, a $10,000 long-

[4] A loss sustained on the sale of stock is not deductible if the seller acquires substantially identical securities thirty days before or after the sale date.

term loss must be halved to $5,000 before taking a tax deduction. Now you can see why, all else equal, you should strive for long-term gains, but take losses while they're still short-term. But there's still more. What if you have both gains and losses in the same year. What then?

Triumph Through Tax Timing

Given the current tax laws, the best kind of gain is long-term and the best kind of loss is short-term. The worst possible tax situation is when you take long-term gains and short-term losses in the same year because they must be netted against each other before the long-term gains receive any exclusion.

Maybe another example will best illustrate this principle. Let's assume you took a $1,000 short-term loss in 1985 and are contemplating taking a $1,000 long-term capital gain. You have two possibilities: (1)take the gain now (1985) or (2)delay recognizing the gain until next year. Table 53 presents the income tax repercussions of each alternative.

Table 53

Short-Term Loss Combined with Long-Term Gains

	First Possibility	Second Possibility
Short-term loss, 1985	($1,000)	($1,000)
Long-term gain, 1985	1,000	—
Net taxable income, 1985	—0—	($1,000)
Taxes (savings), 1985	None	($400)
Long-term gain, 1986	—	$1,000
60% exclusion, 1986	—	600
Taxable income, 1986	—	400
Taxes, 1986	—	160
Net tax savings, 1985–86	None	$240

As you can clearly see, under the first possibility, the short-term loss and long-term gain occur in the same year and therefore completely cancel out. The bottom line: absolutely no net tax effect.

With the second possibility, however, your $1,000 short-term loss stands along in 1985, thus reducing taxable income by the same amount. If you have a 40 percent marginal tax bracket, you save $400 on your 1985 tax bill. Then, in 1986, when you recognize the $1,000 long-term gain, here's what happens. The 60 percent statutory exemption reduces the gain to a taxable $400. Applying your 40 percent marginal tax rate produces a $160 tax liability. Now look at the overall impact: a $400 tax reduction in 1985 versus an only $160 tax hike the next year—an overall $240 tax savings versus no tax savings if you took the gain and loss in the same year. The difference is obvious. By taking a long-term gain in a year when you also have a short-term loss, you waste the valuable 60 percent long-term gain exemption.

As you can plainly see, your bottom-line return can be vastly influenced by the tax repercussions of capital gains and losses. At this point we summarize our prior discussion by listing four important tax techniques:

1. Don't realize capital gains but do realize capital losses as soon as possible.

2. If capital gains are to be realized, delay the realization until there is a long-term gain.

3. Realize capital losses to offset any capital gains.

4. If capital gains are to be realized, they should be taken in low tax years.

Tax Postponement

Most of us prefer to postpone the payment of income taxes for as long as possible. After all, the longer you delay a tax payment, the longer you have the use of those funds. And remember, time equals money. The longer you have the use of funds, the more dramatic will be the compounding process. Sure, eventually you must pay taxes on all gains, but why pay before necessary? The next paragraphs briefly outline five key ways to postpone (or eliminate) taxes on capital gains.

1. Don't Sell

A taxable capital gain occurs only if you recognize that gain. In most instances you recognize the gain by selling the appreciated asset. If you don't sell, then no taxable gain results. Therefore, an asset can soar in value without creating a tax liability as long as you don't sell. Your portfolio increases without being subjected to the ravages of taxes.

One final caveat: Don't hang on to an asset just to avoid taxes. If you no longer relish the investment merits of the asset, it's probably best to sell and pay the taxes rather than run the risk of the asset's price declining. Never let tax considerations totally dominate an investment decision.

2. Stepped-up Basis

You may be thinking, "But if I never sell, then eventually those shares will be included in my estate when I die. Doesn't this create a horrendous income tax situation?" No, not at all. In fact, your death actually eliminates the income tax predicament.

Now don't misread us. We certainly don't advocate your dying just to remedy an income tax problem. But, as the old adage goes, there are only two certainties in life. That's right, death and taxes. So, just in the event of your untimely demise, let's guarantee that your heirs, not Uncle Sam, benefit to the fullest.

Here's the tax break. When anyone dies, that person's assets are revalued at the date of death (or, alternatively, six months from date of death) so that the assets are assigned a new "stepped-up" cost basis for the heirs. Therefore, say, some IBM shares were bought long ago at a $30-per-share cost. When those same shares are inherited, then a new cost basis is assigned which reflects the current market price at the date of death (or six months thence). Let's assume IBM's price is $100 when the death occurs. If the heir immediately sells at $100, no capital gains tax liability occurs because the cost basis was stepped up to $100. However, if the shares had been sold at $100 by the original owner, the resulting $70-per-share capital gain would create a sizable tax liability.

So popular is the stepped-up basis rule that when Congress eliminated this tax break in 1978, the public outcry was so vocal that the rule was soon reinstated.

3. Short Sale Against the Box

Selling short against the box is the process of selling borrowed securities while at the same time you own securities identical to those you borrowed and sold.[5] We realize this sounds confusing so we'll provide a brief example for the sake of clarity.

You own 100 shares of Exxon common stock, which you bought several years ago for $20 per share. The price has doubled to $40 and you desire to sell except for one problem: your current 1985 tax bracket is very high. Actually you would rather take the gain now but pay taxes next year when you figure your tax rate will be lower. Here's how you accomplish your objective. Don't sell your 100 shares of Exxon. Rather, you should borrow from your broker another 100 shares of Exxon which you sell today at $40 per share.[6] You haven't sold *your* 100 shares so no taxes are due. On January 2, 1986, you deliver your original 100 shares to your broker to replace the borrowed shares. For income tax purposes, January 2, 1986, is your effective sale date because that is the first day you gave up *your* Exxon shares. The net result: you are not responsible for taxes on your Exxon sale until 1986 even though you actually "locked in" the $40 price in 1985. You guaranteed your gain but still pushed the tax bite back into a lower bracket year.

As you see, this technique may be used to lock in a profit based upon current stock prices without having to recognize the gain currently for tax purposes. The short sale is not recognized for tax purposes until the investor closes out the short position, usually in the subsequent year, by delivering identical shares to the broker.

4. *Purchase of Puts*

A put option is a contract to sell 100 shares of a particular stock at a set price (called the strike price) within a specified period of time. The key point about this contract is that it is carried out only if you desire; that's why it's called an option. You must pay a price (called the premium) to purchase a put contract. Puts trade regularly on the five organized options exchanges and can be readily acquired through your broker.

Puts are often used as a way to speculate on a sudden decline in a stock's price. There are, however, other ways to benefit from puts. We shall describe how to use puts to improve your tax position. An example will illustrate a put's usefulness.

Assume, for example, that you own shares of an appreciated stock. Your stock has already appreciated to your price objective and thus you desire to sell. However, your tax bracket is unusually high this year so any capital gains you

---

[5] A short sale occurs when you borrow a stock from a second party and sell it to a third party. Eventually you must buy back shares of the stock and then return the shares to the lender.

[6] This sale represents a short sale because you are selling borrowed shares.

realize will be taxed at the maximum rate. You do not want to pay high taxes this year, but you also do not desire to risk a price decline in your shares by waiting until next year to sell. A put option may be just the thing for you. By acquiring a put, you protect against a severe stock decline because if your stock's market price falls, you can sell your shares at the put's fixed strike price (which, of course, will be higher than the new market price).

Thus, a put protects you against a precipitous price decline: you are guaranteed that you can sell your shares at a price no lower than the put's strike price. In this manner you can eliminate much of the downside risk of your stock without having to sell.

What if your stock's price rises? That's even better. You still reap the rewards because you are *not* required to sell your shares at the put's strike price; such a sale is optional to you. You merely let your put expire worthless. The premium you lost can be viewed as an insurance cost.

There is one primary drawback of puts. They are not available on most stocks, especially many of the smaller stocks which are so crucial to the success of the Hyperprofits investment strategy.

5. *Charitable Contributions*

You can permanently avoid the recognition of a gain on an appreciated stock by donating it to a qualifying charitable organization. With certain exceptions, the amount of the tax deduction will be the fair market value of the donated security (providing the long-term holding period has been met).

Let's return to the earlier example where you own 100 shares of Exxon (your cost = $2,000; current market value = $4,000). If you donate those shares to a qualifying charity, you can take a $4,000 tax deduction. If you're in a 40 percent tax bracket, that deduction will reduce your tax by $1,600 ($4,000 × .40).

But what if you first sold the Exxon shares and then donated the proceeds to the charity? An entirely different situation emerges because in this instance you must pay capital gains taxes. Your long-term gain ($2,000) would produce $800 of taxable income after the 60 percent exclusion. Then, you must pay $320 in taxes as a result of your 40 percent tax bracket. Therefore, a $4,000 gift to your charity would now cost $4,320 (the $4,000 donation plus the $320 tax). One caveat: you must have owned the donated securities more than six months to receive the full tax deduction.

If you plan to make charitable donations, use appreciated properties whenever possible. This is an effective way to avoid capital gains taxes and get the most mileage out of your contributions.

Paying More Taxes and Liking It

Any successful investor is eventually confronted with the unpleasant duty of paying income taxes. So despised are taxes that many otherwise rational investors toss their money into flimsy tax shelters promising extraordinary tax savings. The problem is that often these exotic shelters are acquired merely to reduce taxes, not to maximize investment returns.

The Hyperprofits system of investing is not designed to reduce your taxes. In fact, by using Hyperprofits your tax bill will probably increase. But, in the process, your bottom-line investment returns will increase even more dramatically. Please heed our advice: first manage your investments and then manage your taxes—not vice versa.

In this chapter we have introduced several tax-savings techniques which can be used in concert with the Hyperprofits investment plan. These techniques are not all-inclusive—there are even more available. As you become a more active investor, you will want to consult with your tax accountant to best manage your tax situation. But, remember, your primary goal is to make money through intelligent investing. The reduction or avoidance of income taxes must be kept in proper perspective, that is, an incidental objective which emerges from your successful investment activities.

In the next chapter, we will introduce something that is really exciting. Throughout this book, we've documented the excellent historical profit performance of the Hyperprofits investment strategy. But what about the future? That's what the next chapter discusses. We plan to show you why the future prospects for stocks and, more specifically, Hyperprofits appear so promising.

Appendix A

Brokerage Firms Offering Self-Directed IRA Plans

Broker[1]	Initial Expense	Annual Expense	Typical Commission[2]
Full-Service:			
Dean Witter	$20	$20	$54.15
E. F. Hutton	None	25	55.00
Paine Webber	25	20	53.50
Prudential Bache	25	50	53.00
Shearson American Express	None	50	53.50
Discount:			
Rose & Co.			25.00
MPACT Brokers			45.00
Charles Schwab			45.00
Andrew Peck			47.00

[1] The toll-free numbers of these firms can be obtained from directory assistance, (800) 555-1212.

[2] Based on 100-share transaction at $20 per share. The commission reductions available through discount brokers become more substantial for larger transactions.

A New Era of Stock Market Prosperity

Throughout this book, you have witnessed the profit-generating capabilities of Hyperprofits. Yet we have made very little mention of the impact of bull and bear markets on the performance of the system. Why? Because our research convincingly shows that you don't need to worry about it. By sticking with Hyperprofits over the long run, through thick and thin, you can achieve your desired financial goals. Remember that the 32.3 percent average annual profit return for Hyperprofits stocks was generated in the 1970s, a relatively poor stock market period.

So you can see why it is not necessary for you to be a market prognosticator. Nevertheless, one vital fact which emerged from our extensive research of the Hyperprofits system is this: Hyperprofits makes the most money in strong markets. In this chapter, we will explain why the second half of the 1980s will, in fact, be a new era of stock market prosperity. The implication of this is clear. In all likelihood, Hyperprofits will generate even more wealth-building power in the last half of the decade than it did in the seventies. Why we firmly believe this is the subject of this chapter. After you have read this chapter, see if you aren't as optimistic about this future opportunity as we are.

What Is the Stock Market?

A rejuvenated stock market greeted investors during the early years of the 1980s. At the beginning of the decade the Dow Jones Industrial Average rested at 838.74. The Dow's slumber was short-lived, however, as a massive stock-buying spree propelled this popular average to 1258.64 at year's end 1983. This

50 percent increase in only four years reveals that during the first part of this decade the stock market clearly was the right place for your money.

That's all well and fine except for one problem: those glamorous years now belong to history and thus the fact that stocks performed admirably doesn't put one red cent in your pocket. In this chapter we venture beyond the first half of the decade and explain why stocks are still an ideal place for your money.

Before we show why the outlook for the stock market is so favorable, let's first pause to answer a fundamental question: What is the stock market? Now that we are nearing the end of our journey through it, we think it's only fair to tell you what it is. "Stock market" is a term you hear almost daily. You can hardly turn on your radio or TV set without hearing mention of the day's market performance. But do you really know what the stock market is? We are convinced that most investors cannot answer this important question in the affirmative.

In the most complete sense the stock market represents the broad arena for the trading (buying and selling) for *all* common stocks. So when you ask, "How's the market doing?" you are really questioning the average performance of *all* common stocks.

No problem so far until you consider that no one actually knows how many publicly traded stocks exist at any given point in time. We know there are at least 30,000, and probably closer to 40,000, publicly traded common stocks in the United States alone—not to mention the thousands of Japanese, British, German, and other foreign stocks. Most, of course, are very small companies which trade in the over-the-counter market. The New York Stock Exchange, for example, trades only approximately 2,000 securities—some of which are not even common stocks.[1]

With so many different stocks you can readily see the complications involved in tracking the entire market's performance. Even with today's high-powered computers this is no simple task. As a result, the market index was devised to solve the almost insurmountable chore of monitoring the performance of tens of thousands of stocks. A market index measures the performance of a (one hopes) representative group of common stocks and assumes that these stocks' price movements accurately reflect the overall market's fluctuations. In this way a market index acts as a proxy for the overall stock market.

---

[1] The New York Stock Exchange has listed a number of preferred stocks, warrants, rights, trusts, and even a limited partnership in addition to common stocks.

You Can't Buy the Dow Jones

Everyone's heard about the Dow Jones Industrial Average (the Dow). It's the most widely quoted market index by far and, as such, is often used to gauge the performance of the overall stock market. You can't call up your broker and buy shares of the Dow; there's no such tangible item. The Dow is merely an "average" of several stocks.

The real question becomes, How accurately does the Dow measure the entire market's performance? Because it is a market index, the Dow's primary value lies in its ability to track the movements of stocks in general. Let's pursue this point a little further. To be a reliable barometer of the entire stock market's performance, you would think that the Dow incorporated the movements of numerous individual issues. But no, that is not the case—not even close. The Dow presently consists of only thirty different stocks as shown in Table 54.[2] Do you believe these thirty stocks accurately reflect the actions of all stocks— maybe as many as 40,000 more? Doubtful, isn't it? Now look closely at the list of Dow companies. A common thread emerges. These firms are all very large "blue chips." Every one is listed on the New York Stock Exchange. Even the "smallest" one (Inco) reported 1983 revenues in excess of $1 billion. Nowhere does a truly small or even a medium-sized company appear. Really the Dow only measures how the often stodgy corporate giants are doing.

Table 54

The Dow Jones Industrials, 1983

Company	Revenues[1]	Average[2] P/E	Closing Price
Allied Corp.	10,022	7.8	$64.250
Alcoa	5,263	19.1	44.875

[2] The Dow Jones Industrial Average first appeared in 1896 and consisted of only twelve "blue chips." Today's Dow contains only two of the original dozen (American Brands and General Electric). The ten originals which no longer appear in the Dow are American Cotton Oil, American Sugar, Chicago Gas, Distilling and Cattle Feeding, Laclede Gas, National Lead, North American, Tennessee Coal and Iron, U.S. Leather Preferred, and U.S. Rubber.

Company	Revenues[1]	Average[2] P/E	Closing Price
American Brands	7,093	7.6	59.250
American Can	3,346	12.5	46.875
American Express	9,770	15.5	32.625
American Telephone	67,599	7.8	61.500
Bethlehem Steel	4,898	NC	28.500
Du Pont	35,378	10.6	52.000
Eastman Kodak	10,170	22.1	76.125
Exxon	88,561	6.0	37.375
General Electric	26,797	11.9	58.625
General Foods	8,600	7.4	51.375
General Motors	74,582	5.8	74.375
Goodyear	9,736	9.4	30.375
Inco	1,173	NC	14.625
IBM	40,180	12.7	122.000
International Harvester	3,601	NC	11.500
International Paper	4,357	11.7	59.000
Merck & Co.	3,246	14.9	90.375
Minnesota Mining	7,039	14.4	82.500
Owens-Illinois	3,422	13.2	37.375
Procter & Gamble	12,452	10.5	56.875
Sears, Roebuck	35,883	9.9	37.125
Standard Oil—California	27,243	7.3	34.625
Texaco	40,068	7.2	35.875
Union Carbide	9,001	21.3	62.750
U.S. Steel	17,523	NC	30.375
United Technology	14,669	9.1	72.500

Westinghouse	9,533	9.3	54.750
Woolworth	5,456	9.3	35.125
Sum of Market Prices			1548.13
Common Divisor			1.230
Average, December 31, 1983			1258.64

[1] In millions of dollars.

[2] NC—not calculable because of negative earnings per share.

No, you can't buy the Dow Jones; it's only a market index. But as you know, our contention throughout the book is, Who would want to buy the Dow Jones in the first place? Consisting only of mature corporate giants, this average is destined for investment mediocrity. What you want is spectacular performance—not mediocre results. That's what Hyperprofits is all about. We won't steer you into Dow-type companies. Rather, Hyperprofits directs your funds into the smaller, more poised-for-profits stocks.

Standard & Poor's to the Rescue

You've seen the drawbacks of the Dow: it observes only thirty blue chips while ignoring the other 40,000 or so stocks. The Standard & Poor's 500 improves on this deficiency by monitoring 500 different stocks (the Dow Jones 30 plus 470 more). Without a doubt the S&P 500 is the index that the heavy-weight financial institutions observe the most. A professional's performance is often compared to the S&P 500 to determine how he or she is doing.

Naturally, if the professionals closely observe this index, then it must accurately reflect the entire market's performance. Wrong again! The S&P 500, although improving on the Dow, still covers only 500 stocks (and 488 of those are listed on the New York Stock Exchange). What about the other 39,500 or so? Furthermore, the S&P 500 uses a special weighting process that gives substantially heavier emphasis to the really big stocks.[3] Clearly, this widely

[3] S&P does not merely observe the price of each stock; rather it uses a firm's entire market value. IBM, the largest issue in the index (or anywhere else for that matter), had a $63 billion market value at June 30, 1984. When compared to Pabst Brewing's $45 million total market value, you can see that IBM is approximately 1,400 times more influential than Pabst in affecting the S&P 500's movements.

touted index is biased toward big. But, Hyperprofits is geared to capitalize on the small stocks' performance and thus has little relationship to the S&P 500.

So, Again, What Is the Market?

We have argued that two major drawbacks prevent the most popular market indexes from properly gauging the overall stock market's performance. To summarize, these dual deficiencies are:

1. The popular indexes observe only the stocks of large corporations.

2. The larger the firm, typically the heavier its weighting in calculating the index.

Just to illustrate how dramatic these biases can be, consider one additional market index, the American Stock Exchange index. This index comprises only common stocks listed on the smaller American Stock Exchange (the Amex). The Amex index is not influenced by the corporate titans like IBM, Sears, and Exxon. To the contrary, the Amex index is affected only by the movements of smaller stocks—those securities listed on the Amex which are typically too small to qualify for Big Board trading.

Nonetheless, the Amex index measures the "market's" performance. But you suspect that the market it gauges is significantly different from the one the Dow Jones monitors. Figure 3 confirms your suspicions. Although some similarities exist, overall the Dow and Amex are two very different creatures. No greater testimony to their differences can be found than the performances of these markets during 1977. In that year alone, the Amex soared 31.7 percent while the Dow fell 17.2 percent. So once again we ask: Just what is the market?

We have concluded that the stock market represents many different things to many different people. No single market index truly captures the entire market's performance. Nevertheless, the overall market largely influences investors' buy and sell activities. Therefore, we must remain sensitive to the market's outlook.

The remainder of this chapter is devoted to developing a market outlook for the last half of the eighties. Admittedly, we fall back to the use of some of the popular indexes to measure overall market performance. As long as you understand the limitations of these indexes, we believe that you can develop a feel for the direction of the overall stock market.

What's most crucial is that you don't try to play the market, darting in

Figure 3
Stock Market Performance
Quarterly, 1970–1983

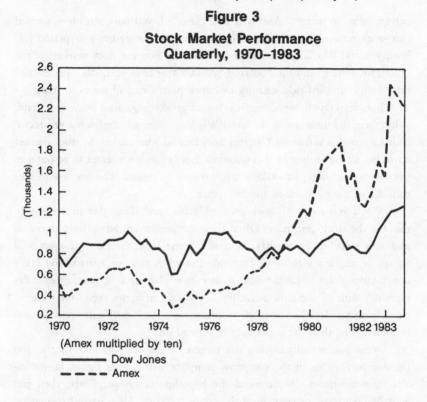

(Amex multiplied by ten)

——— Dow Jones

- - - - Amex

and out in an attempt to beat the Dow Jones, S&P 500, Amex, or any other popular index. Rather, you must discipline yourself to take a longer-term investment approach in which you first establish that a favorable market climate exists and, second, employ the scientifically validated Hyperprofits investment strategy to select individual issues. The adherence to this approach will enable you to harvest financial rewards beyond your highest hopes. As you finish this book, we are confident that you will have become a believer in stocks and, more specifically, Hyperprofits.

The Perfect Inflation Hedge

Let us continue the line of reasoning which leads us to conclude that the market is on the brink of a boom. After a quarter century of reaping unusually attractive stock market returns, investors in the late sixties anointed stocks "the perfect inflation hedge." And why not? After all, you have already witnessed that stock returns far outstripped inflation in the twenty-five-year period following World War II. Investors fondly recall the buoyant stock markets of the "Fabulous Fifties" and the "Soaring Sixties." Year after year, stock prices continued their upward ride, causing investors' portfolios and hopes to soar.

But, deep down, we all realize that all good things must come to an end. Why, then, did investors in the late 1960s place so much confidence on stocks' ability to combat inflation? The real story behind what makes the stock market move lies in the answer to this question. But before we attempt to respond to this important query, let's take a quick detour to explain why one would ever consider owning a stock in the first place.

When you think of stock ownership, the first thing that may come to mind is the stock certificate. Often these certificates are attractively engraved and very colorful. Frequently an artistic scene from Greek mythology will appear or maybe a scantily clad nymph. But when you buy a stock, you really aren't buying the certificate—no matter how glamorous it may appear. Remember, some of the most attractively adorned certificates ever were those of now defunct railroad companies. In many cases these certificates now possess no more value than the paper they're printed on.

What you're really buying is a piece of a corporation. That's right, you become part owner of the company, complete with voting rights. If, for instance, you acquire 100 shares of the hypothetical Prosper Corp., then you actually own some percentage of the entire company. How is your ownership percentage determined? Simply by dividing the number of shares you own by the total number of existing Prosper shares. If 1 million Prosper shares exist, then you own one hundredth of 1 percent (.0001) of the company (calculated by dividing your 100 shares by the 1 million outstanding). You participate in the company's profits based upon that percentage. So, if Prosper earns $10 million this year, your proportionate share equals $1,000 ($10 million times .0001). As the company's profits rise, your profit share increases as well.

Now you see the picture. As Prosper prospers, so do you. Right? One would certainly think so. Isn't it logical to presume that as a company's profits increase so does the value of a share of its stock? If so, as long as management does its job by directing the company to higher and higher profits each year, the stockholder should be rewarded. Makes sense, doesn't it? Well, that's exactly the way investors saw it in the late 1960s. Produce more profits and your stock's price will climb.

So This Is Perfect?

How tempting can an investment be? With a twenty-five-year history of far outpacing inflation, stocks appeared destined to occupy the number one slot on the investors' hit parade for a long time. If corporate managers do their jobs, profit increases are bound to keep up with inflationary pressures. Is there anything else necessary to ensure stock market prosperity?

Enter the 1970s. As glamourous as the post–World War II era was for stocks, the seventies were just the opposite. Actually the mighty bull stampede began to fade in 1968 at the conclusion of a frenetic new-issue craze that saw the stocks of unseasoned (and often unprofitable) companies ascend to astronomical heights. As investors eventually returned to their senses, stock prices began to plummet. The greatest demise in stock prices since the Great Depression was under way. A study by Salomon Brothers, the prestigious investment banker, revealed that during the period from 1968 to the end of the following decade, common stocks performed worse than any other kind of investment. Table 55 displays these startling results.

Table 55

Performance of Assorted Investments
1968–1979

Rank	Investment	Compound Annual Growth Rate in Value
1	Gold	19.4%
2	Chinese ceramics	19.1
3	Stamps	18.9
4	Rare books	15.7
5	Silver	13.7
6	Coins	12.7
7	Old master paintings	12.5

Rank	Investment	Compound Annual Growth Rate in Value
8	Diamonds	11.8
9	Farmland	11.3
10	Single-family home	9.6
11	Inflation (C.P.I.)	6.5
12	Corporate bonds	5.8
13	Common stocks	3.1

Source: Salomon Brothers.

Yes, the so-called perfect inflation hedge provided a compound annual return less than half the average yearly inflation rate (as gauged by the Consumer Price Index). Perfect inflation hedge? Far from it! If in 1968 you had invested $1,000 in a diversified portfolio of common stocks (say a no-load mutual fund), you would have seen the value of your portfolio creep to only $1,400 by year's end 1979. Unfortunately, however, the same basket of goods and services which would have cost you a thousand bucks in 1968 would set you back twice that amount by the end of 1979. The net result: investing in average common stocks would have caused you to lose 30 percent of your purchasing power from 1968 to 1979. That's hardly a solid testimony to the inflation-hedging capabilities of stocks.

Meanwhile, virtually every other investment group performed admirably during this period. The average single-family home, for example, nearly tripled in value, rare books quintupled, and gold increased more than sevenfold. All of these tangibles, of course, proved to be exceptional inflation hedges.

Only stocks and, to a lesser extent, bonds were unable to effectively protect your assets against the ravages of inflation. Because bonds have a fixed interest rate, it's not surprising that they performed poorly: a bond has no chance to increase its yield as inflation rises. But stocks are entirely different. One of the main attractions of stocks is that stock returns, unlike those of bonds, can increase. And to the extent that these returns grow in line with inflation, you would think that stocks would consequently be superb inflation hedges.

But we know that stocks performed miserably during the seventies. So what happened? Did corporate managers fall down on the job, not keeping corporate earnings growth in line with inflationary increases? Certainly languishing profits, if that was the case, would account for this pathetic stock market performance.

Corporate Managers Perform

Without a doubt the 1970s were extremely troublesome times for all Americans—corporate managers included. The Vietnam War, spiraling interest rates, the Watergate scandal, the largest corporate bankruptcy ever (Penn Central), a crippling energy crisis, the resignation under pressure of a president (and a vice-president, too), and the highest inflation rate of the century. Need we say more? All these events combined to make life difficult for the corporate executive. And these represent only the first half of the decade! How could anyone fault corporate officials for not performing well during this abominable time?

Well, let's pause to determine exactly how corporations fared during the trying seventies. Believe it or not, the growth in corporate profits (the S&P 500 companies) slightly outdistanced inflation during the 1970s.[4] Hard to believe, isn't it? During one of the most troublesome periods in our history, American managers performed admirably. Apparently corporations were able to raise product prices fast enough to offset the cost increases brought about by inflationary forces. When the going got tough, corporate managers delivered.

But where does this leave the stock investor? Recall that the late sixties' gospel was that common stocks are the perfect inflation hedge. The reason? Because competent corporate executives should be able to pass on any inflation-induced cost increases to the customer and thus index profits to the inflation rate.

The fact that corporate profits continued to move upward at a pace greater than the inflation rate suggests that those late sixties soothsayers were at least half right. Indeed, corporations were able to produce profit increases that completely offset inflationary expansion.

Unfortunately, these market prognosticators were grossly mistaken about the other half of their contention. That is, stock prices did not move along with corporate profits. Rather, stock prices dropped throughout the decade

---

[4] The earnings per share of the S&P 500 companies grew from $1.49 in 1969 to $3.79 in 1979 —an annual compound growth rate in excess of 9 percent.

even though profits flourished. One lesson vividly emerges from the experience of the 1970s: You can't be just half right about the stock market and still reap handsome financial rewards.

Multiplication—That's the Name of the Game

Now, this is perplexing to say the least. Corporate profits grew at a faster pace than inflation during the 1970s—just what optimistic stock market disciples had prescribed as the proper medicine for healthy gains. If earnings were attractive inflation hedges, then shouldn't stock returns likewise compare favorably?

Well, we already know the answer. Stock returns were paled by the inflation rate. So what's the explanation for this apparent contradiction? To answer this important question, let's break a stock's price down into its two main components. We've already talked about one component, earnings per share. But what about the other? That second factor captures exactly how investors value those earnings per share. This factor is none other than our old friend the price–earnings ratio, which plays such an intimate role in Hyperprofits. By multiplying a company's current P/E times the firm's most recent annual earnings per share, you can determine the market price of the firm's common stock.

Therefore, the following simple equation explains how a stock's market price is calculated:

$$\text{Market price} = \text{earnings per share} \times \text{P/E}$$

Maybe an example will best illustrate the importance of the P/E concept. Say, for example, that our fictitious Prosper Corp. earned $5 per share in the current year. The stock's price is then determined by multiplying those earnings times the stock's P/E. A P/E of 12 would cause the stock to sell at $60 per share. A lower P/E would produce a lower stock price, and vice versa for a higher P/E. You can see why some investors refer to the P/E as the "multiplier." All else equal, the higher the multiplier, the greater the stock price.

You might think that stocks would always sell at approximately the same P/E. Indeed, for years a P/E of 10 was considered "normal." Such P/E constancy would allow you to accurately determine the market value of stocks. If a company's earnings per share rises, the stock's price would rise accordingly as long as its P/E stays the same.

But the real truth is that P/Es fluctuate with amazing frequency and over a wide range. Take the S&P 500 index. Over the 1960–84 period, the S&P's average annual P/E ranged from a low of 7.1 in 1979 to a high of 20.8 in 1961. As you can see in Figure 4, the highest yearly average P/E was nearly triple the lowest. How important is this difference in P/Es? The following example should provide an answer. Assume that our Prosper Corp., an average company, reported $5.00 earnings per share in each of 1961 and 1979. The net result: a share of Prosper's stock, assuming it received an average P/E, would have sold at $104 in 1961, but only $36 in 1979. Same earnings, but certainly not the same stock price. The entire price difference is attributable to a change in the P/E. Amazing, isn't it? Now you can see the potentially dramatic impact that a changing P/E can have on a stock's value.

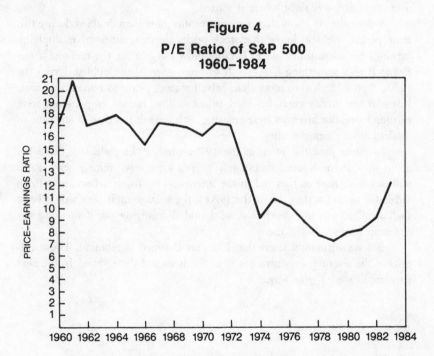

Figure 4
P/E Ratio of S&P 500
1960–1984

We can't overemphasize the importance of the P/E ratio in affecting stock prices. It is imperative that you, the investor, have a grasp of this crucial concept. If it seems clear, then please read on. But if it's still a little hazy, you might take a few seconds to reread the last several paragraphs. We assure you that this will not be a wasted effort.

Earning More but Enjoying It Less

One of the most remarkable stock market coincidences occurred on December 31, 1979—the last day of trading for the decade. On that date, the DJIA closed at 839 (rounded to the nearest point)—*exactly* the same price at which it began the decade. Yes, for ten years the Dow thrashed around, rising as high as 1052 (1973) and crashing as low as 578 (1974). But when it was all over, the DJIA was right where it started.

Yet we already know that corporate profits more than doubled during this same period. We also know that stock prices are determined by multiplying earnings per share times the P/E ratio. Now can you see the message about P/Es? It goes something like this: If earnings more than doubled during the 1970s, then P/Es had to more than halve for stock prices to remain the same. Investors saw profits spiral, but stock prices wallow. Indeed, corporations were earning more, but investors were enjoying such growth less than at any time in modern stock market history.

Investors paid the price in the 1970s when P/Es collapsed, but what about the current decade? Fortunately, there's some very exciting news. P/Es will *not* misbehave as they did in the seventies—far from it. Because if P/Es did halve again (as they did in the 1970s), the average multiplier would be at such a ridiculously low depth that we should all mortgage our homes and buy common stocks—lots of them.

But we adamantly assert that P/Es are destined to rebound. Those culprits of the seventies may turn out to be the heroes of the eighties. In the next paragraphs we tell you why.

25 Percent, Anyone?

How would you like to earn 25 percent yearly on your money without exposing your funds to more than average risk? Sounds tempting, doesn't it? Well, that's what the *average* company would be earning for you if P/Es continue to trend the same way that they did during the seventies. The average stock's P/E at year-end 1979 was approximately 8—less than half the 1969

P/E (refer back to Figure 2). If that trend continues, the average P/E at the 1980s' end would be only 4.

So where do we get 25 percent? Simple: a P/E of 4 *is* a 25 percent return. Confused? Don't be concerned, so are most investors. A closer look at the P/E will eliminate any confusion. So here we go.

Let's explore a make-believe situation. Suppose the market's level did fall so incredibly low that the average P/E was equal to 4. That means that for every dollar a typical company earns, its stock will sell for four times that amount, e.g., $1 earnings = $4 price. Or, stated another way, the $4 price you pay would entitle you to $1 of the company's profits. See what we mean? The $1 profit earned on your share represents a 25 percent return on your $4 investment ($1 ÷ $4 = 25 percent).

Securities analysts have a name for this special return. They refer to it as the earnings yield. We've seen that a stock with a P/E of 4 has a 25 percent earnings yield, but what about other stocks? How is their earnings yield calculated? Again, the answer is straightforward. An earnings yield is computed by dividing a firm's earnings per share by the current market price of its stock. To summarize, the following equation shows how the earnings yield is calculated[5]:

Earnings yield = earnings per share ÷ market price

Frankly, we believe that earnings yields are easier to understand than P/Es. Maybe you feel the same. Try one more example. What if our friends at Prosper Corp. report $2 earnings per share for 1984 and Prosper stock sells at $16 per share? You know that Prosper's P/E is 8, but what is Prosper's earnings yield? Sure, the answer is 12.5 percent ($2 ÷ $16). Just to make absolutely sure that you understand earnings yields, we provide Table 56, which shows representative P/Es and their corresponding earnings yields.

[5] Another way to calculate a stock's earnings yield is by taking the reciprocal of the stock's P/E ratio. For example, a P/E of 8 would translate to a 12½ percent earnings yield (1 ÷ 8 = 12.5 percent). In this sense, as earnings yields rise, P/E must fall (and vice versa).

Table 56

P/Es and Corresponding Earnings Yields

P/E	Earnings Yield
6	16.7%
8	12.5
10	10.0
12	8.5
14	7.1
16	6.3

We hope you have successfully grasped this important concept because in the next section we describe why earnings yields are so important in determining the outlook for stocks.

Inflating Earnings Yields

Now that you know something about the crucial role of P/Es and their inverse, earnings yields, in determining stock prices, let's next find out what influences causes these key factors. Probably the most powerful force affecting overall stock prices in recent times has been inflation. Unexpectedly high inflation rates have wreaked havoc on many investors' portfolios. For one thing, corporate profits must rise as rapidly as the inflation rate for investors to prosper. If inflation outpaces profit growth, then an investor loses ground because his or her purchasing power deteriorates.

Even if corporate profits grow as fast as inflation, stock investors still may not benefit. And you already know why. Because inflation exerts a tremendous pressure on P/E ratios. "Why?" you ask. A little stock market history will serve to place this all in perspective.

Let's return to the beginning of the prior decade. The 1970 inflation rate was 5.9 percent. The average P/E ratio that year was 16.2, which translates to an average earnings yield equal 6.17 percent (1 ÷ 16.2). Makes sense, doesn't it? Investors correctly demanded a sufficient earnings yield on common stocks to compensate for inflation. You certainly wouldn't be content to achieve an earnings yield of only 4 percent, for example, if the inflation rate were considerably higher. Here's the main lesson to be learned: rational investors demand a sufficient return to offset inflation. As inflation advances so do investors demands.

Now let's jump to the decade's end. Inflation by 1979 had skyrocketed to 11.3 percent—approximately double the experience of the early 1970s. Of course, owing to this inflationary spiral the earnings yield of 1970 was no longer appropriate. To offset inflation you would expect investors to demand a much higher return. Well, that's exactly what happened. The average 1979 earnings yield was 13.89 percent—slightly more than double the 1970 figure and, more importantly, a small premium over the 1979 inflation rate. So you see, earnings yields and inflation moved together during this period.

This is an important lesson, to say the least. Inflation rates largely determine earnings yields. As a general rule, overall corporate earnings yields slightly exceed the rate of inflation (from 1968 to 1983 the average annual earnings yield exceeded the yearly inflation rate by an average of 2.17 percent). Figure 5 graphically displays this relationship. It's easy to see that inflation and earnings yield typically move in the same direction. That's why inflation is such a vital consideration in determining market movements.

Rising inflation caused earnings yields to expand. As a natural consequence, P/E ratios fell. The 1970 average P/E was a relatively lofty 16.2 when compared to 1979's average of 7.2. It's no wonder that stock prices struggled during the seventies. The inflation-induced P/E collapse was truly awesome. Let's summarize our discussion by advancing an important stock market theorem:

All else equal, earnings yields move in the same, and P/Es in the opposite, direction of inflation.

If you expect inflation to explode, that bodes bad news for common stocks. On the other hand, inflation under control suggests stock market prosperity. Now you can see why stock prices soared in 1982–83—the inflation rate decline allowed P/Es to expand significantly. So much for stock market history. Although history provides a crucial basis for understanding what causes stock prices to move, it does not put money in your pocket. In the next section we take a big step forward by applying what we have learned to the future for the stock market.

Figure 5
Inflation and Earnings Yields
1968–1983

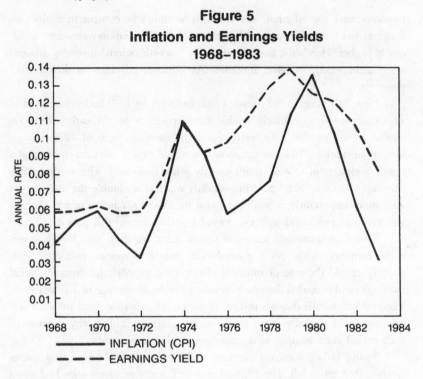

INFLATION (CPI)
--- EARNINGS YIELD

Scenarios for the Eighties

We've traveled a lot of stock market territory in a very short time. Now let's piece all this together. We introduced the Hyperprofits system of wealth-building. Over long periods of time we showed that strict adherence to the Hyperprofits investment technique enables you to attain financial independence.

Through good markets and bad, the patient investor wins convincingly by using this scientifically validated system. But there's more. Hyperprofits is especially rewarding if used when the overall market is climbing. That's part of the secret to Hyperprofits: it generates exceptional returns when the market climate is sunny. That's why we're investing so much of your time and ours to show convincingly that the current market climate is bright.

Now for the outlook for the second half of the eighties. Admittedly, we have no crystal ball. Rather, we must rely on the study of historical relationships and the estimation of future trends. In so doing we believe that we can provide you with strong evidence supporting the long-run viability of common stocks. You already know that those particular stocks singled out by the Hyperprofits method can produce even greater gains.

The stock market's future performance depends on the actions of two underlying factors. Yes, you guessed them: the growth of corporate profits and the level of price–earnings ratios. If we can project these two factors with some reasonable degree of accuracy, then we can forecast the general trend of the overall market.

Inflation, of course, has a substantial influence on both these factors. We admit that we don't know the course of inflation during the remainder of the 1980s. Therefore, let's observe a broad range of inflationary possibilities:

> Very high inflation = 10 percent annually
> High inflation   = 7¹/₂ percent annually
> Moderate inflation = 6 percent annually
> Low inflation   = 4 percent annually

What does each of these potential outcomes spell for the performance of the stock market? In addressing this question we first focus on the likely impact on corporate P/E ratios. We're confident that investors will continue to demand an earnings yield that exceeds the inflation rate. For this analysis we assume that investors will be satisfied with a 3 percent premium above the observed inflation rate. This assumed premium exceeds the 2.16 percent average premium experienced over the 1968–83 period, so we're actually being very generous in our assumption. Thus, if 6 percent inflation occurs, a 9 percent earnings yield would be appropriate. Likewise, 10 percent inflation translates to a 13 percent earnings yield.

Now for the important part. What does all this mean for price–earnings ratios? By referring to Table 57, you can see the effect. Obviously, the higher the required earnings yield, the lower the P/E. If our "very high" inflation scenario unfolds, an average P/E equaling only 7.7 may emerge. But the occurrence of our "low" inflation scenario would produce an estimated P/E of 14.3. Both of those P/Es represent a significant change from the average P/E of approximately 10 at the beginning of 1985. What a difference inflation makes in affecting how much investors are willing to pay for corporate earnings!

What about earnings per share, the other half of the stock price equation? *The Value Line Investment Survey* estimates the combined earnings per share of the thirty Dow Jones stocks will total $222.60 by the 1986–88 period. Let's assume that for now we agree. What happens to stock prices? The answer is

Table 57

Scenarios for the Eighties

Inflationary Scenario	Estimated Inflation Rate	Dow Jones Earnings Per Share[1]	Estimated Earnings Yield[2]	Corresponding P/E Ratio[3]	Dow Jones Average Resulting[4]
Very high	10.0%	$222.60	13.0%	7.7X	1714.02
High	7.5	222.60	10.5	9.5	2114.70
Moderate	6.0	222.60	9.0	11.1	2470.86
Low	4.0	222.60	7.0	14.3	3183.18

[1]*The Value Line Investment Survey* estimate for 1986–88, April 13, 1984.

[2]Assumes 3 percent premium over inflation rate.

[3]The reciprocal of the estimated earnings yield (E/P), e.g., 1 ÷ E/P.

[4]Determined by multiplying the Dow's earnings per share (EPS) times the estimated P/E.

clearly depicted in Table 57. By multiplying the estimated P/E times the projected EPS for the market, we can forecast the level of the Dow.

Now you can see why we're so optimistic about the stock market. Even under our *worst* inflationary scenario, we estimate the Dow will hit 1714.02. That's substantially higher than the Dow's all-time peak. But if low inflation persists throughout the eighties, be prepared for a bull market of staggering proportions. A sustained annual inflation rate of 4 percent could produce a sizable enough P/E expansion to thrust the Dow over the seemingly mythical mark of 3000.

We readily concede that 4 percent sustained inflation isn't likely, nor is a 3000 Dow reading. But what we're most enthusiastic about is the notion that even if relatively poor conditions emerge, the stock market could still perform well. We envision a favorable market climate under all four of our hypothesized inflationary scenarios. Barring runaway inflation or a severe depression, the market appears poised for success and ready to accommodate the Hyperprofits investment strategy.

Could we be wrong? Of course, there's a chance, even though we don't believe it's a significant one. There's that possibility that *Value Line* is too optimistic in its earnings forecasts or the chance that inflation will flare up beyond our high case of 10 percent. Just to be sure that we're aware of the extreme downside, let's journey a little further down the financial trail.

Devil's Advocate

We've painted a rosy picture for the stock market, but what if we're wrong? Could our forecasts be too optimistic? Let's play devil's advocate for a moment and assume that things really fall apart.

What if inflation roars up to the 14 percent annual level, for instance, and holds there? Further, corporate managers are unable to produce sufficient profit growth to match that rate. We know that historically managers have been able to keep profit growth in line with inflation, but let's assume otherwise just to be cautious. What if profit growth is only half the inflation rate? We doubt that this will ever happen, but remember we're playing devil's advocate. Could this scenario spell a real disaster for the stock investor?

Our reasoning suggests that even under these dire circumstances no disaster will occur. Here's our logic. If the Dow's earnings per share increase only 7 percent yearly (half the assumed inflation rate), the 1987 Dow earnings per share will equal $172.12—much less than *Value Line*'s $222.60 estimate for the 1986–88 period. To further complicate matters, the estimated Dow P/E will plummet. In this instance, stock investors will demand a premium return over the inflation rate; let's stick with 3 percent. Thus, the 1987 earnings yield will approximate 17 percent—the highest level in the post–World War II period. This corresponds to a meager 5.9 P/E ratio (1 ÷ .17)—less than half the postwar P/E average of 13.6 and the lowest since the Great Depression.

Now for the answer. Under these absolutely horrid assumptions the Dow would sell at approximately 1015—only slightly less than the current level.[6] And this case assumes runaway inflation, the inability of corporations to maintain satisfactory profit growth, and the demise of price–earnings ratios to the lowest level in modern history. With this kind of minimal downside, surely it is not difficult to convince yourself that committing funds to this exceptional investment arena is a wise decision. Why is this important? Because our research reveals that the Hyperprofits system of stock selection definitely performs best during bull markets. If we are correct in our optimism about stocks, we believe that Hyperprofits could provide even more exceptional results than have occurred in the recent past.

Now you know the whole story, from the high profit potential of the Hyperprofits system to the optimistic future outlook for stocks in general. Just one important issue remains. That is, which stocks will afford you a flying start into the Hyperprofits wealth-building program? In the next chapter, we will address this key issue head-on.

[6] The 1015 Dow Jones estimate is determined by multiplying the Dow's estimated earnings per share ($172.12) times the projected P/E (5.9).

Putting Hyperprofits into Motion

You are now armed with the knowledge necessary to place Hyperprofits in motion. You also have paused to consider the likely stock market outlook for the remainder of this decade. You know that during attractive market periods Hyperprofits stocks perform exceptionally well and, as a result, your personal wealth grows remarkably; the magic of compounding makes sure of that.

Although you are equipped to build your own Hyperprofits portfolio, you still may be hesitant to put the system into motion. If this is the case, we hope to reduce your reluctance by constructing a sample Hyperprofits portfolio for you. Using data obtained from *The Media General Financial Weekly*, we determined the three Hyperprofits pillars for thousands of stocks. From these stocks we selected ten Hyperprofits qualifiers for presentation in this chapter. Each of these stocks met the rigid Hyperprofits investment standards at the time we made these selections.

Look Before You Leap

You may think that we have conveniently designed a model Hyperprofits portfolio for you so that all you have to do is instruct your broker to buy these stocks for your portfolio. Unfortunately it's not that simple. You must remember that these selections were made as we wrote this book, several months before you read the book. Thus, before you leap to buy these specific stocks, keep the following in mind:

1. These Hyperprofits selections were picked at year end 1984, the time at which we were writing this chapter. We realize that by the time you

read this book, some of the stocks pillar values may have changed. Thus, we are not suggesting that you immediately go out and buy these ten stocks. To do so would violate the Hyperprofits investment system. Rather, before purchasing any stock, you must verify that all three pillars fall within the recommended Hyperprofits boundaries. To the extent that a Hyperprofits candidate still qualifies, then you may proceed with the purchase.

2. We have presented ten stocks which participate in ten different industries. A portfolio consisting of only these stocks would be adequately diversified. But you must determine exactly how a specific stock blends into your own portfolio; proper diversification is a must. You may find, for example, that one of these stocks is too closely related to a stock you already own.

3. We present only ten Hyperprofits stocks. In reality many more attractive Hyperprofits stocks exist. We attempted only to show you several diverse selections, not necessarily to pick the very best Hyperprofits stocks. Through your own research and analysis, you may discover other stocks which you feel are even more enticing.

If, after heeding the above cautions, any of the stocks we present still seem attractive, then you can proceed.

Ten Hyperprofits Candidates

So much for the red flags! Now let's get down to business. As we promised, we now present a brief sketch of each of these ten sample Hyperprofits stocks. We have facilitated your entry into this fascinating investment arena by computer-scanning the 4,300-stock Media General universe for attractive Hyperprofits issues.

For each company we determined the value of each of the three Hyperprofits pillars as of December 31, 1984. We believe that our sample portfolio contains widely diverse stocks. Each company participates in a different industry. Company size (MV) ranges from as low as only $6 million to a high of $69 million. Likewise, the PER and DPE pillars vary considerably across these stocks.

Two factors, however, appear to be consistent for all ten stocks: (1) they *all* have attractive Hyperprofits pillars, and (2) they *all* sell at relatively low prices per share. Enough said? Let's now move on to the Hyperprofits candidates.

CARRIAGE INDUSTRIES (CARG)

Price: $4.25	Current P/E: 3.4
1984 price range: $4–7	Historical P/E: 6.0
1984 EPS: $1.24*	Industry P/E: 7.5
Shares outstanding: 4.2 million	Marketplace: O-T-C

* Year ended July 1, 1984

Hyperprofits Pillars

PER	DPE	MV
.45	.57	18

Carriage Industries is a carpet manufacturing company. Most of the company's revenues and profits come from its Carriage Carpet division, which manufactures carpeting for such specialty markets as factory-manufactured housing and recreational vehicles. Based on fiscal 1984 earnings per share, Carriage has a P/E of only 3.4.

Carriage is not a typical Hyperprofits selection because the stock did not trade publicly until August 1, 1984. As a result, Carriage's DPE is based on a shorter P/E history. We selected Carriage to illustrate the flexibility of the Hyperprofits system. Even though Carriage has not traded publicly for a long time, we discovered that during the company's brief public history the P/E has averaged approximately 6.0. That means that Carriage's DPE comes in at only .57—well within the recommended Hyperprofits range.

Indeed, Carriage is not a unique situation. Many attractive small companies have begun to trade publicly for the first time only recently. We hesitate to delete these stocks from consideration, especially since many have not been around long enough to catch the eye of the institutional investors. Therefore, if the Hyperprofits pillars are strong enough for a new company, we would not hesitate to buy.

DAMSON OIL (DAM)

Price: $4.00	Current P/E: 3.3
1984 price range: $4–10	Historical P/E: 20.2
1984 EPS: $1.23	Industry P/E: 21.0
Shares outstanding: 7.7 million	Marketplace: Amex

Hyperprofits Pillars

PER	DPE	MV
.16	.16	31

Damson Oil is engaged in the oil and gas production business. In addition, the company serves as the general partner for numerous limited partnerships through which individual investors may participate in the company's oil and gas exploration and development activities.

In 1984, Damson acquired Dorchester Gas Corp. and thus substantially increased the firm's profit potential. Although the 1983–84 period was a poor one for most oil and gas companies, Damson continued to report high profits. In fact, the firm's 1984 earnings per share were the highest in the company's history.

Damson's stock price, however, is another story. The current $4 share price is the lowest in over five years. Of course, rising earnings and a falling stock price translate to a low P/E ratio and that's exactly the case for Damson. At its current level, Damson's 3.3 P/E is only approximately one fifth of its historical average. Further, Damson's P/E is very low when compared to its industry average P/E, as evidenced by the firm's PER of only .16. And finally, Damson definitely qualifies as a small firm: its MV totals $31 million, well below the $75 million Hyperprofits cutoff.

DICEON ELECTRONICS (DICN)[1]

Price: $11.75	Current P/E: 10.5
1984 price range: $11–18	Historical P/E: 24.2

---

[1] We thank S.M.U. students Eric Josjo and Thomas Mouch for assistance in analyzing Diceon Electronics.

1984 EPS: $1.12*   Industry P/E: 16.0

Shares outstanding: 5.5 million   Marketplace: O-T-C

* Year ended September 30, 1984.

Hyperprofits Pillars

PER	DPE	MV
.66	.43	65

Diceon Electronics manufactures and sells multilayer printed circuit boards. Although competition is stiff, Diceon has been able to achieve a 57.3 percent average annual growth rate in sales since its founding in 1980. More important, this rapid sales growth translates to an explosion in profits. The $1.12 earnings per share reported in 1984 was the highest in the company's history (more than double the 1983 amount) and is expected to grow at least 20 percent annually for the next few years.

Diceon's success may be largely attributed to the ability to produce state-of-the-art products which meet exacting customer specifications. Diceon, for example, is one of the few companies capable of making advanced twenty-two-layer circuit boards. As a result, Diceon's customers consist of the most technically advanced and stable companies in the United States.

You may have noted that Diceon's P/E ratio is approximately the same as the overall stock market's P/E. This is a prime example of a company that would be overlooked by the traditional low-P/E strategy. However, because Diceon participates in the typically high-multiple electronics components industry, its P/E relative to the industry norm is very attractive, as evidenced by its PER of .66. Further, its DPE of .43 is even more enticing and its $65 million capitalization falls within the recommended MV boundaries.

HEI, INC. (HEII)

Price: $3.75   Current P/E: 8.9

1984 price range: $3–9   Historical P/E: 17.1

1984 EPS: $0.42*   Industry P/E: 15.5

Shares outstanding: 1.4 million   Marketplace: O-T-C

* Year ended August 31, 1984.

Hyperprofits Pillars

PER	DPE	MV
.57	.52	5

HEI manufactures custom optoelectronic components. Like many high-technology stocks, HEI's share price declined by approximately two thirds in 1984. The current price of $3.75 represents only a small rebound from HEI's all-time low price of $3.25.

The severe share price decline can be attributed to two primary factors:

1. HEI's 1984 EPS declined 16 percent versus the previous year's amount, and

2. The entire marketplace for high technology stocks was in shambles during 1984.

The real consideration revolves around whether the stock price overreacted too much on the negative side.

An objective look at HEI's present position indicates that the stock may have overreacted to these two happenings and could be poised for a price rebound. At the current share price, HEI has a 8.9 P/E—approximately the same as the P/E for the entire market. But, remember, Hyperprofits asks about a stock's P/E relative to its industry average P/E. And, in this instance the appropriate industry sports a very high P/E norm of 15.5.

As a result, HEI's P/E, although in line with the overall market P/E, is very low for the high-technology industry. This fact is documented by HEI's .57 PER figure. Likewise, because the company's current P/E is substantially below its historical P/E average of 17.1, a low DPE (.52) also emerges. Finally, with only 1.4 million common shares outstanding, HEI really stacks up as a small firm: its current MV is only slightly more than $5 million.

HOMESTEAD FINANCIAL (HFL)

Price: $11.63	Current P/E: 3.8
1984 price range: $9–21	Historical P/E: 10.8

1984 EPS: $3.05   Industry P/E: 9.9

Shares outstanding: 4.5 million   Marketplace: NYSE

Hyperprofits Pillars

PER	DPE	MV
.38	.35	52

Homestead Financial participates in the much maligned savings and loan industry in California. As the result of high and volatile interest rates, investors have shied away from S&L stocks in general and Homestead Financial in specific.

Homestead is not a typical Hyperprofits stock because it trades on the New York Stock Exchange. Yes, that's right; this stock resides on the Big Board. We know what you're thinking: "I thought Hyperprofits selected only small stocks, while the NYSE houses only large companies. How can this be?" Let's respond to that question.

At first blush Homestead appears to be a large company. For example, the company has total assets of approximately one half billion dollars—hardly a small sum. But, as you may recall, in Chapter 4 we established that market value, not assets, is the appropriate figure through which we determine a firm's size. Now look at Homestead's measurements: its 4.5 million shares create a $52 million MV. Amazing, isn't it? A company with assets totaling almost one half billion dollars is valued at only $52 million.

While Homestead is not the smallest firm around, it is well within our $75 million Hyperprofits MV cutoff. So you see, in Hyperprofits terms Homestead Financial is a small firm. Homestead also stacks up extremely well on Pillars 1 and 2. Why? Because its current P/E of only 3.8 is considerably below the stock's historical average P/E and the S&L industry P/E norm. The result: Homestead has PER and DPE ratios, respectively, of .38 and .35. Indeed, this "small" firm qualifies as a Hyperprofits pick.

OVERLAND EXPRESS (OVER)

Price: $10.75   Current P/E: 5.9

1984 price range: $10–26   Historical P/E: 13.0

1984 EPS: $1.83   Industry P/E: 10.3

Shares outstanding: 1.7 million   Marketplace: O-T-C

Hyperprofits Pillars

PER	DPE	MV
.57	.45	18

This Minnesota-based company offers long-haul trucking services transporting general commodities throughout the forty-eight contiguous states. Overland experienced rapid earnings growth from 1980 to 1982, as EPS soared from $0.71 to $1.72 (142% increase). Accordingly, Overland's stock price advanced as high as $26¼ in 1984.

Primarily owing to a slowdown in earnings growth (1984 earnings were less than 10 percent higher than the 1982 amount), Overland's stock price began to sag, falling as low as $9¾ per share in late 1984. Could this price decline represent an overreaction by fickle investors? Let's take a look at Overland's Hyperprofits' pillars in an attempt to answer this question.

At its current $10.75 share price, Overland has a 5.9 P/E. This figure compares to the company's 15 P/E at the 1984 peak price and to the firm's historical average P/E of 13. Also, Overland's P/E is very modest when compared to the trucking industry's 10.3 P/E. The net result, of course, translates into a very low Hyperprofits Pillar 1 (PER = .57) and Pillar 2 (DPE = .45).

This stock also qualifies on the final count, the market value pillar. At the current price, Overland's total MV is only $18 million, thus easily qualifying as a small firm. Interestingly, earlier in 1984 at the stock's highest price, Overland's MV was approximately $45 million—two and a half times its present market value.

ST. JUDE MEDICAL (STJM)

Price: $8.75   Current P/E: 7.8

1984 price range: $8–19   Historical P/E: 40.9

1984 EPS: $1.12   Industry P/E: 14.6

Shares outstanding: 4.7 million   Marketplace: O-T-C

Hyperprofits Pillars

PER	DPE	MV
.53	.19	41

St. Jude Medical produces an implantable heart valve and engages in the research and development of other cardiovascular implantable and electronic diagnostic products. The company has experienced consistent and rapid earnings growth, as evidenced by its EPS advance from $0.29 in 1980 to $1.11 in 1984.

Stock price, however, has not kept pace with earnings growth. Surprisingly, St. Jude stockholders have observed the firm's stock price falling from a 1984 high of $19¼ (the stock sold at an even higher $29¼ in 1983) to its present $8¾ price. The bad news for those stockholders who suffered through this substantial price decay may translate to good news for new shareholders who acquire St. Jude at the current low price.

Here's why. The price decline coupled with continued earnings growth means that the firm's P/E dropped to an all-time low. The current 7.8 P/E is paled in comparison to the 40.9 historical average P/E. The result, of course, is that St. Jude's DPE is a minuscule .19. The company's P/E also is only approximately half that of its industry P/E norm, as evidenced by its .53 PER. And, finally, the company comfortably qualifies on the MV count: its 4.7 million shares have a total market value of $41 million.

SEA GALLEY STORES (SEAG)

Price: $7.38

1984 price range: $7–11

1984 EPS: $2.05

Shares outstanding: 3.9 million

Current P/E: 3.6

Historical P/E: 18.8

Industry P/E: 16.9

Marketplace: O-T-C

Hyperprofits Pillars

PER	DPE	MV
.21	.19	29

Sea Galley Stores operates over fifty full-service seafood restaurants in the United States, primarily on the West Coast. Growth has been rapid as evidenced by the increase in net sales from only $13.4 million in 1979 to nearly $100 million annually at the present time—a more than sevenfold increase.

As you probably guessed, Sea Galley's stock price also soared during the early 1980s, attaining a high price of $18 per share. Since then, however, the stock's price has floundered and currently sells at its lowest level in over two years. The reason for this poor performance is that the company experienced a very poor 1983 when it lost 46 cents per common share. Profits have sailed skyward since as shown in the information above, but the P/E has yet to rebound. The result is that Sea Galley ranks as a top Hyperprofits pick. Its DPE (.19) and PER (.21) are exceptionally low, and of course the firm's $29 million MV easily qualifies it as a small company.

ULTRASYSTEMS, INC. (ULTR)

Price: $9.00   Current P/E: 9.7

1984 price range: $9–21   Historical P/E: 30.3

1984 EPS: $0.93*   Industry P/E: 19.2

Shares outstanding: 7.7 million   Marketplace: O-T-C

* Fiscal year ended January 31, 1985

Hyperprofits Pillars

PER	DPE	MV
.51	.32	69

Ultrasystems, Inc. operates chiefly through two primary subsidiaries, an engineering and construction segment which accounted for 70 percent of fiscal 1984 revenue and a defense and space system segment which accounted for 29.4 percent of 1984 revenues.

The company has recorded solid increases in revenues and profits during the eighties. For example, Ultrasystems 1980 revenues totaled only $15 million versus over $100 million for the recent fiscal year ending January 31, 1985. Meanwhile, earnings per share have skyrocketed from only $0.08 for the fiscal year ending January 31, 1981 to the current $0.93 amount. Further, EPSs have increased each year during the eighties at a compound rate exceeding 80 percent per year.

Even with this outstanding track record, Ultrasystems stock has been far from a top performer. Its current $9 share price is the lowest in several years. As a result, Ultrasystems sports a current P/E ratio which is considerably below its historical average P/E and the industry average P/E. The PER (.51) and DPE (.32) of this stock are exceptionally low and the firm's MV of $69 million falls within the Hyperprofits attractive range.

XEBEC (XEBC)

Price: $4.00	Current P/E: 5.1
1984 price range: $4–20	Historical P/E: 47.0
1984 EPS: $0.79	Industry P/E: 13.7
Shares outstanding: 23 million	Marketplace: O-T-C

Hyperprofits Pillars

PER	DPE	MV
.36	.11	52

XEBEC is the leading manufacturer of the Winchester disk drive controller. The company's controllers are designed primarily for use in small business and personal computers. As a result, XEBEC has the opportunity to participate in this popular and fast-growing market.

XEBEC's earnings per share exploded from $0.39 in 1983 to an estimated $1.05 in 1984. On the other hand, XEBEC's stock price fell from a 1984 high of $20 per share to a year-end low of $4 per share. Based on the firm's $0.79 EPS for the twelve-month period ended September 30, 1984, XEBEC's current P/E is only 5.1—a mere fraction of its traditionally high P/E ratio of 47. Also, XEBEC's P/E is considerably lower than its industry-counterpart P/E of 13.7. Therefore, both XEBEC's PER (.36) and DPE (.11) are exceptionally low.

The company's 13 million shares outstanding translate to a firm market value equaling $52 million—once again not exactly the smallest Hyperprofits stock, but nonetheless qualifying as an acceptable small-MV stock. We believe XEBEC's strong PER and DPE pillars make it an attractive Hyperprofits selection.

There you have it—ten representative Hyperprofits stocks from ten different industries. While we make no guarantee of the future performance of these ten stocks, we do believe that they represent attractively positioned Hyperprofits selections. In Table 58 we summarize the reasons why these ten securities appear poised for Hyperprofits.

Staying in Motion

Let's assume that you have identified several stocks whose pillar values are attractive. Some stocks may come from the ten sample securities we presented, while others may be your own selections. To begin your Hyperprofits investment program as soon as possible you decide to purchase enough of these securities to build a well-diversified portfolio. Is your job complete? By now, you know that the answer to that question is an emphatic "No." A successful approach to Hyperprofits requires the periodic rebalancing of your portfolio. The failure to review your holdings on a regular basis exposes you to those "foolish" investment risks we discussed in Chapter 2. Even Hyperprofits isn't sufficient to overcome a foolish approach to risk.

Therefore, as we discussed in Chapter 7, you must at a minimum review your Hyperprofits holdings every six months. Any number of unexpected things can occur which change your stocks' pillar values. You must be on top of these changes and ready to react in order to capture the full advantages of the Hyperprofits investment system. No, Hyperprofits is not a sit-back-and-get-rich scheme: it requires your periodic attention and analysis. We simply cannot emphasize this point enough.

A Final Touch

We believe that the ten Hyperprofits stocks presented in this chapter will give you a good idea regarding how to put the Hyperprofits system into motion. We hope you were able to detect the reasons for which we selected each stock and why the stocks, when combined, create an attractive portfolio. These are very important considerations because eventually you must make your own selections from the huge universe of different stocks. Our current picks provide only a guideline for you to follow in constructing your own Hyperprofits portfolio. The rest is up to you.

Table 58

The Ten Hyperprofits Candidates

Company	Industry	Stock* Price	The Pillars*		
			PER	DPE	MV
Carriage Industries	Carpet manufacturing	$ 4.25	.45	.57	18
Damson Oil	Energy	4.00	.16	.16	31
Diceon Electronics	Electronics	11.75	.66	.43	65
HEI, Inc.	Optical technology	3.75	.57	.52	5
Homestead Financial	Savings and loan	11.63	.38	.35	52
Overland Express	Trucking	10.75	.57	.45	18
St. Jude Medical	Medical technology	8.75	.53	.19	41
Sea Galley Stores	Restaurant	7.38	.21	.19	29
Ultrasystems, Inc.	Construction; defense	9.00	.51	.32	69
XEBEC	Computer components	4.00	.36	.11	52

*As of December 31, 1984.

11

Hyperprofits: The Final Answer

You must admit that we've covered a lot of ground in our journey through Hyperprofits. We sincerely hope that we've provided an enjoyable tour for you. We would hate to think that learning how to invest successfully would be a boring experience. We would also like you to know, as we conclude, that we found it a genuine pleasure to present our story to you. Since you've been exposed to so many different concepts, we thought it would prove helpful to summarize by presenting a brief sketch of the main ideas and how they fit together. We will do this first. In addition, we will make some concluding comments which we believe you will find interesting.

Make Your Day

Hyperprofits is a validated investment system which, when adhered to properly over a sustained period of time, has the potential to yield an extraordinary profit return on your invested dollar. By coupling the system with the miraculous effects of compounding, you have the opportunity to transform a relatively small sum of savings into a very substantial estate. We have assumed throughout that you might start with, say, $5,000 to $10,000 and build from this base alone. In reality, you would probably be adding some new savings to the plan each year. Over a ten-to-15-year horizon, this would create an effect all the more dramatic.

For example, let's say your initial investment is $7,500 and you utilize Hyperprofits in your IRA plan, supplementing your program by an additional $2,000 per year. Then, assuming the historical Hyperprofits return, your gross estate before brokerage costs and taxes would grow to $878,685.51 after fifteen years.[1] So you can see that adding a reasonable amount of capital to your plan each year will pay big dividends in the final analysis. The beauty of it is, as we pointed out earlier, that if you designate Hyperprofits as your IRA account, you won't have to pay taxes during the building phase of your program. Therefore, you will achieve the maximum impact of compounding.

Sudden Impact

Hyperprofits will not make you wealthy overnight, nor is it risk-free. Over short periods, the value of your portfolio will fluctuate up and down. The merit of the system is that it stacks the odds in your favor. This puts the law of large numbers to work for you. What does this mean? It means that the more money you add to the system, the more stocks you are able to accumulate, and the longer you stay invested with the system, the smaller and smaller is the risk element. As risk diminishes, the closer your profit performance will conform to the high average returns characteristic of the system. Remember that in order to build wealth you must bear a certain degree of calculated intelligent risk.

In a Nutshell

When you set the Hyperprofits system in motion for yourself, you are employing some of the soundest and most proven investment techniques known. You have seen that the low-P/E method is one of the most solid and validated foundations for investing ever devised. Low-P/E stocks correspond to low-expectation companies. People don't think much of the future of these firms. It sounds contrary, but this is precisely why these stocks can be so profitable. Because expectations are low, you can acquire them at cheap prices.

Now, let's suppose the future turns out to be as bleak as anticipated. Then what was expected has come true. Since nothing surprising has occurred, there is little reason for the price to fall further. Hence, low-P/E stocks tend to hedge against poor company performance. On the other hand, what if the future materializes in brighter fashion than expected? This is a surprise. Now the stock is more valuable than people thought; therefore, its price shoots up to correct for this. So low-P/E stocks incorporate the dual benefit of being more

[1] Because an IRA allows tax-free accumulations, we have assumed no taxes in calculating this sum. We also ignore brokerage commissions.

resistant to price declines while offering a higher chance for pleasant surprises. Therein lies their merit.

While the low-P/E strategy appears to yield attractive profits, empirical findings show that these are not great profits, the stuff that fortunes are made of. Here's where the three pillars of Hyperprofits come to the rescue. Pillar 1, the P/E relative or PER, says that a stock's P/E ratio is more accurately measured with respect to its own particular industry than to the mixture of all industries which comprise the total market. Doesn't it make more sense to compare a computer stock with other computer stocks than to compare it to bank stocks or utility stocks? For banks, the P/E ratio of a particular computer stock might be just average, but in relation to other computer stocks, it might be quite low. Hence, such a stock could be a major bargain within its own realm but completely overlooked by the low P/E strategy.

Pillar 2, the discounted P/E or DPE, adds another dimension to our picture. Suppose that a stock's P/E is low, but we discover that it has been traditionally low for a long period of time. What does this imply? We have learned that such a stock may deserve low expectations. If so, the chance of an upward price surge is small.

In contrast, a stock which finds itself in an unusually low P/E position with respect to its own historical background is likely to be the victim of a temporary setback. The revelation of some bad news may well trigger an overreaction on the part of the investing public. An explosion of selling interest can plummet a stock's price well below its true value. In such cases, there is a strong likelihood that the stock will rebound to its true value in a reasonable period of time. When it does, you want to be along for the profitable ride.

Pillar 2 is our means of identifying and measuring the strength of this phenomenon. You have seen that our research findings confirm the notion that both Pillars 1 and 2 do, in fact, yield high investment returns. Moreover, they work together. The two in concert are superior to either one alone.

But we found that there is yet a third piece to the puzzle, namely, Pillar 3, firm size. Small firms offer at least two major advantages. First, they often possess much higher growth potential than do large firms. Can you imagine General Motors tripling its business? Not likely. What about small firms? It happens all the time.

The second advantage of small firms to you is that they are largely inaccessible to the giant institutional investors. There just isn't enough stock available to accommodate the huge investment demands of most institutions. Professional analysts scour the stock universe night and day to uncover bargains in big-company stocks. And when they are uncovered, institutions are lightning-quick to capitalize on them.

But what about small firms? Bargains can arise in this sphere and end up just sitting there untouched because the pros simply aren't interested. So here you have a realm in which you can compete with the pros and compete very successfully.

And it works. By coupling the first two pillars with Pillar 3, we validated the fact that your profit returns could be elevated to an even higher pinnacle. There you have it, the Hyperprofits system in a nutshell.

You have learned where to get the necessary data and a step-by-step procedure for managing Hyperprofits. We have suggested a number of ways of maximizing your net profit by paying only those taxes which you legally owe. Earlier we mentioned one of the most important of these, the self-directed IRA.

Of special importance to your wealth-building program is the future of the stock market itself. Although Hyperprofits was demonstrated to perform very well over any market cycle, recall that it performs even better in bull markets. Our analysis of the future of the market showed that under a number of reasonable scenarios, the market will, indeed, be a stellar performer in the second half of the 1980s. We firmly believe that our opportunity is now at hand.

To facilitate your seizing this opportunity, we have provided you with some high-potential Hyperprofits selections as of the time of this writing. But remember, nothing stands still. Be sure to carefully evaluate the data at the time you read this before buying any of these picks.

What's in It for Me?

After having seen all this, you might ask the question, Why are we writing this book? If Hyperprofits is as good as the research findings show, why bother to write this book? Why not just invest in it? Good questions. The answer is, we *do* have our money invested in Hyperprofits. We have formed our own Hyperprofits portfolio with a bank custodian to handle the account. If you review some of the tables presented throughout the book, you will see something important. The more money you put into the system, the better off you will be after the magic of compounding has had time to cast its potent spell.

Frankly, by sharing this knowledge with you, we hope to invest even more money in Hyperprofits. We view this book as the best of both worlds. It allows us to increase our own investment and at the same time affords you the opportunity to share in the rich rewards offered by Hyperprofits. We think this makes good sense for all of us.

Let George Do It

You have seen that sources of data exist which allow you to implement and manage the Hyperprofits system. Nevertheless, we know that there are some people who will say, "Hey, I'd like to participate in the benefits of the system, but I would prefer not to spend any time or effort on it. Why can't I have a professional do it for me?"

We can certainly appreciate these sentiments. If you are one of these people, we will be happy to try to direct you to an appropriate money manager or mutual fund. In addition, we hope to make available to you future updates on the performance of the system as well as any refinements we develop in the system itself. If you would like to receive information from us, please use the return page provided at the end of the chapter. We wish to assist you in whatever ways we can. Happy investing!

I would like to receive information on:

☐   Appropriate professional management

☐   Updates on Hyperprofits

☐   Hyperprofits computer software

Name: _____

Address: _____

City and state: _____ ZIP: _____

Phone: _____

Send to: Hyperprofits
          P.O. Box 821292
          Dallas, Texas 75382-1292

Glossary

American Stock Exchange—A national exchange for the trading of marketable securities (primarily common stocks); also known as the Amex. Most companies whose stocks trade on the Amex are not large enough to qualify for New York Stock Exchange listing.

Bear market—A time period during which stock prices in general are declining.

Bill—A short-term debt instrument (original maturity of one year or less). Most bills are issued by the U.S. Treasury and are considered to be the lowest-risk security available.

Blue Chip—The stock of a large, established company with a relatively stable history of growth and dividend payments. Most blue chips trade on the New York Stock Exchange.

Bond—A long-term debt instrument. Bonds are issued by the U.S. Treasury, corporations, and municipalities and usually have a fixed rate of interest and a set maturity date.

Bull market—A time period during which stock prices in general are rising.

Common stock—Stock that represents the ownership interest in a corporation. Each share of common stock has a pro rata claim to corporate profits and voting rights on important corporate matters. Prices of common stock shares may fluctuate considerably depending on the fortunes of the company.

Compounding—The process of reinvesting the earnings from an investment so that those earnings will generate future earnings. Earnings, when compounded, grow much more rapidly than noncompounded earnings (e.g., when the investor does not reinvest).

Convertible—A specialized type of bond or preferred stock which is exchangeable into the common stock of the issuing company.

Discounted Price–Earnings Ratio—The second Hyperprofits Pillar; also known as the DPE. The DPE compares a company's current P/E to its historical average P/E. On average, the lower the current P/E versus the historical P/E, the better the Hyperprofits potential.

Diversification—Spreading investments over several different securities so that no single security can dominate the performance of the portfolio. The Hyperprofits system requires the implementation of diversification to protect the investor from excessive risk.

Dividend—A share of a company's profits which is distributed in cash to shareholders in direct proportion to the number of shares owned.

Dow Jones Industrial Average—A measure of the performance of thirty selected common stocks, mostly blue chips. The Dow is not a complete market indicator because it ignores the performance of small companies.

DPE—*See* Discounted price–earnings ratio.

Earnings per share—The amount of net profits a company earns for one share of its common stock; calculated by dividing total net profits by the number of common shares outstanding.

Earnings yield—The amount of net profits (earnings) per share earned as a percentage of the market price of a share of stock; the reciprocal of the price–earnings ratio.

Efficient market—A totally efficient market assumes that all stocks are fairly priced and thus no one can earn superior stock profits. The Hyperprofits system asserts that although many stocks are efficiently priced, there may be "inefficiencies" among small stocks.

Exchange—A centralized location for the trading of certain stocks that have been approved for trading on the exchange. *See also* American Stock Exchange; New York Stock Exchange.

Growth company—A company whose earnings per share are growing at a rate much faster than that of the average company.

Growth stock—A common stock whose price appreciates faster than that of the overall stock market.

Market value (MV)—The third Hyperprofits pillar. MV is the total worth of all common shares of a company; determined by multiplying the current price of a company's stock by the number of common shares outstanding.

Multiplier—Another name for the price–earnings (P/E) ratio.

Mutual Fund—An investment company which pools the funds of many investors and invests in a diversified portfolio of marketable securities. Each investor owns a proportion of the overall portfolio.

MV—*See* Market value.

NASDAQ Index—A market index which measures the average performance of over-the-counter stocks. Unlike the Dow Jones or S&P 500, this index reveals how small-firm stocks are doing.

New York Stock Exchange—The national exchange where the shares of most very large companies are bought and sold; also known as "the Big Board."

Over the counter (OTC)—The nationwide marketplace where nonexchange-listed securities are traded. Most OTC stocks are smaller than those traded on the American and New York stock exchanges.

P/E ratio—*See* Price–earnings ratio.

PER—*See* Price–earnings relative.

Pillar—An ingredient of the Hyperprofits system. Hyperprofits is the synthesis of three investment pillars: the price–earnings relative (PER), the discounted P/E ratio (DPE), and the market value of the firm (MV).

Preferred stock—Stock that does not participate in the growth of the issuing corporation. Preferred stock typically has a constant dividend payment and no voting rights.

Price–earnings relative—The first Hyperprofits pillar; also known as the PER. The PER is calculated by dividing a company's P/E by the average P/E for the companies in the same industry. A low PER is a desirable Hyperprofits trait.

Price–earnings ratio (P/E)—The price of a share of common stock divided by the annual earnings per share of the company; also known as the P/E ratio or the multiplier.

Risk—The possibility of not earning the amount of return that you originally expected. The riskier the security, the higher the rate of return you should expect to earn. Hyperprofits distinguishes between prudent risk and foolish risk.

Short sale—The process of borrowing a stock from a second party and selling it to a third party with the intention of eventually buying back the stock at a lower price and returning it to the lender.

Small company—A company whose market value (MV) is small in comparison to other companies. Hyperprofits considers a company with an MV of $75 million or less to be a small company.

Standard & Poor's 500—A stock market index which measures the performance of 500 selected companies. Although the S&P 500 improves on the Dow Jones Industrial Average, it still overlooks the performance of small companies.